Media, Identity, and Struggle in Twenty-First-Century China

How are different groups of people such as sex workers, migrant workers, rural cadres, and homosexuals represented in China's media? How accurately do representations created by the media reflect the lived experiences of Chinese people? Do Chinese people accept the representations and messages disseminated by the media? Can they use the media to portray their own interests? How are media practices in China changing? Have new technologies and increased access to international media opened up new spaces for struggle in China?

The essays in this volume address these questions by using a combination of ethnography and textual analysis and by exploring representation in and usage of a range of media including instant messaging, the internet, television, films, magazines, and newspapers. The essays highlight the richness, diversity, and sometimes contradictory tendencies of the meanings and consequences of media representations in China. The authors caution against approaches that take the representations created by the media in China at face value and against oversimplified assumptions about the motivations and agency of players in the complex struggles that occur between the media, the Chinese state, and Chinese citizens.

Articles in this book were published as a special feature in two issues of *Critical Asian Studies*: Vol. 39, No. 1 (March 2007) and Vol. 39, number 2 (June 2007).

Rachel Murphy is senior lecturer in East Asian Studies at the University of Bristol. She received her PhD in sociology from the University of Cambridge in 1999. She is author of *How Migrant Labor Is Changing Rural China* and coeditor of *Chinese Citizenship: Views from the Margins*. Her articles have appeared in *China Quarterly, Population and Development Review,* and *Journal of Peasant Studies*.

Vanessa L. Fong is an assistant professor in Harvard University's Graduate School of Education. She is the author of *Only Hope: Coming of Age under China's One-Child Policy*, which won the Francis Hsu Prize in Asian Studies, and coeditor of *Chinese Citizenship: Views from the Margins and Women in Republican China*. She received her PhD in anthropology from Harvard University in 2002.

MEDIA, IDENTITY, AND STRUGGLE IN TWENTY-FIRST-CENTURY CHINA

Edited by Rachel Murphy and Vanessa L. Fong,
with an introduction by Vanessa L. Fong

LONDON AND NEW YORK

First published 2009 by Routledge
2 Park Square, Milton Park, Abingdon, Oxon, OX14 4RN

Simultaneously published in the USA and Canada
by Routledge
270 Madison Ave, New York NY 10016

Routledge is an imprint of the Taylor & Francis Group, an informa business

Transferred to Digital Printing 2009

© 2009 BCAS, Inc.

Typeset in the USA by BCAS, Inc.

All rights reserved. No part of this book may be reprinted or reproduced or utilised in any form or by any electronic, mechanical, or other means, now known or hereafter invented, including photocopying and recording, or in any information storage or retrieval system, without permission in writing from the publishers.

British Library Cataloguing in Publication Data
A catalogue record for this book is available from the British Library

ISBN10: 0-415-46058-1 (hbk)
ISBN10: 0-415-57468-4 (pbk)

ISBN13: 978-0-415-46058-3 (hbk)
ISBN13: 978-0-415-57468-6 (pbk)

CONTENTS

	Abstracts	v
	Introduction Vanessa L. Fong	1
1.	Performing Media-Constructed Images for First-Class Citizenship: Political Struggles of Rural Migrant Hostesses in Dalian Tiantian Zheng	6
2.	Migrant Workers in the Pearl River Delta: Discourse and Narratives about Work as Sites of Struggle Eric Florence	27
3.	The Paradox of the State-Run Media Promoting Poor Governance in China: Case Studies of a Party Newspaper and an Anticorruption Film Rachel Murphy	46
4.	Querying Queer Theory: Debating Male-Male Prostitution in the Chinese Media Elaine Jeffreys	66
5.	The Internet and the Fragmentation of Chinese Society Jens Damm	83
6.	SMS, Communication, and Citizenship in China's Information Society Kevin Latham	96
7.	The New Chinese Citizen and CETV Yingchi Chu	110
	Notes	122
	References	141
	Contributors	163
	Index	165

DEDICATION

This book is dedicated to Vivienne Shue, Leverhulme Professor of Contemporary China Studies and director of the Contemporary China Studies Programme (CCSP) at Oxford. This is one of several contemporary China projects to be developed under the auspices of CCSP and the editors are most grateful for her encouragement and help and for program support throughout.

The editors also acknowledge assistance from a British Academy international networks grant.

ABSTRACTS

Performing Media-Constructed Images for First-Class Citizenship: Political Struggles of Rural Migrant Hostesses in Dalian

Tiantian Zheng

This article addresses how the state, the market, and intellectual discourse in China construct the sexually promiscuous, dangerous, and threatening rural migrant woman as second-class citizen in opposition to the civilized, demure, and moral city woman who is pictured as a first-class citizen. Rural migrant women's bodies are thus the battleground for the formation of the hegemonic cultural norms. The author describes the ways in which rural migrant hostesses imbue media-constructed stigmatized sexuality with new meanings. Foregrounding hostesses' interactions with clients in the karaoke bar sex industry, the author argues that hostesses perform represented images to redistribute clients' resources and procure legitimate cultural and political first-class citizenship. Their political struggle both challenges and contests media constructions about themselves.

Migrant Workers in the Pearl River Delta: Discourse and Narratives about Work as Sites of Struggle

Eric Florence

With the introduction of capitalist labor relations into China certain attitudes, competencies, and values associated with global capitalism seem to be increasingly valorized. This article analyzes the values and principles ascribed to migrant workers as part of practices linked to modes of government. The author confronts the dominant form of cultural construction of migrant workers through the Shenzhen official press with migrant workers' own narratives about their experience of work (*dagong*) in the city as the narratives are mediated through two different sites, namely, participant observation, interviews with rural migrants, and a body of unpublished letters to the editor acquired from several magazines dedicated to migrant workers. The article sheds light on the ways in which migrant workers' narratives confirm or, on the contrary, contest the pivotal elements of the hegemonic construction. Three different narratives that migrant workers produce about their own lives and about Shenzhen are examined. These narratives range from affirmations of dominant discourses about migrant workers and expressions of disillusionment about such discourses, to strategic uses of dominant discourses to justify the claims made by migrant workers.

The Paradox of the State-Run Media Promoting Poor Governance in China: Case Studies of a Party Newspaper and an Anticorruption Film
Rachel Murphy

This essay draws on the analysis of media texts and ethnographic fieldwork to present case studies of the production, distribution, and consumption of two kinds of media products in China that are used for educating cadres about official policies, law and morality, namely, a Party-produced prefectural newspaper and an anticorruption film. Such pedagogic media products merit study because they are consumed by a huge audience of cadres who are entrusted with interpreting and implementing state policy and with carrying out the daily work of the different institutions that make up the Party-state. The case studies show that the internal circulation of pedagogic media products within the Party-state apparatus works in two ways to reinforce "organizational involution," which causes poor governance. First, the content of the media products and their methods of distribution buttress the norms and institutional practices that entrench unchallenged power, corruption, and official malfeasance within the system. Examples include the role of top-down administrative fiat in determining the content of the media products and the ways in which individuals and institutions are compelled to purchase materials and participate in pedagogic activities to secure their positions. Second, state pedagogy deflects attention away from the structural failings of the Party-state system. The pedagogic products enable the Party-state to portray itself as the leading crusader in the fight against corruption, despite the corrupting consequences of its continuing unsupervised monopoly on power. Meanwhile, self-improvement exhortations in the media texts sidestep the question of systemic political reform.

Querying Queer Theory: Debating Male-Male Prostitution in the Chinese Media
Elaine Jeffreys

This article examines media publicity surrounding the case of Li Ning — a 34-year-old native of Nanjing City, Jiangsu Province, who made legal history in the People's Republic of China (PRC) on 17 October 2004 when he was sentenced to eight years jail and fined 60,000 yuan for organizing male-male prostitution services in a recreational business enterprise. Reportedly the first conviction of its kind, the case proved to be controversial for three reasons. First, it prompted legal debate over the nature of China's recent shift to a "rule of law" and associated conceptions of due legal process and individual and sexual rights. Second, it intimated that homosocial prostitution — male-male prostitution in which neither participant may self-identify as homosexual — is an integral but frequently neglected component of China's burgeoning, albeit banned, sex industry. Finally, it raised questions regarding the perceived appropriate parameters of same-sex sexual conduct in a country facing rapidly increasing rates of HIV/AIDS infection. An examination of media coverage of these concerns suggests that accusations of official homophobia in the PRC are overstated: they elide the specificity of debates on homosexuality in present-day China due to their overarching concern with Western understandings of sexuality as constitutive of selfhood and (rightful) sociopolitical identity.

The Internet and the Fragmentation of Chinese Society
Jens Damm

Research on the internet in China typically focuses on questions of censorship, the blocking of websites, the democratizing effects of the medium, and the use of the internet by dissident groups. In much of this research, a deterministic view of technology prevails: the inherent features of the internet such as ubiquitous access and the fact that "everybody can easily become his or her own publisher and participate in many-to-many communications" are assumed to be leading automatically to specific societal and political developments. These developments are seen as taking place along a fixed line only dependent on technological innovations, a characteristic of an earlier view of modernization that was also found in Marxist and Leninist perspectives. This simplistic view is inadequate for two reasons. First, it portrays the Chinese internet user as fundamentally different from his/her Western counterpart. Second, it ignores the rise of urban and consumerist lifestyles, which have changed Chinese society during recent decades and resulted in less interest in conventional politics, more fragmentation, and a stronger focus on identity politics.

SMS, Communication, and Citizenship in China's Information Society
Kevin Latham

China has entered a new information age that calls for a reconsideration of some key presuppositions about the relationship between Chinese media, communication, society, and culture. These include stereotypes that dominate representations and understandings of China such as the appealing, though too simple, model of propaganda versus free speech and political repression versus democracy or those anticipating the emergence of a more or less Habermasian "public sphere." Taking the example of mobile phone short messaging services (SMS), this article investigates the transforming relationships between Chinese media, power, political subjectivity, and citizenship. SMS now constitutes an important new set of communication practices in China. It is more widely used than the internet and by a more diverse section of the population. In early 2005 per person, fifteen times more SMS messages than emails were being sent in China. Putting forward the idea of "orderly" and "disorderly" media it is suggested that while the Party voices its own rhetorics from the past, many people, particularly in the large metropolitan centres, are driving their own alternative visions of the future and forcing the authorities to engage with entirely new kinds of media practices that pose quite different challenges to those of the past.

The New Chinese Citizen and CETV
Yingchi Chu

This article addresses the ways in which the leading Chinese TV Education provider, CETV, negotiates its role within the parameters of government policy, media industry constraints, media mandates, technological innovation, program reform, public ratings, and increasing audience participation. The author argues that mainly as a result of a radically new horizon of audience expectations, a new kind of participatory citizen is gradually emerging in China. In this process, the article submits, TV programming and program reform can be taken as a reliable indicator of change, since they must balance top-down government directives and bottom-up, popular demand that is measurable in direct audience input and public ratings. The author corroborates this claim through a brief analysis of documentary programs that are being designed more and more to maximize public participation, concluding that while we cannot yet speak of a proper public media sphere in China, there is ample evidence of the training of dialogic and polyphonic interaction that will be able to serve as a formal and practical precondition for more extended public debate. Certainly, the trend toward a participatory style in much recent CETV programming, and at many other TV stations, is unlikely to be reversible. What we are seeing is the birth of a new, TV-trained citizen who will aim to extend the privileges of participation toward contributing to a more fully political forum.

MEDIA, IDENTITY, AND STRUGGLE IN TWENTY-FIRST-CENTURY CHINA

Introduction

Vanessa L. Fong

How accurately do representations created by the media in China reflect the lived experiences of Chinese people? Do Chinese people accept the messages disseminated by the media to which they are exposed? How much control does the Chinese state have over information flows? How are media practices in China changing? How do Chinese people use the media to pursue their own interests? Have new technologies and increased access to international media opened up new spaces for political struggle in China? The papers in this volume use a combination of ethnography and textual analysis to address these questions.

As post-Mao economic reforms have encouraged the flourishing of new media technologies such as the internet and text messaging,[1] allowed the content of news and entertainment to be increasingly driven by consumer demand,[2] and removed many of the barriers between the international media and Chinese citizens,[3] the Chinese state is finding it difficult to control the flow of information into, out of, and within China. As Mayfair Yang has observed, global information flows have liberated Chinese citizens from the centralized power of the Chinese state, even while drawing them and the Chinese state itself toward global capitalism.[4] In an effort to retain its relevance and influence in the globalized, market-driven society its reforms have created, the Chinese state has tried to shift its approach from one that emphasizes top-down governmental pronouncements to one that emphasizes the cultivation of "high-quality" (*gao suzhi*) Chinese citizens who willingly accept state discipline and voluntarily participate in the state's ideological projects.[5] Yet a gap remains between representations produced by the state-controlled media in China and the interests, identities, and experiences of the Chinese people who consume these representations.[6] The papers in this volume explore the causes and consequences of this gap.

Drawing on analyses of media images as well as on participant observation among rural migrant Chinese hostesses, Tiantian Zheng's article looks at how these hostesses simultaneously performed and resisted media depictions of themselves as hypersexualized second-class citizens. Media vehicles ranging from pornography magazines and soap operas to state-sponsored education campaigns and academic scholarship portray rural migrant women as sexually powerful but morally weak seducers. During sex work, the hostesses Zheng studied sang provocative songs and dressed and acted like the dependent, hypersexual images the media in China produced about them in order to gain profit and sometimes social and political assistance from their male clients. At the same time, however, hostesses maintained emotional distance from their performances, and made fun of these performances in offstage spaces where they constructed "true" and "ideal" identities that were stronger, more calculating, and more in control than the weak, lustful, dependent characters they played during sex work. By protecting these "true" and "ideal" identities from the identities foisted upon them by the media, hostesses resisted the shame and helplessness often associated with sex work.

Like the hostesses that Zheng studied, the migrant workers at the center of Eric Florence's article seemed ambivalent about the extent to which they buy into media portrayals of their lives. Based on his analysis of letters that were sent to the editors of several migrant magazines but rejected for publication, as well as on his own interviews with rural migrant workers in southern China, Florence examines the relationship between narratives the media in China produce about migrant workers and the narratives Chinese migrant workers present about their own lives. Migrant workers' narratives ranged from affirmations of dominant media discourses about migrant workers, to expressions of disillusionment about such discourses and strategic uses of dominant media discourses to justify protests about the harsh conditions in which migrants labor. Some migrant worker narratives affirmed dominant media discourses by expressing faith in claims about how the successful transformation of the self depends on individual striving, and how the fair and competitive environment of "the South" can liberate migrant workers' potential. Other migrant worker narratives, however, lamented the fact that the dominant media discourse's promises of fairness and opportunity were empty. Some narratives even explicitly demanded that the Chinese state live up to its socialist and/or neoliberal promises. Florence argues that the discrepancies between dominant media discourses about migrant workers' lives and migrant workers' own narratives about their lives contribute to the controversy and sensitivity surrounding issues of migrant labor in China.

The gap between media discourses and lived realities is also central to Rachel Murphy's article, which describes how the media in China help entrench unchallenged power and official abuses while deflecting attention away from the structural failings of the Chinese state. She illustrates this process with a case study of the dissemination, content, and reception of a state-approved anticorruption film entitled *The Life and Death Decision*. This film enjoyed enormous commercial success, as it was widely shown as part of Communist Party anticorruption education efforts. In this film, the righteous cadre protagonist must decide between allowing a whitewash to protect the corrupt activities of his wife and his mentor, or sacrificing his wife and his mentor by revealing the truth and saving China from corruption. After much agonizing, he decides on the latter course. Murphy demonstrates the failure of the film as an anticorruption measure through an analysis of cadres' critiques of both the film's relation to reality and the flaws in the anticorruption measures promoted by the film. Cadres who viewed the film said that no real cadres could be as good, idealistic, or naïve as the film's protagonist. These cadres also suggested that the film's message about the power of virtuous individuals to stop corruption was flawed because reliance on individual virtue was not nearly as effective as reliance on systemic checks and balances, which are lacking both in the film and in real life. Moreover, they argued that the film's recommended strategy of having righteous whistleblowers stop corruption with the help of righteous superiors affords too little protection to whistleblowers to be effective in real life. Murphy argues that even well-intended media productions like this film help to create a gap between official media discourses and lived realities that discourages commitment to a greater socialist good.

Diverse viewpoints are now represented among the media in China, as demonstrated by Elaine Jeffreys, who finds a wide range of conflicting perspectives presented by journalists and commentators in Chinese newspapers, magazines, and websites about the case of gay male prostitution. Based on her analysis of the vigorous debates that took place in these media, Jeffreys suggests that Western assumptions about homophobia in the People's Republic of China (PRC) are unwarranted. Instead of universally condemning homosexuality as many Western observers might predict, journalists and commentators in China have engaged in heated debates over whether the punishment of an organizer of gay male prostitution was overly harsh due to homophobia, which many of them considered unfair and harmful to efforts to move toward a judicial system bound by the "rule of law." Though they drew on international media images of homosexuality as a global phenomenon, Chinese journalists and commentators did not assume (as many Western theorists do) that homosexuality was an inherent yet repressed identity. On the contrary, Chinese journalists and commentators grounded their perspectives on Chinese views of homosexual identification as negotiable within conceptions of "face" and "status" that invoked both the family and the nation as forces that are constitutive of one's social being.

The expansion and increasingly market-driven nature of the media in China has opened up new spaces for audience participation, but Jens Damm cautions against focusing too much on how these spaces serve as arenas for political dissent. Damm argues that Western research on the effects of the internet on China has too often focused on questions of censorship and cyber-dissidents and not enough on how the internet is being used to promote commerce and sociality. The latter are actually more important to Chinese internet users, most of whom are relatively wealthy and well-educated elites who are much more interested in using the internet to do business or socialize than they are in cyber-dissent. The most interesting and important effects of the internet on Chinese society, Damm argues, lie not in the creation of public spaces for political activism, but rather in the creation of public spaces for business, play, sexuality, and private life.

Kevin Latham's article, however, suggests that ostensibly apolitical uses of "disorderly" media such as cell phone text messages, phone calls, faxes, and the internet conceal tremendous subversive potential. Orderly media, such as newspapers and radio and television broadcasts, can be closed down, taken off the air, taken over, run directly, monitored more closely, or guided in some other way. But it is impossible to know when disorderly media will be used, what will be said, by whom, to whom, and for what purposes, and they cannot easily be switched off, controlled, or made safe by centralized supervisory authorities. Ironically, Chinese leaders have focused most of their attention on orderly media, while assuming that disorderly media do not pose a threat because their purposes are primarily social or commercial. Under these circumstances, the flourishing of disorderly media in China means that information is not as much under state control in China as either Westerners or Chinese officials believe.

As it faces increasing competition from other, more democratic media such as short messaging services (SMS) and the internet, even state-run television stations have had to become responsive to audience demands. Yingchi Chu argues that this increased responsiveness is not just a means to increase media profitability, but also part of the Chinese state's strategy for creating "high-quality" citizens who can become active participants rather than passive recipients of state pedagogy. Chu looks at CETV (the leading educational television station in China) and the role it plays in making Chinese citizenship more democratic and participatory. She argues that the reforms the CETV management has initiated contribute to the production of a new kind of high-quality citizen who is able to participate in state directives in a more democratic way than was possible in the past. The Chinese state's new emphasis on cultivating high-quality citizens has resulted in the replacement of monological and voice-over–dominated shows with participatory strategies such as panel discussions, interviews, consumer response, talk-show formats, audience participation, and electronic feedback.

Chinese government officials and international observers alike have recognized the potential that new media technologies hold for democratizing or destabilizing Chinese society. In early 2007, the Chinese government instituted a ban on the opening of new internet cafes and the use of virtual money to buy "material products,"[7] shortly after relaxing and then reinstating a ban on Wikipedia.[8] Meanwhile, Western journalists alternated between condemning the Chinese government for heavy-handed censorship[9] and predicting that restive Chinese citizens empowered by new media technologies such as the internet will soon wrest power away from the Chinese government.[10] Yet a closer look at how Chinese citizens actually use new media technologies suggests that such technologies may not be nearly as subversive as Chinese officials lament and Western journalists hope, nor as vulnerable to censorship as Chinese officials hope and Western journalists lament. The articles in this volume look at how an increasingly demanding and sophisticated citizenry and increasingly open and flexible media technologies and discourses have transformed each other.

The papers in this volume suggest that relationships between Chinese citizens and the media representations they produce and consume are growing more complicated as marketization, globalization, and new technologies transform power dynamics in sometimes unexpected ways. As James C. Scott has argued, dominant discourses can carry an enormous variety of meanings, including those that are used in ways subversive to the intentions of the dominant.[11] The papers highlight the richness, diversity, and sometimes contradictory tendencies of the meanings and consequences of media representations in China, and caution against approaches that take representations created by the media in China at face value as well as oversimplified assumptions about the motivations and agency of players in the complex struggles that take place between the media, the Chinese state, and Chinese citizens.

❑

1

PERFORMING MEDIA-CONSTRUCTED IMAGES FOR FIRST-CLASS CITIZENSHIP

Political Struggles of Rural Migrant Hostesses in Dalian

Tiantian Zheng

LOUD WESTERN MUSIC FILLED MY EARS as I stepped into the "Romance Dream," a karaoke bar in Dalian. Two friends accompanied me, a high-level official in the municipal government and a businessman, both regular customers. At the door, a beautiful woman dressed in a cheongsam greeted us with a bow and ushered us inside. As I made my way into the main lobby, my nose tickled from the pungent odor of cosmetics. Images from an American x-rated video flickered on a wide-screen TV. Over a hundred *zuotai xiaojie* (literally, women who sit on the stage) stood poised in eager anticipation of the male customers. Each woman was heavily made up and fancily dressed, each head topped with an elaborate coiffure. The *Mami* (Madam or "mother"), clad in sheer black tights, selected a dozen of the women by pointing with the antenna of her walkie-talkie and led them into the VIP rooms located on the second floor. There, a lucky few would be chosen by customers as escorts for the night.

Within the fifty-plus years of Communist rule, China's sex industry has gone from bust to boom. During the Maoist era, the Communist Party attempted to level previous class distinctions and promote its egalitarian ideology by eliminating all forms of conspicuous consumption and "reactionary" leisure activities including the consumption of commercial sex.[1] The time, form, and content of leisure activities fell under the scrutiny and supervision of the state, and leisure itself was conceptualized as a form of collective action. In political study classes, unsanctioned leisure activities were denounced as capitalist behavior, and state propaganda advocated the ethos of "hard work and simple living."[2]

Since 1978, the state's pro-consumption stance has opened the way for the reemergence of nightclubs and other leisure sites. To avoid any residual negative connotations left over from the previous era when nightclubs, dance halls, and bars were condemned as emblems of a non-proletarian and decadent bourgeois lifestyle, nightclubs in the current post-Mao period are referred to as karaoke bars, karaoke plazas, or *liange ting* (literally, "singing practice halls"). These new consumption sites are prominent in the more economically prosperous SEZs (Special Economic Zones).[3] Visitors are mainly middle-aged businessmen, government officials, police officers, and foreign investors. Clients can partake of the services offered by hostesses and at the same time engage in "social interactions" (*yingchou*) that help cement "relationships" (*guanxi*) with their business partners or their patrons in the government.[4] Hostesses play an indispensable role in the rituals of these male-centered worlds of business and politics.[5]

The Chinese government calls hostesses or escorts who work in karaoke bars "*sanpei xiaojie*," literally, "young women who accompany men in three ways." These "ways" are generally understood to include varying combinations of alcohol consumption, dancing, and singing. Sexual services are an additional, unstated part of the work these women are expected to perform.

These women, mainly seventeen to twenty-three years of age, form a steadily growing contingent of illegal sex workers. Hostesses first emerged in modest numbers at the end of the 1980s. Their numbers expanded rapidly in the mid 1990s as KTV (karaoke) bars became favored sites not just for male recreation but also for transactions between male businessmen and political elites. Paradoxically, the state agents responsible for policing KTV bars comprise one of the main segments of the KTV bar customer base.

The majority of these hostesses come from China's countryside. Of the two hundred hostesses with whom I worked, only four were from cities. They were extremely averse to exposing their rural origins. At the beginning of my field research, hostesses always told me that they were from large, metropolitan cities, such as Dalian, Shanghai, and Anshan. It was only after becoming close friends that they confided to me that they were actually from rural areas on the outskirts of these cities.

During twenty months of fieldwork in Dalian, I lived and worked with the hostesses as a hostess myself.[6] My research sample includes approximately two hundred bar hostesses in ten karaoke bars. I was intensively involved in three karaoke bars categorized respectively as high, middle, and low class. In the first section of this article, I explicate how rural migrants obtain political identities as second-class citizens. In the second section, I discuss how rural migrant women's cultural and social identities are naturalized as derogatory second-class citizens in the media. Their bodies are a site where the imperatives of state politics become legible. In the third section, I pinpoint the creators of this image and the underlying reasons for the creation. I will explore in detail how and why the agents of the state, intellectuals, and markets exercise the power to establish and naturalize the differences between the rural and urban women. In the fourth section, I demonstrate how such a derogatory cultural representation, while tying the hostesses to the constructed identities in a constraining way, paradoxically leaves some room for the hostesses to maneuver. Specifically, I argue that rural migrant hostesses perform this image as a means to accumulate the accoutrements for legitimate first-class citizenship.

Migration and Political Second-Class Citizenship in Post-Mao Dalian

In 1958, the Maoist government initiated the household registration system (HRS), classifying the national population into mutually exclusive urban-rural categories possessing unequal political, economical, social, and legal access.[7] Rural residents found themselves on the losing end of a heavily lopsided distribution of social wealth. Concomitant with the broad-based restructuring of society, the "peasantry" as a derogatory cultural category but revolutionary mainstay was further refined and concretized.[8] The Maoist government portrayal of the countryside in peasant administrative categories involving the HRS and mobility restrictions reinforced the cultural stereotypes of rural identities[9] and segregated and branded the peasants as the reservoir of backward feudalism and superstition and a major obstacle to national development and salvation.

Relaxation of state mobility controls in recent years has allowed rural residents to migrate to urban regions, where they are now labeled the "floating population" (*liudong renkou*).[10] In search of job opportunities and adventure, these migrants have become the "vanguard" in China's largest population movement since 1949 and harbingers of the market economy in the post-1978 era of economic reforms.[11] As China's engagement with the global economy and experiments with economic reform continue, cities highlight the deepening disparities between permanent urban "citizens" (those with urban residence permits) and migrant populations without residence permits.

Market reform has provided a new and powerful justification for the loosening of restrictions on population movement. Starting in the late 1990s, many advocates of the dismantlement of the HRS argued that labor, as a key input to the production process, must be free to relocate in order to realize the market's promise of enhanced efficiency and optimum resource distribution.[12] These calls for reform have materialized into a program of limited and cautious policy experimentation. In the late 1980s, some provinces started selling local urban household registration cards, known as blue cards or blue seals,[13] to migrant workers.[14] Building on and deepening these reforms, the State Council in August 2001 announced a "township household registration system" that allows peasants who own housing and have stable careers and incomes in a township to apply for permanent residency.[15]

Although the state today tolerates a higher degree of population mobility than under the Mao Zedong government, the urban-rural gap is still the main fault line between rich and poor in Chinese society. Inequalities are perpetuated and even aggravated by post-Mao state policies that transfer the brunt of the state and collectives' tax burden onto poor rural households.[16] This situation has not gone unnoticed by peasants themselves. Since 1985, peasants have launched collective protests against taxes, fines, cadre corruption, and the drastic urban-rural income gap. This unrest points to their discontent with local authorities and constitutes one of the major threats to the Chinese Communist Party's power and stability.[17]

With one hundred million rural migrants on the move, modern China's urban landscape is now faced with the management of individuals who by definition are "outsiders" (*waidiren, wailaigong*).[18] Despite their contributions to local and overall economic growth, migrants encounter severe institutional and social discrimination. Blamed for blemishing the appearance of cities and contributing to overcrowding, migrants have become the scapegoats for a multitude of social problems, ranging from crime to urban pollution.[19] As the "losers" in China's market reforms, migrant workers are denied civil, political, and residential rights.[20]

Women account for over 30 percent of the total number of rural-urban migrant laborers.[21] Providers of labor power for the state, they are important social and political actors. Institutional (such as the household registration system) and social discrimination (such as the derogatory category of migrants) forces most female migrants onto the lowest rungs of the labor market, where they commonly work as garbage collectors, restaurant waitresses, domestic maids, factory workers, and bar hostesses.

Migration and Cultural Second-Class Citizenship in Popular Media

Numerous theorists have examined the relationship between discourse and power. One characteristic of discourse identified in these theoretical studies is the naturalized representation of a social group to produce and legitimate a hierarchical social order. Foucault writes, "Discourses are composed of signs; but what they do is more than use these signs to designate things….It is this 'more' that we must reveal and describe."[22] Defined and viewed as "the political economy of communication,"[23] discourse is the place where relations of power are exercised and enacted. In this section, I discuss the ways in which media discourse defines, constrains, and ties rural migrant women to their labeled identities in the coercive discursive regime that affects "their participation in employment, in development programs and in education in profound and immense ways."[24]

Fertility and Uninhibited Sexuality

Concerned that an oversized population is a major impediment to economic growth and an indirect cause of a myriad of social ills that carry the potential for disrupting social stability (e.g., a tight labor market), the Chinese government has made population control a key item on its agenda of economic expansion and continued political dominance.[25]

The state declares rural women's mobility to be a serious threat to government population policy. Women migrants' "floating" lifestyle puts them out of reach of regular monitoring techniques administered through "grassroots" (*jiceng*) government organs — namely, the countryside's village committee and the city's street office (*jiedao banshichu*). Indeed, ruralists are sometimes even accused of purposefully using migration as a way to escape detection.[26]

The government's anxieties are amplified by the perception that rural women are naturally prone to high fertility. Indeed, the media depict the entire countryside as a hotbed of sexual activity driven by raw, animalistic passions.[27] Some scholars lend scientific credence to this view. Based on a nationwide survey of sexual behavior, prominent sex sociologist Liu Dalin claims that there is not only a higher rate of premarital and extramarital sex but also a greater overall frequency of sexual intercourse in the countryside than the city.[28] Rural women's sexuality is implicated as the critical variable for explaining urban-rural differences in sexual behavior:

> Many [rural women] have precocious sexual biology but late-maturing sexual psychology. For many, the period of sexual hunger is too long, but they cannot get married in time [to satisfy this hunger]. Lovers have frequent contact with each other, but their sexual control is weak. If by chance a male shows interest, the female lover, also in the grasp of "an unbearable hunger," will give herself to the man.[29]

In this passage, rural women's sexual promiscuity is portrayed as a product of their carnal urges. Other scholars emphasize rural women's lack of culture to explain their behavior.[30] These two angles — biological and cultural — are not mutually exclusive but rather complementary: Rural women's bodies intensify their sexual urges at the same time that their lack of culture reduces their ability to resist these impulses. This dual-level explanation reflects larger patterns in the discriminatory representations of peasants and national minorities.

Regardless of the approach, however, rural women's sexuality is always implicated as the critical variable that explains the differences in sexual behavior between rural and urban areas. Studies rarely draw attention to men's sexuality, implicitly taking the level of men's sexual desires as a constant across the urban-rural divide. By assuming that all men are equally likely to engage in sexual conduct, responsibility for the countryside's alleged sexual promiscuity is pinned on the rural woman for failing to fulfill the traditional female duty of policing the body and thereby maintaining the community's moral order. The culpability of those women is extenuated only because they are acting under the influence of passions against which they are culturally defenseless.

Even before migration skyrocketed in the earlier 1990s, the *People's Daily* began featuring articles on the dangers of the unchecked fertility of migrant women. The earliest example — a 1988 article entitled, "Concerns about Over-Reproduction" (*chaosheng de danyou*) — helped introduce the issue to the general public: "They [migrant women] bear children above the one-child quota, disturbing the implementation of the family planning policy."[31] Urbanites suddenly awoke to find that their homes and neighborhoods had become a haven for rural fugitives from state reproductive policies.

These twin characteristics of mobility and fertility are condensed in the epithet "over-quota guerrilla force" (*chaosheng youjidui*) — also the title of a comedy skit featured in the 1990 Spring Festival broadcast.[32] In this performance, a rural husband and wife — performed by Huang Hong and Song Dandan, respectively — engage in a humorous dialogue about their reproductive travails. The husband is frustrated by the fact that among the six children to whom his wife has given birth not a single one is a boy. He vows to continue to enlarge his family until his wife successfully produces a son. To create such a large family, the couple has had to evade family-planning officials by wandering nonstop throughout the country. The names of their daughters testify to the breadth of their travels; each child is named after the place in which she was born, including some of China's most exotic and out-of-the-way locations like Hainandao (on China's southernmost tip) and Tulufan (on the eastern border of Xinjiang). Thus, by the early nineties, the Chinese public was well acquainted with the "problem" of migrant women and the increased rate of their fertility.

In the popular media, violence and sexuality are intertwined in the portrayal of rural women in pornographic magazines sold at train stations. These pornographic magazines are meant to satisfy the sexual desires of travelers and city men and to provide economic profits. Because of the state censorship of pornography, these magazines combine violence (rape, abuse, and crime) and sexual descriptions under the camouflage of "legal education." As McClintock argues, "There is every evidence that where sexual reciprocity is censored, sexual violence prevails."[33]

These magazines contain stories of promiscuous, sexually available, and fallen rural women. One article says that the goal of all rural women in a village is to "make love to every male worker in the adjacent village." The women are said to invite the male workers to sleep with them. One rural woman allegedly sleeps with six men per night; some seduce the workers into a one-night stand just for a meal; others have sixty workers waiting in a line to make love to them.[34] Articles also recount stories of rural women who exchange male rural partners every day or make love to men in public parks. They not only engage in the "mad" process, but also cruelly murder the men's wives. The magazines record stories of rural women murdering other women for a male lover, or seducing every driver who comes to the village. They even wait on the roads, targeting drivers to satisfy their primitive sexual desires.[35]

One article goes as far as to describe a rural woman's pleasurable experience of being raped in the fields.[36] In the story, a strange man forcibly drags the woman into a sorghum heap. At first she impulsively tries to free herself. However, when she sees the beautiful moon and experiences bodily pleasure, she stops resisting and starts cooperating with the rapist. She says, "The moon is so beautiful and the village is so far away. This seems to be the will of God."[37] She enjoys sexual gratification "in the moon and the wild sorghum field." She is even thankful for what the rapist has done to her body. She says repeatedly, "It is so good to have a body." Her intense physical and spiritual pleasure make the rape not criminal, but even acceptable, enjoyable, and pleasurable to her.

This article blends the peasant woman's sexuality with the nature of moonlight and the wild sorghum field. According to the article, this rape scene fits quite well with the woman's belief in the "chaotic female and male sexual relationship." It suggests that for rural women, men and women are not human beings, but merely sexual animals. Because of their alleged enjoyment of rape and abuse, rural women with animal instincts are thus the most ideal sexually available and sexually driven objects for the male readers.

Whereas pornographic magazines depict rural women as promiscuous to stimulate and satisfy male readers' sexual desires, the state media tries to control and manage rural women's alleged unbridled sexuality. A forty-episode TV drama called *Red Spider* provides a lively media education.[38] This TV series relates the stories of the short lives of ten female criminals. These women "used to have their own dreams and ideals, but chose a road to their ruin, for which they were severely punished." This TV drama is designed to "warn women to respect high morals, family responsibilities and social consciences and to lead healthy lives." Female criminals are compared to "red spiders," with "red" signifying "female," and "spider" signifying "poisonous," "dangerous," and "vicious." These women's criminal experiences are dramatized in the play by focusing on their locked handcuffs and tearful confessions before execution.

One of the episodes describes a vicious rural woman named Lan Hua. Lan is bought into her husband's village with 5,000 yuan, and later gives birth to a son. She is involved with a married man, Zhu, from the same village. Because of her extramarital affairs, Lan's husband severely abuses her at home. Unable to bear the physical abuse, she deliberately irritates her husband every day by recounting her sex escapades with her lover. Infuriated, her husband eventually succumbs to a fatal disease and passes away. After his death, Lan murders both her own seven-year-old son and her husband's brother because of their attempts to meddle in her affairs with her lover, Zhu. Irrational and dependent, Lan asks Zhu to take her away. In the end, Lan is arrested and executed because, as a police officer observes, "immoral love leads to death."

In this TV play, Lan is portrayed as a slave to her sexuality and emotions. In reality, this image has become so influential that the Chinese police officer arrested and nearly executed one innocent peasant woman in 1997. Before any investigation or interviews were conducted, this peasant woman was presumed to have conspired with her "extramarital lover" to murder her own husband.[39] After several years of petitioning the Supreme Court, her case was finally cleared. Other recorded cases involve rural women being brutally beaten up or mistakenly arrested by police on charges of prostitution.[40] In these cases, a demonstration of their virginity is necessary for their release. A loss of virginity signifies moral failing and prostitution.[41] Lan's case in this play not only reinforces the stereotype of rural women, but also warns other rural women to protect their sexuality and morality.

Disrupting Urban Family Stability

Migrant women as opportunistic home-breakers represent a special threat to urban society. The media record countless divorces caused by infidelity of husbands with migrant women. Some wives even set out to murder the migrant women who, they allege, have bewitched their husbands.[42]

Migrant and urban women are seen as pitted against each other in a contest over the hearts and bodies of urban men. Reports inevitably side with the urban women while demonizing migrant women as tricky "foxes." In these accounts, the migrant women's overpowering desire for material pleasure and social status makes them likely candidates for urban men's "second wives" (*ernai*). Migrant women are described as "running rampant across the country, disturbing urban men's hearts and creating turmoil in their harmonious families."[43] Urban women are urged to stay alert for signs of their husbands' adultery and to take measures to keep their men at home.[44]

Urban men are also admonished to remain vigilant against migrant women. Reports portray migrant women as the carriers of HIV/AIDS and sexually transmitted diseases (STDs) and the most dangerous and criminal segment of the population.[45] The *Red Spider* television series shows the ill fortune that awaits city men who get involved with migrant women. One episode tells the story of an entrepreneur, Li, who buys a villa for his second wife, Hui. Hui eventually murders Li. The graphic scenes of torture and violence inflicted by Hui forcefully warn urban men to stay away from migrant women.

The fear of marital instability — both real and perceived — has engendered great anxiety and even outright hostility toward migrant women. These sentiments coalesced to push the All-China Women's Federation (*fulian*), other women's groups, and individual irate women to fight for legal penalties against "third parties" (*disanzhe*) — the formal term for mistress — into revisions of the marriage law (2002). Although legislators ultimately rejected the proposed provisions, the Chinese government, through the judiciary branch, has made clear its disapproval of migrant women's illicit relations with urban men. In a series of cases, Chinese courts have supported claims by adulterers and their wives (sometimes even in conjunction) that have stripped second wives of property rights to presents and cash gifts given by male patrons before the dissolution of the extramarital affair. The majority of these decisions are based on flimsy legal reasoning that only serve to highlight the extralegal considerations that inform case outcomes. Indeed, in one such instance, the judge — unable to find a legal basis for his ruling — was forced to rely on the very vague and seldom-invoked principle of "public order and good customs" (*gongxu liangsu*) to justify depriving a second wife of her ownership to property bestowed on her by her deceased lover. (The ruling also blatantly infringes on the deceased's right to dispose of his property postmortem.)

Migrant women are warned to learn from others' transgressions and become respectable candidates for marriage. The TV serial play on migrant women titled *Maids from the Outside (Wai lai mei)* is a major cautionary tale.[46] It contrasts two types of migrant women: pure versus sexually permissive. In the play, Fang sleeps with the leader of her factory for a promotion. In the end, however, Fang becomes pregnant, loses her position, and is abandoned; she has nothing but a protruding belly, a sign of her immorality. Adding to her humiliation, Fang becomes the laughingstock of her factory. Another migrant woman, Xiuying, descends into prostitution. She is severely humiliated in public by a client's wife and eventually ends up in prison. In contrast to these two fallen women, Yulan intensely guards her sexuality. She forbids her boyfriend to even hold her hands or kiss her before marriage. Her repression of sexual desire is awarded with happiness — she is the only one in her migrant group to wed happily. In this play, the portrayal of two different outcomes in the lives of two types of migrant women suggests that only the pure will eventually be qualified to become wives and be rewarded with happy marriages.

The popular media represent migrant women in pornographic magazines as men's easy sexual prey. These magazines include pictures of half-naked migrant women posturing enticingly and salaciously for the male reader's gaze. Both the story and the migrant woman's body on display deliberately make the urban male readers the "surveyors" of the "surveyed" migrant woman.[47] Women are portrayed as objects to be raped, abandoned, and sexually abused as "dirty prostitutes." They are transformed by city men from simple and pure peasant girls into fallen and shameless prostitutes.[48] Their moral degradation is commodified as a selling point — a source of the male readers' satisfaction. This commodification helps instigate and promote men's sexual demands and violence toward migrant women.[49]

Destabilizing the Party

The most common stories about rural migrant women who work as migrant hostesses articulate a crisis of national morality and a political regime in a period of transition. Described as an "unstable element," these rural migrant women disrupt the rhetoric of women as the bearers of traditional culture. Signifying social "vice" and disease, they destabilize social order and wreck urban families.

Not only urban families but also the party and state are seen to be at risk from the transgressive sexuality of rural migrant women. They are believed to be at the core of corruption in China's officialdom. Reports tell of government officials who, to satisfy the insatiable appetite of their second wives for money and power, are forced to embezzle and otherwise abuse their powers of office. One newspaper report alleged that over 60 percent of government corruption is attributable to the sexual entanglements of officials with rural migrant hostesses.[50]

These women's ability to seduce men is described as an almost magical power to enthrall and delude — for example, "the power of female allure" (*zise de liliang*) and "the weapon of beauties" (*meili de wuqi*).[51] According to these accounts, powerful men are the most likely to be targeted for seduction. The rural migrant hostess uses her body to secure favors, ranging from cash gifts to government jobs. This form of exchange — referred to as "sexual bribery" (*xing huilu*) — is seen as even more dangerous than bribes of money. As the *China Youth Daily* reports: "Some leaders and cadre faced with the temptation of money have no problem refusing, but, when faced with a woman's allure (*nuse*), start stumbling over themselves."[52] The article's author urgently calls for lawmakers to stamp out this harmful phenomenon by formally recognizing "power-sex transactions" (*quanse jiaohuan*) as a form of bribery punishable under criminal law.

Reports from newspapers, Party periodicals, and other publications have been compiled into "internal documents" that serve as study materials for weekly political classes organized by government units.[53] Officials are admonished to remain vigilant against the seductive powers of hostesses and to hold steadfast to Party principles of public service and dedication. As reports dramatically illustrate, failure to abide by these guidelines comes at the penalty of ruined careers, broken families, and prison sentences. This reputation has earned hostesses the unflattering title of "beautiful disaster makers" (*hongyan huoshui*) — a concept similar to that of the "sirens" of Greek mythology — who led good men down the path to destruction.[54]

One such example, which made national headlines, involves the ill-fated love affair between a rural migrant woman, Chen Li, and a government official, Jiao Junxian. They first met at a bar in which Chen worked as a hostess. Chen, who is described as always being envious of the extravagant lifestyle of cadres' lovers, supposedly used her womanly charms to put Jiao under her spell. Before long, Chen asked Jiao to find her a job in the government, which he did apparently without any question. Chen was made director of three bureaus (Culture, Broadcasting, and Press) and one department (Propaganda) in the Economic Development Zone (*kaifa qu*). Chen, however, remained unsatisfied. With her appetite for power whetted, she demanded that Jiao assign her peasant relatives to other, highly coveted posts in government units. She soon became notorious throughout the district for her brazen abuse of political office and flagrant disregard for the public. Chen's instant rise to power, however, provoked the jealousy of other local officials. After a failed attempt to assassinate an informant against her, Chen's official misconduct and illicit relationship with Jiao were eventually unearthed. Jiao was brought up on charges of "political deceit" (*zhengzhi qipian*), stripped of his political office and Party membership, and put under house arrest.[55] This and other similar cases were publicized in order to urge government officials to be wary of hostesses.[56]

Image Creators and Control of Sexuality

The state asserts its *cultural* control in what Siu calls "state involution"[57] and constructs a culturally hegemonic urban population by reducing rural residents to inferior second-class status. The power of the state today is thus manifested not only through administrative regulations and policies but also through cultural representations, including ones that relate to consumption and body culture, which generate a rural-urban hierarchy. The state's hegemony is constructed and consolidated through the model of demure, sexually controlled, and modest city women. A hierarchical power relationship between the "self" (city) and the "other" (countryside) is formulated by repudiating the "other" of rural and migrant women. Such a representation confines rural and migrant women to stigmatized and marginalized identities and second-class citizenship, affecting in profound ways their participation in employment, education, and social relations.[58]

Chinese intellectuals have a long historical tradition of appointing themselves as the national moral guardians, ruling women's bodies and sexuality.[59] In the present context, they replicate state language about inferior rural migrant women, legitimizing the image construction with scientific and sociological research about the women's "easily transgressive" sexuality being so dangerous and immoral that it has to be regulated and fought against. With the state, intellectuals thus try to police these marginalized women's bodies and sexuality in order to make the women docile and obedient. In this process women are urged to exercise self-control rather than liberate themselves.

Siu has noted that intellectuals in China are caught in an ambivalent relationship with the state, simultaneously subversive and complicit.[60] For instance, the writer Wang Shiwei contested the party's portrayal of peasants as victims.[61] At the same time, many intellectuals still serve as mouthpieces of the state and claim moral and political authority.[62] Pertinent to the issue at hand, Feuerwerker argues that intellectuals attempt to control and police rural and migrant women's morality and sexuality to constitute their own self-identity.[63] Feuerwerker uses the term "other paradigm" to capture the ways in which intellectuals have objectified and represented women and peasants as "others" — "passive, inarticulate, and even to some extent mindless," bringing to "a final end the obsessive dualistic theme of the intellectual vis-à-vis the peasant in modern Chinese literature," which was "inherited and adapted from the traditional self-conception and role of the scholar-official (*shi*) toward the 'people' (*min*), the fictional self-representation of the writer/intellectual and construction of the peasant 'other' in modern Chinese literature."[64]

The state, intellectuals and market in China all make woman's bodies the site for debates over tradition and modernity. In China, especially in the austere Maoist regime, sexual differentiation was negated and women's bodies served as sites for ideological battles. Any woman wearing a feminine dress in the street was likely to be severely attacked, stripped, and humiliated in public. In post-Mao China, feminists led by Li Xiaojiang rejected the Maoist definition of women as workers and replaced it with the model of essentialized woman. They stress women's basic and fundamental bodily differences (sexual and reproductive body) and glorify the life of the consumer housewife devoted to full-time domestic service.[65] The theoretical works of these feminists appear "as nothing less than the ideological justification for a form of national womanhood that is handmaiden to economic boom and frontier capitalism."[66] They emphasize not only the "holy" role of mother and wife, but also the consciousness of "oriental woman" as "restraint [*kezhi*], steadfastness [*jianren*], reserve [*hanxu*], and dignity [*ningzhong*]."[67] Women's agendas and experiences should be subsumed under nationalist imperatives. As Li Xiaojiang maintains, "The first principle of the founding of the human sciences is the principle of nationalism [*minzuxing*]" — "Her female body is displaced by a nationalist agenda and denied the meaning of its specifically female experience, for the nation decides all the meaning for it."[68]

Intellectuals emphasize hostesses' potential for virtuous motherhood. They perceive these women's morality and sexuality as crucial to the nation because the potential power of their sexual transgression can contaminate national and political purity. Having accepted the party goal of restoring communist values in their research, scholars serve as the moral police and social and scientific authority to regulate the transgressive behavior of rural migrant women.[69] In so doing, they have subordinated their science to the goal of the state. They portray hostesses as pathological and biological "sexual misfits" in the national system, against which a "sexual norm" is congealed and constructed.[70] Such a biological model represents the hegemonic control over hostesses' transgressive sexuality. Foucault maintained that in considering transgressive sexuality one must examine not the "level of indulgence or quantity of repression but the form of power that was exercised."[71] Power is manifested in "medicine and regimentation," Foucault argues: one of the four channels of power he lists as different from "simple prohibition."[72] That is, "Instead of aiming to suppress it, the hegemonic discourse gives it analytical, visible, permanent reality implanted in bodies, slipped in beneath modes of conduct, made into a principle of classification and intelligibility, established as raison d'être and a natural order of disorder."[73] Such a "medicalization" of the "sexually peculiar" or "oddities of sex" relies on the embedded-in-bodies characteristics of individuals and the technology of health and pathology. Hostesses' aberrant sexuality actually becomes a "medical and medicalizable object" that needs to be diagnosed as "a dysfunction or symptom, in the depths of the organism, or on the surface of the skin, or among all the signs of behavior."[74]

Such a medical model is utilized to regulate hostesses' morality and sexuality. This endeavor is justified on the grounds that their bodies belong to the state and their "motherhood" determines their transmission of "traditional" values. Intellectuals thus sustain and regain their precarious political power through controlling rural migrant women's morality. Without questioning the state's prerogative to rule these women's bodies, these intellectuals allow women's bodies to be exploited, suppressed, and subjected to the state-building process.[75]

That the market profits from the perceived urban-rural cultural difference is evident in the pornographic materials and beauty/fashion advertisements that capitalize upon the represented cultural characteristics of rural migrant women. The state and the market both construct and constrain the rural migrant women in a representation that "weaves knowledge and power into a coercive structure."[76] (Intellectuals, as we will see below, play a role in this construction.) Labeled as the second-class Other, the women are constructed as the foil against which the model of the first-class urban citizen is naturalized. Completing this othering process helps the state to maintain hegemonic control. According to Butler,

> [The] zone of uninhabitability will constitute the defining limit of the subject's domain; it will constitute that site of dreaded identification against which — and by virtue of which — the domain of the subject will circumscribe its own claim to autonomy and to life. In this sense, then, the subject is constituted through the force of exclusion and abjection, one which produces a constitutive outside to the subject, an abjected outside, which is, after all, "inside" the subject as its own founding repudiation.[77]

Butler argues that the reification of the subject (gender) is a mere historical process of "reiteration, citation and abjection." The rigid category is stabilized as natural through the act of repeated abjection.

Sexuality is a major theme in dominant Chinese discourses about rural migrant women. The term "migrant women" (*dagongmei*), literally "working little sisters," emphasizes the sexuality and youth of migrant women workers. "Little sister" (*mei*) is a term often used to signify a female lover of low social status who can be easily exploited. In many media depictions of rural migrant women, these women's desire for money and urban status causes them to become sex objects for urban men.

Rural migrant women's sexuality is often depicted as promiscuous and licentious. Reinforcing this aspect of their sexuality provides sexual pleasure for male readers.[78] Detailed descriptions of sexual conduct, visual imagery, and violence in media stories allow male readers to conduct and fantasize the sexual ways in which they could control, exploit, possess, and abuse women's bodies as sexual objects.[79] As Segal observes, "The powerful have always not only sexually exploited the relatively powerless, but also projected sexuality itself on to those they see as least powerful — particularly the apparently dangerous, troubling and 'dirty' aspects of sex."[80] As the objects and the subjects of desire, hostesses are identified with both sexual agency and victimization. They magnify their own sexual desires to manipulate city men and reach their goals, materially and politically. Men's attempts to impose, control, and define their sexuality only highlight men's unsafe and inadequate sexual status: "It seems that men are *least* sure of their power over women, and *most* fearful of women's self-sufficiency and autonomy, precisely in their sexual encounters with them."[81]

Foucault writes that the "policing of sex is an important component in maintaining the unmitigated power of the central state."[82] In its anti-vice political campaigns the state polices migrant women's fertility and sexuality as part of a national project that emphasizes civility and purity. Thus, the state maintains control.[83] According to Partha Chatterjee, the nation is situated on the body of the women as "chaste, dutiful, daughterly or maternal."[84] Women's sexuality and bodies must be kept under strict control because women, as the bearers of national virtue and tradition, metaphorically mark the boundaries of a nation.[85] In China, men's physical prowess and women's reproductive duties are considered their main capacities — an emphasis on "social alliance" rather than sexuality.[86] Women's special nurturing and reproductive role is considered crucial in the transmission of virtues to the next generation and to the moral well-being of the nation.

To conclude, the othering process is accomplished by the marginalization and degradation of the dangerous social group of rural migrant women. In particular, their "threatening" and "contaminating" sexuality and their desire to "occupy" and "transgress" the urban space constitute the state's biggest concern. The state's call for migrants' return to their rural hometowns becomes the central message.[87] When this message fails to work and migrant women choose to stay rather than leave the city, the state has to re-intensify the boundary between the moral, demure, and modest urban woman and the sexually unbridled, rural migrant women.

Performing Constructed Images

As illustrated above, media discourse powerfully locks in rural migrant women as static political and cultural second-class citizens. Do they have any way out? Foucault, Bourdieu, and Derrida remind us that individual motivations count for nil or almost nil in this scheme. Moore, however, argues that resistance does not need to be "discursive, coherent or conscious."[88] In fact, if one cannot resist outside the dominant discourse or structure, one can at least displace oneself within it. Women can refuse the construction of gender by approaching it "deviously and ironically," or "refer to it endlessly," or, a shift in meaning can result from a "reordering of practical activities."[89] One of the major ways to contest the discourse is to interpret and reinterpret.[90] In this section, I argue that hostesses' resistance takes place within this hegemonic structure, epitomized by their performance of the represented images.

Based on Foucault's work, Butler contends that there is no inner essential self; it is only through performance that identities are made in a hierarchical relationship.[91] As such, performance is both a constitutive and political act. More specifically, Butler theorizes gender as a performance or an enactment of cultural norms. In other words, female and male opposition become naturalized and reified as people repeatedly act out, perform, or cite the conventions of maleness and femaleness. Thus, Butler pinpoints the theatrical agency of the drags who, through performing a hyperbolic version of "female," parody the naturalized gender dichotomy and ultimately call it into question.

In ethnographic studies, scholars such as Manalansan,[92] Ruhlen,[93] and Schein[94] use performance theory to highlight the subjects' agency to challenge the hegemonic imperative. Manalansan, in his study of Filipino gay men in the United States, argues that they form varied body strategies around the prevailing Orientalist notions to address and confront Orientalist sentiments, ideas, and images in daily life. Some perform the role of passive Oriental female partners in sexual acts with Caucasian lovers. However, they are not passive or demure partners in everyday life, as one interviewee, Java, points out, "when he and his lover got into fights, his big lover was usually the one in tears afterward." They see their performance as a way to manipulate or "play with the world," to "confuse, distract, and fool the public."[95] Their performance is an everyday struggle and it is "in this space where the oftentimes unnoticed and unwitting acts of resistance occurred." Parallel to the Filipino gay men, the Korean feminists in Ruhlen's study also perform and self-Orientalize the negative characterizations of Orientals with defiant intentions. By wearing the traditional *hanbok* (Korean dress), they shroud their potentially threatening feminist activism under the guise of traditional and properly demure Korean women. As a result, the audience's affirmation will enable them to interrogate and challenge their secondary status. Schein also discusses how the Miao minorities in China perform and celebrate the feminized and traditional image through commodifying and marketing this image. In all of these three cases, disadvantaged subjects, while performing, contest the stereotypes of race, gender, and class imposed upon them to reject second-class citizenship.

Similarly, hostesses perform the constructed negative images imposed upon them as a survival strategy and a means of resistance within a hierarchical relationship. Their performance is a self-conscious negotiation with the hegemonic imperative and a vehicle or space in which to imagine a belonging and a first-class citizenship.

The job of the bar hostess is to serve her clients. In exchange, the client compensates the hostess with money. Within this seemingly simple exchange relationship, however, hostesses are in constant negotiation with male customers. Hostesses attempt to extract from their clients additional benefits that go beyond the basic, flat rate fee for their services. These perquisites include tips and gifts and, most important, access to the customers' social networks.

One of my informants, a twenty-year-old rural woman from Hunan, explained to me that the key to being a successful hostess is the ability to establish a stable relationship with the customer and then to exploit him. To reach this goal, as she and many other hostesses emphasized, the hostess needs to play on the customer's *expectations* and *stereotypes* of how a hostess should act.

Consider this scene I witnessed in a KTV room during my fieldwork: Around twenty women, sent in by Mami, lined up before several male clients in a KTV suite. The male customers, casually sitting on a sofa, inspected the women from left to right, with critical expressions on their faces. Eager to be chosen, the women struck provocative poses to gain the men's attention. They played with hair and winked at the clients. In the middle of this examination process, Mami pulled one hostess over to the front and said, "What about this one? She's got big eyes!" A customer pointed at the woman and said, "Big eyes mean big vagina!" followed by fits of laughter from the other customers. At these words, the woman quietly retreated into the group. This embarrassing remark did not stop Mami. "We also have one with tight buttocks. She will surely serve you well!" She called out, "Come over here, Tight Buttocks! Come to the front, Tight Buttocks!" At these words, I saw a pretty woman in a tight cheongsam move to the front. A male customer raised one finger at her, motioning her to come over. At this gesture, the woman almost leaped to the man's side and hung on to his arm. Another customer pointed at a plump woman in the group and shouted at her, "Hey, are those breasts fake or real?" The hostess responded by gently shaking her full figure. The customer, apparently unsatisfied, turned to all the women and cried out, "Whose breasts are the largest? Who wants her breast to be fondled? Come and sit beside me!"

In this scene, the hostesses perform in a hypersexual manner with provocative poses and salacious winking in response to clients' licentious remarks. Such a hypersexual image projects the rural women's cultural portrait as sexually promiscuous and available. As shown in this scene, one hostess, despite the customer's insulting comments about her breasts, continued her erotic performance to gain the customer's favor. The woman with "tight buttocks" demonstrated her willingness to be sexually dominated by jumping into the embrace of the customer.

To lure clients, hostesses present a hypersexual and lustful image by winking at the clients, wearing revealing clothes, and assuming seductive postures. They purr, laugh, scream, or moan when clients prey on their bodies, and they sing songs to seduce clients and convey their "devotion." For instance, a hostess chose a song titled "Why do you love other women behind my back? (*Weishenmo ni beizhe wo ai bieren*)" As she was singing the song, she fondled her client, leaned her whole body over him, and coquettishly asked him, "My husband [*laogong*], why do you make love to other women behind my back?"

Outside of KTV bars, hostesses send tantalizing phone messages to their clients, such as "Making love is fun. A woman with large breasts is like a tiger or a wolf. A woman with flat breasts has unfathomably superior techniques. Let's make love...." Hostesses commonly boast to each other about the "whore-like sexuality" (*sao*) that their clients love most.

By allowing their bodies to be **sexually fragmented and erotically staged for** marketing, hostesses refuse the state's attempt to regulate rural women's promiscuous and transgressive sexuality and to control their sexuality for purely reproductive purposes. Hostesses perform media images of their hypersexuality in order to extract profit from male clients.

Internalizing the Performance?

Wendy Chapkis argues that the construction of "multiple identities" is a general characteristic of all sex workers ("prostitutes").[96] She argues that sex workers change identities in order to "manage" their emotions in the process of sexual labor. Identity switching allows sex workers to both summon and contain emotions at will. In other words, sex workers' multiple identities function as a defense mechanism to protect themselves from the harmful psychological ramifications of their work.

Like the sex workers in Chapkis's account, the hostesses I knew perform the roles of different characters in the course of serving clients. As Chapkis notes, character shifting is part of a conscious strategy that is linked to the performance of their labor. However, unlike the hostesses in Chapkis's account, the hostesses I knew maintained a stable, unified identity as against their multiple work roles. Therefore, I avoid Chapkis's psychology-based terminology ("identity") in favor of a language of performance ("character").

Do hostesses identify with the characters they act out in their sex work, as Chapkis argues they do? From my observations, hostesses maintain a clear and stable distinction between their "true" self and the characters that they portray as part of their erotic services. Some of the several factors that contribute to this character detachment lie in the objective circumstances of the karaoke bar sex industry; others reflect a conscious attempt on the part of hostesses to distance themselves from the "weak" and "passive" characters of their erotic performances.

While on stage, hostesses must fulfill client expectations of rural women's "nature" by acting out their image as portrayed in state and media representations, but offstage they reverse their position by performing the role of clients. They repeat client's abusive commentary and even reenact episodes of sexual aggression. On a several occasions, I witnessed hostesses remove one another's bras and fondle one another's breasts. Such activities would sometimes peak into mimicked rape scenes. Hostesses would sometimes ride on top of one another, ordering the other to shout and scream.

By parodying the acts that demean them, the hostesses turn the tables and demonstrate the foolishness and ineptitude of the clients. In reducing the stature of the clients and constructing the absurdity of the situation, the women portray themselves as superior. Mimicking their client's sex acts both reflects and helps to create a separate space within which they can construct a "true" and "ideal" identity as distinguished from the characters they act out on stage. By "true," I mean that hostesses subjectively understand their offstage identity as being real *in relation to* the set of characters they portray on stage. By "ideal," I mean that this offstage identity is in many ways preferable to their onstage characters. Hostesses see their offstage self as their true identity because it offers a stronger, more independent self-image than their onstage characters. Thus, the existence of this offstage space serves as the basis for hostesses' interpretation of their on- and offstage selves as respectively fake and real. Below I explore in detail the specific ways in which this understanding takes shape.

Hostesses see character playing as a way to "cheat" (*pianqu*) clients out of more money and acquire extra benefits.[97] I put "cheat" in quotation marks, because this is the hostesses' own construction of the nature of these transactions. The view of clients as "cash cows" to be exploited is a constant theme in offstage conversations.

An alternate interpretation would be that these extra benefits are a proportional compensation for their labor output, a larger than average tip, for example, indicating that the hostess has performed better than average. There are two reasons why hostesses do not adopt this second interpretation or why it is less available as a way of understanding these transactions. First, sexual labor is socially not prestigious, thus negating any sense of accomplishment from doing a "good job." Second, casting themselves as "cheaters" gives hostesses the sense that they have gained the upper hand in a transaction relationship in which they are subject to severe abuse. The idea that they "got something for nothing" is both a source of comfort for the abuse they endure in the course of services and seems to prove that they are still able to exert some measure of control over male clients.

Clients' abusive treatment toward hostesses contributes to the sense that character playing is a façade to disguise their profit-making aims. Clients both physically (pinching, punching) and mentally (denigrating and objectifying commentary) abuse hostesses during onstage services and in their out-of-bar interactions. This treatment naturally engenders resentment and even outright hatred against clients. At the same time, hostesses cannot show any resistance because they have to satisfy clients in order to maximize their profits. The inability to forthrightly give voice to these sentiments leads to a strong sense of division between their true and false selves. As one hostess explained, this condition is the "bitterness" of a hostess's life:

> I don't like men. I hate them. To get their money's worth, they torture you until you can't stand it any more. They curse you and treat you as if you weren't a human being. We have to take all this with a smile. Do you know what kind of feeling that is? Only a hostess can understand. It's like we hostesses have two faces — one real face and one fake face. The fake face tries very hard to cheat men's money. It is all fake.

This quote demonstrates how clients' behavior creates powerful emotions that are denied expression by the economics of the server-client relationship. The disjuncture between what is thought or felt and what is expressed leads to a bright-line distinction between the hostess's true self and the falseness of their character playing — the "two faces" of the hostess.

The following poem written by and circulated among hostesses concisely combines the themes discussed in this section, namely, the falseness of hostesses' performances, instrumental purposes, and antipathy toward clients:

> Entering the karaoke room,
> We smile our brightest smile.
> Sitting by the clients,
> We act as if we are their most obedient wives.
> But as soon as the tip lands in our hands —
> Screw you![98]

While hostesses gain a sense of empowerment from "cheating" clients, they are still at the mercy of clients' whims, as one hostess's comments illustrate:

> If you do not tolerate these small things [i.e., clients' abusive treatment], you will encounter a big mess [*xiaoburen ze daluan*]. Hold your nose and do whatever he says. Always be compliant. Never act against his will. Then, he will definitely give you a 200 yuan tip. Otherwise, you will suffer the worst consequences.

Hostesses reduce characters to a repertoire of acting techniques that are then studied with conscious mental effort. Getting the part down does not mean "becoming one" with the character; it is simply a matter of technical skill. Certain techniques, practiced over and over again, become established "tools of the trade" that are handed down from veteran to novice hostesses. Winking techniques (*feiyan*) are one such example. Hostesses summarize this technique as follows: "Slightly closing your left eye seduces a man's soul. Slightly closing your right eye conveys your devotion. Slightly closing your two eyes means you agree to have sex with him." Thus hostesses encounter characters not as fully fleshed out "identities" as in Chapkis's analysis but as a collection of separate techniques to be studied and applied in their work.

Cultural Legitimacy and Flexible Citizenship

In *Flexible Citizenship* Aihwa Ong delineates the cultural strategy of flexible citizenship of the overseas Chinese business elite.[99] Some purchase houses and send their children to prestigious universities in the United States. Others rely on *guanxi* — personal and kinship networks — to earn rights of residence in Australia, Canada, and the United States. As such, their economic power is converted into social and cultural capital. At times when it meets the obstacle of symbolic racial hierarchies already established in the American places of residence, some use philanthropy, particularly to the arts and to universities, as a strategy to gain social prestige and acceptance and offset white resistance to Asian mobility.

Similarly, hostesses convert their economic power and guanxi with clients to cultural legitimacy and first-class citizenship. Considering their job to be both a sacrifice and a steppingstone to their goals, almost every hostess derives some degree of social and cultural advantage from her relationships with clients.

Such cultural legitimacy includes travel, marriage to clients, further education, and business investment opportunities.

My hostess friend Hong learned English, typing, and computer science from her client boyfriend Chen. Chen even offered her a computer to practice with. She told me that having Chen as a free instructor instead of paying for classes saved her a great deal of money. Ever since she learned to type and send email, we have been using the internet to update one another about changes in our lives. During my research in Dalian, I also witnessed quite a few hostesses who paid for classes to learn occupational skills such as tailoring, hairdressing, and beautification.

Hostesses also enjoy increasing physical mobility. Clients often drive hostesses around the city or take them along on sightseeing trips. Hostess Zhang used to show me stacks of photographs taken in Shanghai, Beijing, Shenyang, and other major cities she had visited. Hostesses not only traveled with clients, but also traveled in groups or at times, alone. During my research in the karaoke bars, four hostesses traveled to Beijing to meet an internet friend who studied at the Chinese Politics and Law University. My friends Huang and Li traveled to Shanghai alone for different purposes. Huang went to temples in Shanghai to pray for good fortune in the New Year; Li went to Shanghai to meet with her hostess friends who were working there. While physical mobility is hard to achieve for most in China today, hostesses' economic power and their relationships with clients give them easy access to travel.

Some hostesses managed to procure first-class political citizenship. It is by no means rare for their clients who are officials to issue them free temporary resident cards or urban household registration cards (*hukou*). This transforms them into legitimate first-class citizens. For instance, my friend Yu went out with a client who was an official. He arranged for her temporary resident card to be stamped for a whole year free of charge. Another hostess, Han, had an urban household registration card issued to her for free. She was then holding two registration cards, one rural and one urban. She was very proud and deemed herself "a very successful woman."

Wealthy clients kept a great number of hostesses and some of these hostesses became not only "legitimate urbanites with urban residency cards," but also entrepreneurial owners of businesses such as sauna bars, gift shops, karaoke bars, and restaurants. Six of the two hundred hostesses I studied were able to move beyond their profession through marriage to their clients. For instance, hostess Han was married to the treasury director of a prestigious hotel in Dalian. Before marriage, Han earned enough money to buy two houses, one for her family in her rural hometown in Heilongjiang, the other in Dalian. She told me that nine people in her family were supported by her income alone: her parents and seven other brothers and sisters. Han gave her brother 25,000 yuan as a wedding present and similar amounts to her sisters upon the birth of their children. She has now been married for more than two years and runs a hair salon bought by her husband in Shenzhen.

Clients commonly introduce hostesses to new job opportunities, including work in other industries such as beauty parlors. While in Dalian, I helped out during the day at a small clothing boutique run by a former hostess, Zhang. At the time we were introduced, Zhang had already been retired from hostessing for a few months. Her ability to open the store and keep it afloat, however, crucially depended on the financial backing of her lover, whom she had met while working at the KTV bar. Money from her lover also made it possible for her to maintain her former fashion habits. Clothing remained a central preoccupation for Zhang even though she was no longer subject to the occupational demands of hostessing. Her particular clothing practices, however, had been altered to fit in with her new environment. Zhang was now surrounded not by other hostesses but by city women who worked in the surrounding stores in the same shopping plaza. Her old wardrobe from her days at the bar would have scandalized these women and instantly revealed her former identity as a sex worker, exposing Zhang to discrimination, harassment, and most likely eviction. The threat of exposure was intensified by the talk of other vendors who claimed to be able to detect hostesses by their unseemly garb.

By looking for those elements that remain constant across these changes, we can tell which aspects of hostesses' clothing are nonnegotiable and therefore most likely tied up with their sense of identity and self. Zhang toned down her look but tellingly without discarding the hostesses' characteristic penchant for foreign fashion. In particular, Zhang switched from the sexy fashions of Korean clothes to cute Japanese fashions.

Zhang would sometimes take advantage of my presence at her boutique to slip out during lulls in business and do some shopping of her own. After one such shopping excursion, Zhang returned dressed head to toe in a cute, Japanese-style outfit. The centerpiece of the outfit was a form-fitting, pink t-shirt with the Hello-Kitty cartoon emblazoned across the chest. Zhang introduced the outfit to the other vendors, emphasizing above all that she was wearing genuine imported Japanese clothes. Her strategy worked. Zhang was awash with accolades from the other vendors. "It's so cute!" (*zhen keai*), they chorused.

Zhang's case illustrates how some retired hostesses are transformed into legitimate first-class citizens through the acquisition of a legitimate economic identity. In this case, her body became a site where appropriate fashion could legitimate her first-class citizenship. As another hostess, Sun, proudly boasted to me, "My boyfriend always says that I do not look like a rural woman at all. When I walk on the street, police cannot tell that I am from the countryside so they don't ask me for my temporary resident card any more." Like other migrants in the city, Sun had previously been required to show her temporary resident card on the street and this caused her to live in constant fear and anxiety. By not being harassed by the police, Sun had passed the most important test of the legitimacy of her first-class citizenship.

Hostesses' resistance and performance of their constructed image during sex work helps them redistribute urban men's political, economic, and social resources and obtain legitimate first-class citizenship. Hostesses fake, ridicule, and rebel against their representation in the media. Indeed, media representations become tools for hostesses' political, cultural, and economic gain. The expressive freedom enjoyed by hostesses in their offstage lives allows them to construct a "true" and "ideal" self. If the onstage hostess is a weak and vulnerable victim, the offstage hostess is a strong and aggressive manipulator. Boundary-maintenance performance in sexual transaction helps hostesses subvert gender and rural-urban political and cultural hierarchy by gleaning first-class citizenship from urban men. The high status hostesses achieve, however, is always at risk because of the entrenched stigma attached to their rural origins and sex work.

ACKNOWLEDGMENTS: I would like to thank Vanessa Fong and Rachel Murphy, who so kindly invited me to produce and present the first draft of this article, and *CAS* editor Tom Fenton for his editorial assistance.

❏

2

MIGRANT WORKERS IN THE PEARL RIVER DELTA

Discourse and Narratives about Work as Sites of Struggle

Eric Florence

IN THIS ARTICLE, I FOLLOW MITCHELL DEAN "in studying the forms of truth and knowledge that "inform and arise from the practices of government," as well as the formation of collective and individual identities, i.e., the "statuses, capacities, attributes and orientations…assumed of…those who are to be governed."[1] I confront the dominant form of cultural construction of migrant workers through the Shenzhen official press with migrant workers' own narratives about their experience of work (*dagong*[2]) in the city as they are mediated through two different sites: participant observation (in-depth interviews with about ten to fifteen rural migrants and short, informal interviews in the streets with about seventy to one hundred people) and a body of unpublished letters to the editor sent to several migrant workers' magazines. Drawing on James C. Scott's suggestion that the dominant discourse may be considered "a plastic idiom or dialect that may carry an enormous variety of meanings, including those that are subversive to their use as intended by the dominant,"[3] I will uncover the ways in which migrant workers' narratives confirm or, on the contrary, contest the pivotal elements of the hegemonic construction. I will examine three different narratives that migrant workers produce about their own lives. These narratives range from affirmations of dominant discourses about migrant workers, to expressions of disillusionment about such discourses, to strategic uses of dominant discourses to justify protests about the harsh conditions experienced by migrant workers.

From 1958 onwards, the Chinese Communist Party (CCP) exercised power over the population through the use of "categories." One set of categories differentiated the agricultural from the nonagricultural population (*nongye renkou* vs. *fei nongye renkou*). Those who were designated as agricultural found themselves geographically and socially immobilized. Another set of categories took the form of class labels. The CCP also enacted a series of class-based and political classifications.[4] During the mass movements of the 1950s, these classifications enabled the Party to distinguish between those who would benefit from its largesse and those who would become the targets of struggles (*douzheng*). Those assigned the lowest class labels could find themselves relegated to the bottom of the social hierarchy, facing statutory or political death. As Jean-François Billeter has noted, for almost three decades after 1949 such classifications exerted tremendous consequences on the position of each individual in the social hierarchy and on the nature of the relationship of each individual with the Party whenever mass movements were launched.

But if the functioning of this highly elaborate system of classifications had very concrete material purposes and effects, the system has been bolstered through the mobilization of a series of narrative techniques that aimed at overcoming, inverting, and reinterpreting reality.[5] This reinterpretation has been of critical importance in creating a "new mythos of the polity, a new moral discourse of the nation, and a new hegemonic interpretation of experience." Some of these reinterpretative techniques ("speaking bitterness," literary campaigns, scar literature, mass movements, etc.) have been claimed and institutionalized by the state. As Lisa Rofel has argued, in the Mao era, the CCP had posited within workers and peasants a "subaltern consciousness."[6] By telling their story, using specific categories of knowledge such as class exploitation, individuals were encouraged to locate themselves with regard to the Party, and so became conceived of as new socialist subjects. This also contributed, as Rofel has noted, to the creation of a new public discourse about socialist wealth that emphasized egalitarianism and collectivism. These narrative techniques were mobilized repeatedly during the Maoist era, accompanying major social and political transformations such as the collectivization of agriculture in the mid fifties.

Since the beginning of the reform era in 1978, some of the Party-state-sanctioned classifications and concomitant allocation systems (of space, goods, labor, etc.) have been altered considerably. On the one hand, with the trend toward marketization and the progressive incorporation of the Chinese economy into global capitalism, certain institutional and ideological constraints have been relaxed, e.g., the household registration system (*hukou*) and regulations on employment and trade. Simultaneously, a culture of consumption has spread throughout Chinese society as a tremendous variety of goods, ideas, values, and information saturated Chinese cities against a background of socialist institutions.[7] On the other hand, the Party-state has been keen to allow greater freedom within the society by enacting a series of disciplinary techniques toward specific groups of the population such as rural migrants. Michael Dutton has termed this the "double pincer" movement:

> Peasants are offered to the market as "free" labour...and simultaneously disciplined into the language of the market by the harshness of the alternative (strict laws against vagrancy, prostitution, itinerant suspects, etc.). This double move is a compact signed under two names: one signs "freedom" (the freedom of movement to places of work, the freedom to buy

and sell one's labour, not to mention the freedom to trade), the other signs "restriction" (restriction upon those who can and cannot remain in the cities, restrictions upon acceptable and unacceptable forms of work).[8]

The relative relaxation of state control over people's lives has not meant the end of ideological control, however, but rather its transformation both in the organization of ideological work and in its content. Not only have the media changed, but the Party propaganda organizations and the nature of the propaganda have diversified as well to incorporate market culture. As Geremie Barmé has stressed, some of the Party's slogans and modes of language have been transformed and its "sign systems have been enhanced and enriched."[9]

Major changes have also taken place in the content of state-sponsored representations and discourse since the beginning of post-Mao economic reforms. The stress on class struggle has been supplanted by a state-sponsored discourse on development that has spread throughout society, taking a variety of forms (scientific, journalistic, popular, etc.). As Ann Anagnost has argued, the language of class has been replaced by a teleological narrative that emphasizes a Party-state-led evolution from backwardness to civilization and from poverty to wealth.[10] The notion of the "quality of the population" (*renkou suzhi*) is at the core of this discourse of development. It allows for a shift from a focus on relations of production during the Mao era to a strong emphasis on productivity in the post-Mao era.[11] Rachel Murphy has noted that part of "suzhi" discourse's power was due to its strengthening of "related systems of valuation already embedded within Chinese development, such as town versus country, developed versus backward, prosperous versus poor."[12] In post-Mao China, suzhi has turned into a core element "in order to enact hierarchization," by measuring and coding people's value and utility for economic development.[13]

Along with the abandonment of the use of the language of class, the historical heroes of Maoist socialism (*gongren*) — formerly represented as the "masters of the country" (*guojia de zhuren*) — have been "de-centered" and "reconstituted" as they are now represented on account of their "low quality" as one of the major hindrances to China's quest for modernization. Whereas in the Mao era job stability and predictability were highly valued and constituted a defining feature of the status of workers, with the economic reforms, forms of work, subjectivities, and attitudes related to flexible capitalism have become more and more prized. With this major representational shift[14] and with the popularization of new forms of knowledge that justify social stratification through an essentialization of the self, how do migrant workers in the Pearl River Delta rationalize their successes and failures and how does this relate to dominant forms of rationalization? I address these and other questions in this article.

Considering Lisa Hoffman's Foucauldian argument about the emergence in post-Mao China of "new modes of professionals" (as well as new subjectivities and new forms of labor) "*in relation* to modes of governing" that draw upon a mix of "disciplinary techniques, political education, and market rationalities,"[15] I first pinpoint some key features of the socioeconomic and institutional context of the Pearl River Delta and some aspects of the disciplinary controls that the Delta environment allows. I then turn to the politics of representation of migrant workers by analyzing migrant workers' letters to the editor of a Guangdong Province migrant workers' magazine.

The Pearl River Delta Environment: Observation, Social Control, and Appropriation

As the region that has been at the forefront of China's export-oriented development strategy, the Pearl River Delta has witnessed a parallel increase in (foreign) investments — mainly of Hong Kong origin — and of rural migrant workers.[16] According to conservative estimates, at the end of the nineties, the volume of the "floating population" in the Greater Delta alone reached 10 million, with the most dynamic areas attracting the greatest number of predominantly young female migrant workers.[17] In many cities in the Delta, those in the floating population frequently outnumber the permanent population. In 1999, the municipality of Shenzhen had a floating population of 2,850,000 people, against a permanent population of 1,250,000, while in 1980, 90 percent of the fewer than 100,000 residents of Shenzhen were holders of a permanent household registration.[18] Following the incorporation of the Delta region into the world economy, coastal cities and provinces, as well as county governments in the Pearl River Delta, have become important players in cutthroat competition to offer the best conditions to potential investors in terms of land and low production costs.[19] As a result, even in comparison with countries such as Malaysia or Thailand, migrant workers' salaries have been kept at very low level.[20] Despite the fact that since the end of the eighties the media have focused greater attention on these alarming labor conditions, local governments have struggled to prevent any deterioration of the investment climate.

The sense we get from the letters analyzed below — as well as from much of the sociological and anthropological literature — is that the institutionally induced instability puts great pressure on migrants and pushes them to accept work at lower-than-expected conditions. Migrants are vulnerable both inside and outside the Delta factories. Within the factories, administrative and fiscal decentralization, key components of economic reforms, means that managers have immense leeway in determining working conditions.[21] Scholars who have studied the labor regimes and workplace politics in the Delta factories have depicted the fierce exploitation and often humiliating conditions migrant workers endure in these factories.[22]

I want to stress here, along with Lee Ching-Kwan, Pun Ngai, and Anita Chan, the fact that the macro-institutional features of the urban environment go hand in hand with such disciplinary labor regimes and allow for optimal appropriation of workers' labor. As has been stressed elsewhere, and as confirmed by my own fieldwork and analysis of migrant letters, the environment outside factory walls in the Delta area is highly unstable and precarious.[23] Pun Ngai observes that in Shenzhen the household registration system and labor control mechanisms are well connected. These mechanisms contribute to intensify and conceal "the exploitation of migrant labourers," she argues.[24] Outside factory walls, migrants face two major forms of vulnerability. One pertains to daily necessities such as shelter; another has to do with controls enforced by public security officials.[25] The high costs that living in an urban setting involves, as well as the difficulties of finding a shelter while looking for work, are reportedly major concerns for migrants. Tamara Jacka has stressed that in the interviews she carried out with migrant workers, most of them "were yearning for a little stability and predictability."[26] Several of the unpublished letters written by migrant workers as well as articles published in migrant magazines and in some mainstream newspapers and magazines, describe the feelings of insecurity that migrants confront on the street due to controls, fines, arrests, and the threat of deportation.[27] Anita Chan notes that among ten young migrant workers she interviewed in Shenzhen in 2002, five had been caught by the police, some of them several times, and nine of them knew of people who had been arrested.[28] Many migrants I interviewed in the streets of Guangzhou, Dongguan, Shenzhen, and Foshan from 2001 to 2004, whether legally registered migrant workers, scrap collectors, or wandering monks, expressed frustration about the prejudice they faced in the city. They felt particularly frustrated about having to comply with all sorts of regulations and having to make payoffs. One worker asked, "Are these streets not large enough for us? Are they, after all, not ours too?"[29]

The household registration system and the host of formal and informal, institutional, and discursive practices that go with it make possible an economy of power. Through a process of *observation*[30] and social control, hierarchies of citizenship are produced and the Party-state is able to treat categories of people in a differentiated manner.[31] The degree of intervention by the Party-state in people's private lives in cities varies according to which population category migrant workers belong. Moreover, the category of "rural migrants" ought to be further divided into smaller and more accurate categories according to their status, the kind of jobs they do and the level of prestige attached to their occupations, the nature of their relationship with officials,[32] their "visibility" in the city, etc. In most Chinese cities, each category of rural migrants has been subjected to a high and differentiated degree of state intervention — both formal and informal[33] — in spheres of residence, employment, reproductive practices, etc.[34] By "externalizing"[35] migrant workers, the household registration system and the several certificates and permits required surely help in implementing highly flexible production regimes.

In the remaining section of this article, I analyze the official construction of the "legitimate migrant worker" in three Shenzhen official newspapers[36] with migrant workers' narratives from a body of forty-one unpublished letters to the editor of a migrant magazine and from fieldwork interviews carried out between 2001 and 2004 in several cities of the Pearl River Delta. I start by describing briefly the main features and content of the unpublished letters. Then I examine in-depth three letters that exemplify different modes of articulation of migrant workers' narratives with the official construction of migrant workers.

Migrant Workers' Magazines and the Characteristics of Letters to the Editor

Before examining the unpublished letters, it will be helpful to address briefly the nature and the status of migrant workers magazines in relation to the changes the press and cultural production have undergone over the last decade. Despite a clear trend in transformations toward marketization it must be stressed that the nature of the principles of news and cultural production have not been altered fundamentally: the Chinese media still retain their role as mouthpiece of the Party.[37] Kevin Latham observes that "one of the fundamental responsibilities of news media is [still] to contribute to social change as desired by Party and government."[38] Still, there has been a tremendous diversification of both the press in its written and audiovisual forms and many daily papers in China nowadays look quite like Western tabloids, with much stress on sensationalism and consumption.

In press organs directly under the supervision of Party or municipal authorities, however, rather bald examples of Party propaganda are still common. For instance, in newspapers such as the *Shenzhen Special Zone Daily* articles on model workers and more generally on spiritual civilization are frequently imposed by Party leaders.[39] Zhao Yuezhi shows that even street tabloids that may seem to deviate from dominant or official norms, actually confirm these very norms, even if not in a systematic manner.[40]

Yet, as Barmé has shown, during the nineties, the lines between "the mass culture suffused with ideological traits that may back authoritarian rule and more traditional forms of propaganda" began to blur.[41] Barmé links this blurring to the emergence of young editors, journalists, and writers and to their ambivalent position toward Party propaganda. Migrant magazines[42] offer migrant workers space to narrate their own often contradictory visions of migration, life, and work in China's cities. And they provide a way for migrant workers to build a collective condition and identity. Some magazines are linked to mainstream newspapers or to government or Party authorities while others may not have such straightforward institutional links.[43] In a certain sense, these magazines face constraints that are similar to those that more mainstream types of popular magazines and newspapers face: they have to be responsive to the market and be attractive to their readership and advertisers, while at the same time they must stick to, at least not move too far from, the Party line, especially on sensitive issues like migrant labor. In my interactions with journalists and editors of such magazines, I could sometimes feel a tension between a sincere desire to remain as close as possible to the issues relating most directly to migrant workers' lives and concerns, as well as to raise and discuss questions relating to social hierarchy or to the prejudices that migrant workers face,[44] and, on the other hand, the political injunctions to stress positive or optimistic dimensions of the dagong experience.

Staff of the magazines and political leaders both agreed that the magazines should have a pedagogical function vis-à-vis migrant workers. The authors of several letters I analyzed expressed the thought that the magazines give "a direction to migrant workers" because, as one writer said, "they allow us to better understand how to protect our human rights and our dignity."[45] Magazine journalists and editors were all conscious of a need to give direction: "to give migrant workers an example of how they should act," they would tell me. They did this by selecting stories that showed the successes of migrant workers or, as negative examples, their failings. The Party-sponsored ideological dimension of these magazines can be perceived in their efforts to "educate people." This function they share with the more mainstream media, emphasizing correct attitudes and stressing the social norms associated with them.

The forty-one letters I analyze here describe the writers' lives and work in Delta cities. Thirty-three unpublished letters I obtained feature poems and short stories that refer more indirectly to the workers' "dagong experience" (*dagong jingli*).[46] Of the forty-one letters under scrutiny, thirty-five were written in 2001 and six in 2003. The length of these letters varies from two handwritten pages to more than twenty pages: a total of 174 pages. The authors of the letters all work in Pearl River Delta cities such as Shenzhen, Dongguan, and Guangzhou. Thirty-four of the letters were written by male migrant workers.[47] This is worth noting because while most surveys show that labor migration in China is predominantly masculine, approximately 60 percent of migrant laborers in the Pearl River Delta are women.[48] Compared with articles published in other migrant magazines that discuss romance and dating practices of (female) migrant workers at length, only a few letters in my collection focus on romance. The fact that these letters were rejected, and perhaps not read by the editors, does not distinguish them per se from published letters. The explanations given to me for the rejections included "poor literary style," the content of the letters not conforming to the editorial line of the magazine, and insufficient time to read all of the hundreds of letters received each month.[49] The value of reading these unpublished letters lies in the greater variety of styles and plots they exhibit. The picture they give of the lives of migrant workers in the Delta is also somewhat darker than the one in the published letters, which editors select because they paint a rosier picture of the lives of migrant workers.

Depictions of painful factory labor, long working hours, instances of prejudice and humiliation in the workplace, and other violations of migrant workers' rights are the central, core elements of sixteen of the letters.[50] Feelings of loneliness, of leading a bland existence, of hopelessness, and fears associated with looking for work in a rather unfriendly environment and with potential failure also stand out prominently in most unpublished letters.[51] Two contrasting elements are also reflected upon in several letters: (1) self-achievement or the wish for it through laboring in the city, and (2) disillusionment linked to failure or to the impossibility of fulfilling oneself or one's ideals. Another theme evident in several letters is that of the marginal and precarious conditions of migrant workers in urban settings, including in the dimension of controls (real or potential) by public security agents, fines, and arrests. Some authors also point to rather complex issues such as the relationship between local authorities, the labor inspection bureaus, and the factory managers.[52]

A dimension that emerges in all of the letters is the constraint of China's rural environment. In nine letters the decision to leave the village is explained as being the consequence of one's family being burdened with heavy debts, and with being unable to pay for education or health expenses.[53] Migration, it is clear from these narratives, is not a matter of free choice. Workers are compelled to leave the countryside because of the conditions in which they and their family live.[54] The depictions of these constraints are not general statements about rural conditions but more a *lived reality* that causes intense suffering. In several accounts, the decision to leave the village is explained both as a choice as well as the result of constraints, as suggested by phrases such as "could not help but to leave the village for dagong (*budebu chulai dagong*)."

Let us now further examine three different narrative modes. Each mode exemplifies a specific type of articulation of the narrative with some key elements of the dominant discourse about migrant workers in the Pearl River Delta.

Self-fulfillment and the Environment

This first narrative mode may be seen as an illustration of a widespread acceptance or "internalization" of the dominant mode of rationalization of social mobility and stratification in post-Mao China. By "internalization," I do not mean to imply complete submission to the dominant discourse.[55] Rather, I suggest that the writers of letters mobilize categories that are central to the dominant discourse and that circulate widely throughout society to explain how (well) they have fared.

In one tale, a young male migrant worker starts by explaining how bitter his first experience of work outside the village has been.[56] After six months searching for work, during which time he almost lost hope, he explains what gave him the strength not to give up: "As I was in the street, I realized that there was nobody to care for me....I am a man, I have got my dignity, my thought, my hopes and promises. I do not believe that it is not possible to create one's own sky with one's own hands." He then writes that in facing the tough and dehumanizing environment of factory work he found the resources to overcome his difficulties:

> To be a migrant worker is really like living a non-human life....You get tired to a point that you do not know what the day is and which year next year will be. The factory I worked in was like that. What was even tougher was that every day you would suffer different kinds of humiliations. But it is precisely in this environment that my world outlook has undergone a fundamental change.

In the next paragraph, he tells the story of a female worker who befriended him and who managed to get a good job thanks to her own striving and self-education in English. She suggested that he too should learn new techniques and knowledge. This friend, the author writes, "said that although she was not really smart, by doing some extra efforts, she would manage to be successful, she just needed to struggle consciously and she would eventually be able to create her own space." In the next sections, the letter writer describes what has changed in his world outlook. He now knows that "the dagong life is a tempering process and the one who goes forward with courage will manage to go against the tide. The weak one will only stagnate. A person cannot endlessly be angry at others, and keep saying that his lot is unfair."

The author concludes his letter by addressing migrant workers as a whole:

> In fact, we, "the nation of laborers," start from much lower than many

people....Those who arrive first are those fighters who go forward in difficult circumstances. They are the champions who deserve to be truly respected and whom we may proud of. The "dagong" [experience] is a wealth. Struggle! Nation of laborers! Life of laborers.

In this letter, as well as in some other texts, the author brings together a number of elements, drawing upon the dominant discourse about Shenzhen, the South, and migrant workers in general. In particular, the writer places his faith in the officially espoused view that the successful transformation of the self is made possible thanks to individual striving, the will to master useful knowledge and techniques; the fair and competitive environment of "the South" can liberate migrant workers' potential. Let us discuss these elements and test them against the results of my fieldwork, the literature on the subject, and my analysis of the dominant discourse on migrant workers in the mainstream Shenzhen press.

Several scholars have stressed that despite the fact that factory work very often involves fierce exploitation, prejudice, and injuries to their dignity, it also means opportunities for greater autonomy and potential self-fulfillment, as well as experiences associated with city life and factory work.[57] My own fieldwork shows that migrant workers often depict migration as a chance "to see the world" (*jian shimian*), "to try one's luck in the world" (*chuang yi chuang shijie*), to endeavor to achieve one's plan, and to fulfill oneself. The vocabulary often used by migrant workers in such depictions of their hometown is one of the "negative potential" such as "cannot stay [in the village]" (*daibuzhu*) and "cannot earn money" (*zhuang buliao qian*). In such accounts the village or hometown is contrasted with "the outside world," which is then the site where one may achieve oneself. One of my migrant worker informants nicely summarized this:

"Once out of the valley, there is a sky." Once I was out, thanks to my efforts, I have been able to find a job in the South....So, I find that in the South, there is a vaster world. This vast universe....When you are in the valley, and you look at the sky, it is so small; once out of the valley, I realize how big this sky is. Then I can fulfill myself.[58]

In my analysis of the representation of migrant workers by the Shenzhen's mainstream press, I found an even greater stress on self-fulfillment.[59] In many articles in the *Shenzhen Special Zone Daily* and the *Shenzhen Evening News*, self-fulfillment is associated with the milieu of competition that Shenzhen offers. The idea conveyed in these articles is that self-fulfillment is made possible mainly *thanks* to the adversity found in Shenzhen and its atmosphere of emulation. These two excerpts illustrate this point:

1. When I arrived in the Special zone, I felt immediately that Shenzhen was a city where competition was widespread; I had the feeling that I was not very capable, that I did not know very much. But the zone gave us an environment to grow.[60]

2. The South is very fair, it has provided us migrant workers with an opportunity for fair competition, so that everybody can stand on the same starting line....The South is a place that polishes people's determination. Over here, there are people who succeed, while others fail; there is joy and

there is sorrow. When I fail or when I am in distress, I really want to go back to my place to spend my peaceful life of the past. But when I think over it: I cannot go back, I should not go back. Because I have understood that I love deeply this warm place the South is ![61]

This idea that Shenzhen offers opportunities that enable the individual to progress and contribute to local prosperity is emphasized particularly in articles on model migrant workers, which have been very prominent in the *Shenzhen Special Zone Daily*, especially in 1998.[62] In one such article in March 1994, ten temporary workers were praised for their outstanding achievements for which they were given a permanent resident permit. The model workers obtained their permits thanks to their "painful labor [*jiannan laodong*] and the exceptional results they had achieved [*chuangzao chude chuse chengji*]." The next section of the article emphasized that "if, as them, you are earnest and pragmatic [*jiaotahsidi*], if you try to learn and make progress [*qiuzhi jinqu*], if you are steady and industrious [*qinfen nüli*], if you make contributions [*zuochu gongxian*], perhaps then one day you too will possess a Shenzhen green card." In this as in many other articles in the Shenzhen mainstream newspapers, we observe the stress on notions such as "painful labor," the qualities of pragmatism, steadiness, industriousness, the will to "learn and make progress," and to contribute to economic development. These are the necessary sought-after attributes and competences that may decide somebody's legitimate claim for permanent residence. In the last section of this article, the authors note that not many workers will be able to get a residence permit because Shenzhen is such a small place. But this, as the author shows, should not prevent workers "from expressing their capacities in the future." The author goes on to say: "What is most important is to use fully the advantageous conditions offered by Shenzhen, to take advantage of one's best years of youth [*dahao de qingchun suiyue*], to learn useful knowledge and techniques. This is the intelligent attitude." The author concludes: "One may not have a Shenzhen 'green card,' but what one can surely not fail to possess is to have ideals and aspirations [*lixiang baofu*], knowledge and competences [*zhishi caineng*], as well as dignity [*renge zunyan*]." Shenzhen — no matter what its size — is thus a place, full of opportunities and challenges, where people are supposed to make the most of their potential.

In the unpublished migrant worker's narrative detailed above and in the *Shenzhen Daily* articles, the mobilization of common or similar values and aptitudes such as the worthiness of the dagong experience conceived of as a tempering process, the will to go forward, make progress, and learn new techniques and knowledge, the importance of industriousness and steadiness, as well as the need to keep struggling on one's own in order to grasp the opportunities offered by this nurturing environment can all be observed. These arguments share an individualization of the reasons of success and failure. They do indeed confer the idea that if one happens to fail, it is mainly due to one's own inadequacy and inability to adapt to the environment, suggesting a quasi-linearity from one's efforts to the possibility of success.[63] Let us note also in the Shenzhen official press a cultural construction of youthfulness as a potential for the development of productive forces and for social mobility that ought not to be wasted away in order to be able to improve oneself and grasp opportunities.

The emphasis on striving, on the individual capacity to take advantage of opportunities, is somewhat characteristic of the kinds of pioneer narratives commonly found among migrants around the world. "Successful" individuals may draw on specific cultural repertoires to make sense, explain, or justify their success and other people's failures. Globalization surely allows for a diffusion of such repertoires around the world, and China is no exception, in the sense that, through the media, through modes of (cultural) consumption, and through migration networks, globalization popularizes models of existence, such as the pioneer or self-made man, that carry strong ethical and symbolic content and may contribute to produce subjectivization.[64] Børge Bakken has documented the vast amount of both Chinese and foreign literature on modernization and on the modern personality, as well as the development of the "study of talents" (*rencaixue*) that has flourished in post-Mao China. Commenting on the Chinese literature on personal improvement Bakken noted the pervasiveness of social Darwinism and the emphasis on values such as striving forward, risk taking, innovation, as well as a necessary and nurturing competition that enhances the will to strive.[65]

Such narratives need also to be considered against the background of great structural disparities between China's coastal regions and the inland areas, as well as between the countryside and Chinese cities. After almost three decades of separation between the countryside and cities,[66] geographic mobility takes on strong cultural meanings, as coming to the city for work also becomes a form of cultural appropriation of ideas and goods related to the city. In such highly social and spatial hierarchicalization, the city becomes an "intense object of desire" and urbanity is conceived of as an "artefact of popular culture and of consumption."[67] It is worth noting that in the Chinese case, the Party-state and the urban elite are deeply involved in the reproduction of a discourse of "lack" and in the strengthening of a "hierarchy of desire" and of "cultural hierarchies of opportunity and stagnation."[68] This discourse of lack needs to be considered as part of the Party-state–sponsored discourse on development. In addition to this, for young rural females, leaving the countryside may be a means to get away from family control, to gain autonomy, and to achieve one's plans in terms of marriage and education.[69]

Furthermore, we need to take into account the weight of thirty years of discourse focused on class struggle and on social equality and the importance of political criteria in deciding limited social mobility. Lisa Rofel observes that as the Maoist class system was repudiated, a new moral discourse on wealth and success that stressed the need to let talents flourish emerged in the reform era. Hence, we need to consider that in post-Mao China, standing behind social comments on and rationalizations of social hierarchy is a criticism of Maoist society. "As a means of radical disengagement from Maoist socialism," Rofel argues, "economic reform is also and most significantly a space of imagination."[70] In this perspective, the rhetoric of "being able to grasp opportunities and learn from challenges" is also very much in line with the ethos of economic reform and more generally with the promotion of market socialism with Chinese characteristics: the process of reform offers opportunities that one ought to be able to take advantage of and there are challenges one should be able to face individually. Some have better aptitudes than others and will benefit more quickly from these opportunities, while those who do not possess the appropriate aptitudes, may still relentlessly learn through processes of migration and work in the city.

The above-cited fragments and many Shenzhen press articles emphasize learning practical knowledge and techniques as a means for self-improvement and social mobility, but in several other tales examined here,[71] the authors explain that the main reason for leaving the village was that they could not continue their secondary school education or they could not afford to enter university. Others explained that they decided to "go out for work" (*chulai dagong*) in order to enable one of their siblings to continue with her/his schooling. Thus, we see how the burdensome constraints of the rural environment bear on the life chances of migrant workers. These letters show that leaving the village for work is not so much a matter of voluntary choice as it is a question of financial limits on further study. Feelings of disappointment, sadness, or frustration at being unable to go on studying and having "to go out for work" stand in stark contrast with the rhetoric of migration as a way to acquire knowledge and skills.[72] An overemphasis on the latter conceals the structural obstacles that block the learning process both in the countryside and in the cities. Fieldwork interviews taught me that "time" is a critical factor: migrants who work twelve, fourteen, or sometimes more hours a day simply have no time or energy to study. One worker told me that once he got a job with regular hours then he could start studying.[73] This "acquire knowledge and skills" rhetoric enables some migrant workers to reconcile elements of their reality and to use ideas about the future to make sense of their "dagong conditions."[74]

The success-through-individual-striving narrative in Shenzhen is linked with the representation of Shenzhen as a model of national economic development. Myth-makers contrast the Shenzhen Special Economic Zone (SEZ) with the "economic failures" of Maoism. George T. Crane notes that even if "corruption is real and failure is common,…the predominant imagery of the SEZs, and the meaning they convey to China at large, is prosperity, novelty and liberation."[75] B. Kjellgren contends that as a city built from scratch and as "a laboratory for economic reforms," Shenzhen has been, more than other areas of China, associated closely with economic reforms, with Deng Xiaoping's thought, and with migrants.[76]

In interviews I conducted in the Pearl River Delta and in the letters studied here, migrant workers criticized the harsh workplace discipline and the prejudice and dangers they faced in the city. Their "love and hate" relationship to dagong is contradictory: freeing them from constraints, on the one hand, but plunging them into harsh working conditions, on the other.[77] Constant striving and perseverance are defining features of dagong and of migrant workers' subjectivities. This is no surprise considering their harsh working conditions and the precariousness of their stays in the cities. What is contested, I suggest, and is part of a process of euphemization of class relations, or the naturalization of power,[78] is the idea that hard work leads inevitably to self-fulfillment and social mobility. The feelings of emancipation and self-advancement commonly associated with migration and work in the city are, as Lee Ching-Kwan nicely puts it, contrasted with "their identities as transient residents victimized by discrimination....From shop-floor work allocation to harassment in public areas, migrant workers harbor a strong sense of being subjugated as secondary citizens." Lee concludes: "Against the official rhetoric that personal capacity and effort determine who gets rich first, the standpoint of peasant workers grounded in their experiences is that market socialism does not bring equal opportunity for all. It is not as fair as the state would like to have them believe."[79]

In the next section, I shall demonstrate how processes of euphemization and concealment[80] manifested through the dominant discourse on migrant workers and "the South" may be contested. I argue that this contestation forms part of a struggle to fix the meaning of dagong.

The "Song of Dagong": Acceptance or Disillusionment?

The second narrative mode I explore here is one that emerges in a letter from a 25-year-old migrant worker from Hezhou in Sichuan Province. He starts by saying that he is looking for a better job and hopes to become friends with other migrant workers who, he says, must "surely be in the same situation as me." He writes that he wants to "end this lonely, sad and tasteless life as a single person" and meet the woman of his dreams. He wishes that all workers be able "to realize their dreams and that the magazine will become more and more successful." He accompanies his text with a "personal file" (*geren dangan*) that includes his photograph, his area of origin, and his age. The following are the main sections of his song, "The Single Love Song: The Song of Dagong":

In this world, rich people are everywhere. Why can I not be counted among them? We run around in order to earn money. It is already a long time since we tasted the bitterness of dagong. Among those who dagong, those who fail are everywhere and I am only one of them. Incomes are getting lower and lower and we have to do more and more extra hours. Each worker needs to be aware of this: for money, you should not be scared of having to pay [*weile qian, bie pa fuchu*].

(*Refrain*) To find a light work, an ideal work, a well-paid work that allows me to get rid of poverty. A job with rights and with a status, a work that would have a name, an advantageous job that enables me to raise my status.

There are so many workers, but only a few are happy. They know nothing but suffering. They have offered and paid their best years of youth [*tamen fengxian le fuchu le meihao qingchun*], but there are only a few fruits.

For money, they are wandering about. It is already a long time since they tasted enough of the bitterness of dagong [*chigou le dagong de ku*]. Among the workers, one finds lost people all around, one can not even find a couple of them who manage to fulfill their ideals. Their burden is getting heavier and heavier, the price we pay is getting higher and higher.

Each worker needs to be clear about this: "dagong" means to be unafraid of suffering.
(*Refrain*)
There are so many workers, those who are well off, one can even not find one among them, while those who have offered and paid their best years of spring [youth] are so numerous. Ah....
(*Refrain*)
Sad people are so numerous. I have to go through this with courage. One ought not miss the opportunities, having paid, having lost one's best years of spring [youth] and to sigh with regret. This sad melody of "dagong," this sincere song of suffering and sadness, who will come sing it with me? Ah....

It is tempting to regard this text as resigned acceptance of the optimistic and often celebratory rhetoric about Shenzhen, the South, migrant workers, and their contribution to the economic development of the region. First, note the repeated contrast between *the rich, who succeed, who are happy* [and] *who are able to fulfill their ideals* and those like himself, who fail and are left with *the bitterness of dagong*. Second, the song's author contrasts the contribution of migrant workers with the little they earn for their labors. Throughout the nineties, numerous articles and books praised the steadiness of migrant workers, their painful labor, and their contribution to economic development and local prosperity.[81] Media representations of migrant workers in Shenzhen were positive: "without these migrant workers [*dagongzhe*] Shenzhen would be an empty city" and "migrant workers are the ones who have shaped the modern city we live in."[82] These differ from assessments of the situation in other Chinese cities, where the focus was on the large masses of city-bound migrant workers.[83]

The *Shenzhen Special Zone Daily* contains numerous articles that emphasize the sacrifices of migrant workers: they pay with their "sweat and blood" (*fuchu xuehan*) and "offer their youth respectfully" (*fengxian qingchun*) to Shenzhen.[84] This latter expression is reminiscent of Mao-era China and the Cultural Revolution (1965–76) when the expression "offering their youth respectfully to the country" (*ba qingchun fengxian gei zuguo*) was used to describe the youngsters who were sent to the countryside to educate the "rural masses" and get educated in return. Articles I studied in the *Shenzhen Special Zone Daily* described migrant workers having to make sacrifices for their company and for the zone. In one article, for example, the author explains that the Zhonghuaren Bicycle Company received a large and urgent order from the world's biggest bicycle retail company in the United States to produce thirty thousand bicycles in three days. Thanks to the perseverance and willingness of the Zhonghuaren workers to endure suffering, the author writes, the factory fulfilled the order on time. The author explains:

[The workers] did not do anything extraordinary, they just offered their youth silently to Zhonghuaren....Yesterday, they suddenly awakened Shenzhen with the sound of their feet; they have created the Chinese miracle [*zhonghua qitji*]. Today, they stepped into the new century. They have initiated a more beautiful and more resplendent tomorrow.[85]

The fact that the company for which migrant workers are striving is called "Zhonghuaren," meaning Chinese people, conveniently elides the interests of the company and those of the nation.

I would argue that the author's use of "to offer one's best years of youth" in "The Song of Dagong" could be an expression of disillusionment or despair tainted with irony. Consider James C. Scott's argument that "practices of domination and exploitation typically generate the insults and slights to human dignity that in turn foster a hidden transcript of indignation." It is also possible that the "subordinate" voluntarily strengthens the stereotypes imposed by the dominant, and that such stereotypes may be seen as a form of oppression or, in this specific case, as a kind of epistemic violence, as well as a resource for the subordinate.[86] According to Scott, the relationship between the dominant and the subordinate is a dialogue in which the dialogue "will invariably borrow heavily from the terms of the dominant ideology prevailing in the public transcript."[87] In my interactions with migrant workers, I have *never* heard anyone use the expression "to offer one's youth" or speak of contributions or sacrifices for the zone, for the company, or for the collective interest. On only one occasion did a migrant worker tell me with sarcasm that migrant workers were "making their contribution to the environment" by cycling rather than riding motorcycles, which, of course, they were in no position to buy. By repeatedly contrasting his own condition as well as that of many migrant workers to the dominant discourse about Shenzhen, I suggest that the author of this text is perhaps reacting to an epistemic violence caused by a discourse that celebrates success through individual striving, prosperity, and local economic development, a discourse that largely plays down the intense suffering the workers undergo as well as the fact that upward social mobility is far from being the rule in Shenzhen.[88] Pun Ngai and others have observed how much migrant workers' very bodies are marked by the Pearl River Delta's harsh working conditions.[89] The unpublished letters under scrutiny here convey a weighty feeling of "suffering applied to the bodies" of these authors.[90] I argue that the author of the "Song of Dagong" contrasts his yearning for greater stability and social mobility, decent working conditions, and revenues with a rhetoric that euphemizes the precariousness and the highly contradictory dimensions of his existence.

I noted that individuals I interviewed similarly address pivotal elements of official or dominant discourse by contrasting them with their lived reality and relating them to structural obstacles.

The Achilles' Heel

The last narrative mode I wish to examine in this article relates to Scott's argument about the malleability of the categories of the dominant discourse and the idea that these very categories may be mobilized by subordinate groups and have their meanings changed in order to back the claims or grievances put forward by the subordinates. More precisely, I want to elaborate on Scott's idea that the "basis of the claim to privilege and power creates...the groundwork for a blistering critique of domination on the terms invoked by the elite" and that any "publicly given justification for inequality thus marks out a kind of symbolic

Achilles' heel where the elite is especially vulnerable."[91]

In "The cry of a dagongzai," a five-page letter to the editor, a male migrant worker from Hunan Province describes his efforts to get justice after having been beaten up in the factory in which he was working in Dongguan. He writes about being turned away repeatedly by several official organs such as the police bureau, the village committee, and the labor and management office. As in many other letters, he situates his own experience in the wider reality of migrant workers: He explains that after suffering the beating, he almost got fired by his boss. His workmates suggested that he should take revenge outside the factory or simply swallow his anger and pain. To this advice he replies: "I can't do this because I believe that our society is a society of legality, I need to use the law in order to obtain justice and protect my legitimate rights." In the next section, he explains that after having been turned away by various officials, he eventually decides to go back to the police office only to be told that his case is "just a minor affair that should not be exaggerated." Reacting to this statement, he writes: "But police officer comrades, this is exactly because you disdain to care for so many minor affairs and that you do not treat them rapidly that it engenders revenge by a minority of people and eventually they become the tricky criminal cases of your enquiries and certificate controls."

In the following paragraph, the author explains that he is then dismissed, with his salary unpaid. He writes: "We, the 'migrant workers' [dagongzhe], while we suffer unfair treatments, while we suffer the deterioration of our environment, is there not a single place where we can call for justice when our person has been violated and when our dignity has been injured? I do not believe it and I do not accept it."

He eventually finds a county government official who listens to his plea. "At that moment," he writes, "I was very moved. There are still good officials in our government." He finally abandons his search for justice, since he needs to find work as soon as possible in order to prepare for his daughter's future and ensure that she can continue her schooling. "Although I did not get a satisfactory end in this struggle," he concludes, "at least the alarm has rung for the employer. We, the 'migrant workers,' shall not retreat, scared by your money and your power. As there is a 'truth among the people,' I wish that you treat your employee with benevolence....One should not abandon one's dignity in order to protect one's rice bowl. One needs to be able to use the law as a weapon in order to protect oneself."

In his final paragraph, the author addresses the attitude of public authorities toward migrant workers:

> I am also saying to our administrative organs, to the public servants who educate the people: raise the consciousness of legality, carry out your sacred function with probity, great efficiency, raise your sense of responsibility. For these workers who have left their fields and their families, who have their blood and sweat flowing on the production line,[92] and who wipe their tears silently for reform and opening, and for the wealth and power of the country, please do more real, concrete and good things [*duo ban yixie shishi, haoshi*].

Let us observe first that the letter writer raises a legal issue through calls for the protection of his "legitimate rights." Legality and the rule of law are after all tenets of the government's claim to legitimacy and modernity in the post-Mao era. Even though the labor conditions of migrant workers in the Pearl River Delta have not fundamentally improved and are in many cases harsh, a variety of official, semiofficial and unofficial organs (labor bureaus, trade unions, legal advisors, NGOs, the media, etc.) have all made substantive efforts to better inform migrant workers about their labor rights and to help them claim such rights. Migrant workers' magazines surely play an important part in calling attention to such issues and they often serve as platforms for migrant workers to express their grievances. In some cases of blatant violations of migrant workers' rights, the media have even intervened to help migrant workers obtain compensation or redress for unfair treatment.

Second, the author's description of the attitude of the police concurs with what many studies on migrant workers in urban China have stressed all along: urban authorities require migrant workers to pay fees in order to be allowed into cities, but they provide minimal services in return. Studies show that when problems arise in urban settings, most migrants feel they have no one to turn to for support and often prefer not to go to the police or other officials for help.[93] This letter is a rare example of an open complaint about public security officers, including migrant workers' magazines.

The last-quoted fragment of the letter uses key phrases from ideology sponsored by the Party-state, including an emphasis on legality ("raise the consciousness of legality"), making sacrifices "for reform and opening" (migrant workers who "have their blood and sweat flow on the production line and who wipe their tears silently for reform and opening"), and national construction and modernization ("wealth and power of the country"). Also included is a reference to a major tenet of Deng Xiaoping's thought, *shishiqiushi* or "look for truth in facts," which in this case encourages officials to adopt a correct and pragmatic attitude and do concrete things for the people. This slogan was first intended to contrast wished-for pragmatic attitudes by officials with Mao-era officials' obsession with ideological factors. In this case, however, looking "for truth in facts" is used to question the way police officers have overlooked the prejudicial treatment of migrant workers.

This migrant letter may also be read as an illustration of some features of what Kevin O'Brien, drawing on James C. Scott, has termed "rightful resistance," or a kind of political contention that entails "an innovative use of laws, policies, and other officially promoted values to defy 'disloyal' political and economic elites...to apply pressure on those who have failed to live up to some professed ideal."[94] The author of the letter calls on the Party to take seriously the implications of its rhetoric about sacrifices, rights, pragmatism, etc. Isabelle Thireau and Hua Linshan, in their work on complaints migrant workers have sent to the Shenzhen municipality labor bureau, show how the quest for a sense of justice is articulated around three principles: fundamental justice linked to the human person; fundamental and founding principles of the official ideology; and the 1995 labor rights legislation.[95] Lee writes likewise that, apart from framing their actions in terms of demands for justice, more and more migrant workers use labor regulations set up by the state to further their claims and interests. As she puts it: "These labour regulations and policies offer workers a new cognitive and discursive resource to frame their claims in state-approved idioms."[96]

How are we to relate these narrative modes with larger processes of redefinition of social stratification in late-socialism China? What can we say about the transformation of the Party-state power and about its effects at the beginning of the twenty-first century?

Conclusion

In this paper, I have compared different ways in which migrant workers' narratives relate with dominant discourses about them and about Shenzhen and the "South." Such narratives include a "migrant workers' affirmation" of the dominant discourse, a "reversed echo" reacting to the epistemic violence of such discourse, and the strategic usage of pivotal elements of the dominant discourse that serve to back a series of claims made by migrant workers. In the two latter cases, it is worth noting that the illustrations of (rightful) resistance to dominant ideas and representations of migrant workers and their environment explicitly address the elite: they are public and *not* anonymous, "they seek rather than avoid the attention of the elite."[97]

Drawing on some of James C. Scott's insights, I have shown that categories and principles that are part of the dominant discourse may be mobilized and reworked in order to question the ruling elite on the very enactment of the principles upon which their rule is grounded. One should note however that within this reworking process, it is the *very categories* of the dominant discourse that are used and sometimes contested or reworked by the subordinates, not alternative categories. As Scott has observed, the capacity "to determine (never entirely unilaterally) what is considered the 'public transcript' [in this case the terms that may be debated openly and what they embody] and what is not,...the ability to choose to overlook or ignore an act of insubordination...is a key exercise of power," hence in this "ideological debate about justice and dignity" migrant workers' speech is checked by power relations.[98] The issue of migrant workers' rights may be discussed in migrant workers' magazines for instance, but to a certain extent and only by using specific terms in the debate.[99] Under the control of the Chinese Communist Party, however, the Chinese media do not dare to frame such discussions in terms of "exploitation" or class, since these categories refer to capitalist societies and the moral foundation of the Chinese communist regime was grounded on a rejection of exploitation and capitalist class relations, as well as on the discursive production of "labor" (*laodong*) as "the principal cultural site for the production of identities."[100] The Chinese state demands that Chinese media avoid the categories that once were central in the Party-sponsored "hegemonic interpretation of experience." This is why labor issues, and more specifically forms of labor such as dagong, are so touchy nowadays, and this also accounts for attempts by the Party-state to fix the meaning of this category and the struggles around it.

I have also argued that the very category of dagong is an important site of struggle for fixing its meaning to specific referents. In post-Mao China, dagong has indeed turned into a site of intense state-sponsored cultural construction partly in order to adapt to the conditions of global capitalism, to try to reconcile such forms of labor with the Party-state founding discourse and identity, as well as to shape an acceptable form of relationship between migrant workers and the Party-state. This intense cultural construction may also serve to dilute the potentiality of class antagonism by euphemizing the meaning of dagong and by expanding the ranges of social groups that are said to dagong.[101] In the dominant construction of migrant workers in the Shenzhen press as well as in some instances in migrant workers' letters, dagong refers to a rather linear narrative line or discursive chain: in the face of a tough, competitive *but fair* environment, striving, hard work, self-sacrifice, suffering, enterprising spirit, and self-learning should lead to self-fulfillment and eventually an improvement in productivity and development. The body and soul of the officially constructed migrant worker are fully turned toward production. He is a "legitimate" Shenzhen person only insofar as he contributes to economic development. He embodies the very defining features of the immigrant as underlined by Abdelmayek Sayad, i.e., "mainly a provisional, temporary, and in transit labor force"[102] whose legitimacy is in need of constant justification and defined by how much they contribute to economic development.

ACKNOWLEDGMENTS: I am grateful to Jean-Philippe Béja and Zhao Yuezhi, and also my colleagues Hassan Bousetta, Sonia Gsir, Emmanuelle Le Texier, and Marco Martiniello for their helpful feedback on earlier versions of this text. Rachel Murphy's very close reading and insightful comments have been very useful in the writing of this article. My thanks also go to Guy Massart for the many discussions we have had on the material presented here and on our respective research interests. I remain the only person responsible for any shortcomings.

❑

3

THE PARADOX OF THE STATE-RUN MEDIA PROMOTING POOR GOVERNANCE IN CHINA

Case Studies of a Party Newspaper and an Anticorruption Film

Rachel Murphy

THIS ESSAY EXAMINES MEDIA ITEMS that are produced by China's Party-state to educate cadres about morality, state policies, and rule of law and to improve the public's perception of its governance. These pedagogic media items include books, newspapers, and films commissioned by the Organization Department (Zuzhi bu) and the Publicity Department (Xuanchuan bu). The Organization Department is responsible for Party recruitment, the discipline of cadres, and the management of good relations between the Party and the masses; the Publicity Department supervises the producers and distributors of cultural products and coordinates public cultural activities. The items are produced by state-owned publishers and movie studios and distributed through state and non-state outlets including government institutions, schools, cinemas, and shops.

Despite state claims to the contrary, China's pedagogic media, I argue, reinforces rather than challenges the norms, incentives, and practices that underpin poor governance, a process that can be described as "organizational involution." Borrowing from Lü Xiaobo, organizational involution refers to a historical process whereby organizations rely on a familiar set of self-perpetuating but inefficient operational strategies that prevent more effective formal and informal norms and practices from evolving. Lü uses this concept to challenge the conventional wisdom that power abuses exist in China because of two decades of market reforms and socioeconomic liberalization. He shows instead that official malfeasance inheres in the routines, rituals, and power relations that are embedded within the Party-state apparatus itself.[1] In this article I extend Lü's analysis by arguing that the pedagogic media is a neglected but hugely important mechanism for sustaining organizational involution.

The circulation of pedagogic media in China reinforces organizational involution in two ways. First, the content of the media products and their methods of distribution buttress the norms and practices that entrench unchallenged power and official abuses within the system. For instance, top-down administrative fiat and efforts to cultivate political patronage dictate the content and distribution of these media products, while the incentive structures of media-production organizations discourage individuals and institutions from deviating from the ideology promoted by their superiors. Second, the focus of state pedagogy on individual failings and the need for self-improvement deflects attention away from those structural failings of the Chinese state that encourage and even compel people to partake in poor governance practices. At the same time, the pedagogic products enable the Party-state to portray itself as the champion of good governance and the rule of law despite its unsupervised monopoly on power.

This essay analyzes how the official pedagogic media promote involutionary tendencies, and then illustrates this process through a case study of a patriotic anticorruption film. The data draws on documents, interview material, and field observations that I gathered in 2000 and 2004 from Rivercounty, an agricultural settlement in Jiangxi Province in China's southwest interior and from interviews with media producers in JA Prefecture, the administrative site in which Rivercounty is located. The newspaper and the patriotic anticorruption film are but two examples of a vast volume of media products produced and circulated within China. Even though such media products represent a substantial volume of economic activity and media consumption in China, they have been largely eclipsed in the scholarly literature by interest in the new and more visible and dynamic processes of marketization, diversification, and liberalization.[2] These neglected media products warrant attention because they are consumed by a vast audience charged with interpreting and implementing central state policy and with carrying out the day-to-day operations of the institutions that make up the Party-state. Before turning to the case study, however, it will be helpful to consider in greater detail the process of organizational involution that underpins poor governance in China as well the relationship between the Party-state and the media's coverage of politics.

Poor Governance and Media in China

Attention to the process of organizational involution in China shows that poor governance is not a problem of failed individual ethics as the Party claims.[3] Rather poor governance is a problem of the ways in which the structures and norms of the Party-state apparatus have evolved. As several Chinese scholars show, poor governance practices, in particular corruption, are produced by the Party-state system itself.[4] According to one of these scholars, Lü Xiaobo, two main sources of norms within the system underpin poor governance. The first is informal ties and practices. These became salient in the late 1950s. At this time, Mao had become disillusioned with the failure of bureaucratic routinization and the emergence of an elite governing stratum, and so he shunned Soviet-type institutions in favor of reverting to an emphasis on using education to cultivate cadres' revolutionary fervor and Communist spirit. But the catastrophic consequences of the Great Leap Forward and subsequent political purges associated with this ideologically driven approach demoralized cadres to the extent that they retreated from Communist comradeship and sought protection in particularistic friendships and informal ties. Even though on his ascension to Party leadership Deng Xiaoping aimed to reinstate modern bureaucratic norms, his economic reforms ultimately worked against this by creating opportunities for cadres to benefit from combining their personal connections with the authority that they derived via their bureaucratic posts.[5] Much to the consternation of the general public, since the mid 1990s the particularistic ties of government and Party officials have often been used in "collective corruption." Such corruption involves networks of Party-state protectors and/or instigators and their associates who operate across a range of governmental and commercial organizations at different levels of the hierarchy and in multiple geographic localities to embezzle huge sums of money.[6]

The second source of involution in the Chinese state comes from the persistence of Mao-style mobilization methods that emphasize the attainment of "core tasks" over and above routines and procedures — so ends rather than means.[7] Since the reforms in 1978, the most important core task faced by cadres in rural areas has been that of demonstrating economic development.[8] Whereas previously governance through top-down core tasks was expressed in the language of production quotas and revolutionary goals, in the reform era it has been cast in the language of scientific and modern management.[9] In both pre- and post-reform eras, cadres' desire to compete with their counterparts in other localities and departments for favor from superiors has fueled exaggeration, fabrication, and cover-ups.[10] In post-reform China it has also prompted the extraction of money from local people and the diversion of budgetary funds to projects that serve parochial interests or else showcase for the benefit of political patrons, rather than meet the needs of local people.[11] The focus on visibly demonstrating the achievement of core tasks and the associated logic of "bigger and faster" are among the deepest causes of dissimulation and poor governance in post-reform China.[12]

Informal particularistic ties and a top-down structure in which officials are answerable only to upper levels creates a system in which everyone must demonstrate their loyalty despite knowing that they are playing games of protection, patronage, and subterfuge. As Lü, drawing on the work of Michael Burawoy,[13] observes,

> Socialism compels compliance to its rituals of affirmation and becomes an elaborate game of mutual pretence which everyone sees through but everyone is compelled to play. The Janus-faced behaviour is a product of a regime that requires utmost loyalty and demonstration of performance.[14]

In such a system, even sincere efforts to establish economic projects or to fight corruption may become distorted and devoid of substance. The gap that arises between values/ideals and reality has two results. First, it diminishes the commitment of cadres to the greater socialist good.[15] Such commitment is necessary if a revolutionary organization is to develop along an *evolutionary* course whereby the revolutionary integrity and discipline of cadres is maintained. In the absence of such commitment disillusioned cadres put the interests of their primary groups above those of the regime.[16] Second, the gap between values/ideals and reality prevents the cadres from adopting rational legal discipline. Such rational legal discipline is necessary if a revolutionary organization is to develop along a *devolutionary* path whereby cadres become modern role-conscious and rule-oriented bureaucrats. Instead, in adapting themselves to the system as it actually exists, these individuals become the "disillusioned, status-conscious and undisciplined cadres" of "an indefinitely patrimonial" *involutionary* regime.[17]

The Chinese Party-state does not allow for any institutionalized or impartial supervision of the bureaucracy that could counter the norms and practices that underpin organizational involution. It is therefore no surprise that rather than acting as a watchdog of the system the media serve as an instrument for furthering the Party's agenda of educating individuals about values and self-cultivation. The crucial pedagogic role of the media creates an impetus for subjecting media employees and media products to strict control. This control is for the most part exercised through ideological education coordinated by the Publicity Department and its subordinate departments at provincial, prefectural, county, and township levels. This ideological education takes the form of ongoing mass campaigns, study groups, criticisms, self-criticisms, and ad hoc instructions. Such activities are integral to the regular functioning of a wide range of societal institutions involved with the production and/or distribution of information. Such institutions include Party schools (responsible for short-term cadre training), middle schools and high schools, research institutes, mass organizations (including the Women's Federation, the Communist Youth Corps, trade unions, neighborhood committees, and village self-governing committees), media agencies, and publishers and the military.[18] The Publicity Department also coordinates the ideological education of people who have specific vocations such as state functionaries, chief editors, and news staff, with poor performance sometimes resulting in their dismissals. This control by the Central Publicity Department has been so penetrating that it has been described by a former Chinese professor of journalism as "a dark empire in which the rays of law do not shine" [and] "the stumbling block in the cultural development of Chinese society."[19]

The executive complement to the Publicity Department in the print sector is the State Press and Publications Administration (Guojia xinwen chuban zongshu), a ministerial-level agency established in 1987 with corresponding agencies at provincial and municipal levels.[20] The Administration issues guidelines about news management and occupational codes and requires the registration of all publications and all journalists. This bureaucratization enables publications and publishers to be regulated by the apparently impartial and apolitical logic of professionalism and procedures, a handy pretext for closing down or consolidating wayward agencies and reining in unruly editors.[21]

Clearly, little media coverage of politics in China falls outside of Party-state control.[22] This control is so pervasive precisely because it does not involve simple censorship. Rather it entails mobilizing the media in the service of the

Party-state's pedagogic governing strategy. By focusing attention on the ethical failings of individuals, particularly those at lower levels, this governing strategy deflects attention away from the system's failings. Yet it is precisely the system and its inadequately supervised monopoly on power that ought to be the focus of media attention because, as several scholars and foreign journalists have argued, this lack of supervision and lack of accountability to the people enables China's governance problems to continue.[23]

A Party Newspaper

Party newspapers are managed by Party Committees at different levels of the state apparatus. Their purpose is to educate readers about official ideology and policies. At the national level, the *People's Daily* is the most famous Party newspaper. At provincial and prefectural levels all Party committees produce their own dailies. This section considers the example of the *JA Daily*, which is a newspaper for JA Prefecture. A small paper, it produces four sheets or eight sides of text six days per week and employs ten journalists. The following discussion considers how the *JA Daily*'s content, news-gathering process, and distribution all reinforce the Party-state's unchallenged monopoly on power, contributing to organizational involution.

The content of the *JA Daily* reinforces the Party-state's monopoly of power through both bottom-up and top-down dynamics: upper-level bodies send down guidelines about the ideological and policy content of each issue while lower-level institutions use the newspaper as a forum for winning the favor of superiors by showcasing their compliance with the central Party line. The Party Committee at the same administrative level as the newspaper adheres to instructions from higher level Party Committees in determining the appointments of key editorial staff as well as in delineating editorial guidelines and priority news topics. The Party-state also uses the newspaper for its continued management of the economy through mobilization-style decrees: in accordance with directives from Party Committees and other institutions, key pages of the newspaper are given over to publicizing these decrees,[24] which often appear as transcripts of speeches by national, provincial, prefectural, and even county leaders. The number of such decrees has increased with successive years of fiscal and administrative decentralization. This increase has occurred because various bodies at different levels of the Party-state apparatus have felt the need to issue their own decrees to help them achieve targets for economic growth, modernization, and social stability.

Other more local news coverage appears on subsequent pages of the newspaper and is compiled with the help of county-based informants who are often cadres in township and county publicity bureaus. These cadres may write the articles themselves. Many pay to attend newspaper agency writing courses. Alternatively, for bigger stories, such as the opening of the Rivercounty suspension bridge, local cadres may invite a journalist to visit. Outside journalists also visit when they want to clarify the details of a submitted story or when they are assigned to cover an example of political or economic work in a stipulated locality. The articles that cadres facilitate earn not only political merit, which advances their own career evaluations, but also merits for the work units, which receive the positive publicity. Most articles in the *JA Daily* describe exemplary projects (*dianxing*) that "showcase" how individuals and institutions have achieved political and economic successes. The tremendous pressure on contributors to show that the local governments from which they hail have satisfied all manner of top-down policy requirements and targets means that even though there is bottom-up reporting and professional training, the newspaper seldom voices local interests or investigates local concerns. Where local interests are voiced in letters to the editor, the emphasis is on isolated quality of life issues such as rubbish on the streets or the price of electricity rather than on critiquing policy and implementation.[25]

Stories produced within the confines of these top-down political structures are invariably dry, formulaic, and exaggerated. But as Edward Friedman argues, and as I learned myself from a county official, readers learn how to read between the lines.[26] For example, one county official in Rivercounty told me that although an article praised a township government for using mediation work and economic projects to resolve social disorder and clan fighting, it was nevertheless possible to infer that the particular township was experiencing severe unrest. Not only do readers look between the lines, they also use their understanding of the political imperatives that inform showcasing reports to question the claimed achievements. As an example, whilst in Rivercounty in August 2004, I came across an article in the *JA Daily* about a new public multimedia education center for reproductive health operating in the county's temple gardens. Hoping to visit the center, I showed the article to my mentors who had been dispatched from provincial-, prefectural-, and county-level institutions to accompany me. Their first thought on reading the article was that the education center might not exist. As it turned out, no one in the temple grounds or Rivercounty had heard of the center. I was later told that the center was a large empty room and the person with the key was away. Local cadres were similarly skeptical about economic growth figures reported in the newspaper and explained to me that these are not exact figures but merely an indication of general trends. Notably, many county-level cadres also told me that when they wanted "real" news they turned to the web.

If the Party newspaper does not report "news" then what is its function? As already mentioned, it is to guide cadres in producing their own political and economic achievements in line with policy priorities. Some articles do this by flagging changes in policy direction. For instance, even though the reproductive health media center in Rivercounty was elusive, the article nevertheless signaled to township and county governments that they should start shifting from a focus on enforcing birth-planning quotas to a focus on providing family planning services, information, and resources for clients. Other articles provide township and village cadres with information that can be used in advancing general state policies on economic modernization and development. One example is the column that appears on Wednesdays on page three advising rural cadres and farmers about new crop varieties and how to plant them. When in 2000 the central state realized that its previous meddling in grain markets had caused prices to fall and farmers to shun grain production, its concern was to reduce the area of land under early rice cultivation, so page three featured information about cash crops. Then in 2002/03, in the face of grain shortages, the *JA Daily* ran stories praising county cadres who had stimulated the enthusiasm of the farmers for producing bumper rice yields and page three articles gave advice about how to ensure a good harvest. Notably though, at no stage did any of these articles challenge how the Party-state uses its monopoly on power by criticizing or debating the impact of fluctuations in central agricultural policies on the welfare of people living in villages.

The extent to which the content of Party newspapers reinforces the Party-state's monopoly on power is influenced by local social and economic conditions. In agricultural localities such as JA Prefecture the Party newspaper limits its content to that suggested by the Party. In contrast, in coastal regions such as Shenzhen, Party newspapers offer their readers more varied content. This difference between Party newspapers in the interior provinces and those in the coastal provinces became particularly stark from the early 1990s onwards. This was the time when media decentralization permitted lower-level Party-state institutions across the country to establish their own media enterprises. It was also the time when fiscal decentralization required that media agencies become financially self-reliant. In the coastal regions these changes pushed cash-strapped Party newspaper agencies to respond to the opportunities presented by the fact that their localities were characterized by diverse social and economic interest groups and populations with burgeoning consumer power.[27] They therefore allowed satellite publishers to found popular newspapers and magazines under their auspices. The Party newspaper agencies were then presented with the problem of trying to compete with the newspapers of these satellite publishers for advertisers. This impetus led them to make the content and format of their own newspapers more attractive to readers and to increase their number of pages. According to its chief editor, the *Shenzhen Daily* deals with competition from satellite publishers by adjusting its content so that only the front pages are a Party newspaper, while the subsequent pages are a market newspaper.[28]

Although the pressure to generate revenue has also affected Party newspapers in interior agricultural localities, and their advertising departments have worked hard to solicit advertisements from companies selling agricultural inputs, medicine, and tobacco, the content of these newspapers has nevertheless remained limited to an uncritical communication of the Party's policies and actions. Why has the content of the *JA Daily* looked to satisfy the Party rather than the market? The reason becomes clear when we consider the following notice issued by the Rivercounty Publicity Bureau under the title "Promoting the Construction of Civilisation":

In order to grasp the important political work of subscribing to Party newspapers and Party magazines for the period of 2005, on 28 November 2004 the Rivercounty Publicity Bureau completed the task of subscribing to the "five newspapers and three publications" (*wu bao san kan*). In carrying out this work task, the bureau persisted in prioritizing subscriptions to Party newspapers and publications above all others. It expended all effort in taking the initiative to achieve results in expanding the scope of the subscriptions and collecting the subscription funds. It carried out the subscription work along the lines of private subscription with public subsidy (*si ding gong zhu*). All people subscribe to the *JA Daily*, the *Jiangxi Daily*, the *JA Evening News* and *Monthly Comment*.[29]

In 2004 this subscription work of the county bureaus covered a range of institutions such as village and township government offices, schools, hospitals, and public security bureaus and gained for the *JA Daily* a weekly circulation of 300,000 copies. This is despite central state decrees in both 1992 and in November 2003 banning compulsory newspaper subscriptions! The compulsory purchase of the newspaper is itself a key illustration of how the political system is hijacked by its own tendencies toward organizational involution — in this case, cash-strapped institutions feel obligated to please and financially support their superiors.

Not only is the monopoly of Party-state power expressed through the compulsory dimension of the sales of Party newspapers, it is also expressed by the compulsion involved in cadres' reading of these newspapers. In Rivercounty, at the county and township levels, the County Publicity Bureau issues self-study journals to cadres. The cadres use these journals to record their thoughts about policy documents and Party newspaper articles, relating the content to their own work on a weekly basis. The cadres are even assigned quotas of how many words to write, with the amount increasing with rank. At periodic intervals random samples of these journals are collected by the Rivercounty Publicity Bureau and Organization Bureau for inspection. At one of my visits to the Rivercounty Publicity Bureau in August 2004 around fifty of these journals were laid out on the table for inspection by a team visiting from the prefectural-level Publicity Bureau.

Clearly, the content, newsgathering, distribution, and even reading of the *JA Daily* all fortify the Party-state's monopoly on power. But it is precisely this monopoly on power that needs to be supervised and questioned if governance is to be improved. Rather than acting as a vehicle for reinforcing the rituals, norms, and incentives of the system that underpin organizational evolution, in my view the newspapers would serve governance better if they were to voice local concerns and interests, critique policies and their local impact, expose showcasing and dissimulation, and respond genuinely to the needs of readers. In enhancing their accountability to local people, such an approach to reporting could counteract incentives for officials to showcase to superiors.

Party newspapers are just one example of official media that are produced for circulation within the Party-state apparatus. As mentioned in the introduction to this essay, other official media include books, music, and films. Considering more than one kind of media is helpful in assessing the extent to which the paradox that official media underpins poor governance is a systemically entrenched characteristic of the CCP's pedagogic mode of governance. Subsequent sections consider the use of a film, *The Life and Death Decision,* in the anticorruption education of cadres.

An Anticorruption Film: *The Life and Death Decision*

At the time of its release in 2000, *The Life and Death Decision* (Sheng Si Jueze, hereafter, *The Decision*) was exceptional for being the first film in China in ten years to portray a provincial-level cadre facing corruption charges. The film is typical however of a much wider body of films called "patriotic films" (*aiguo pian*) that the Party-state has produced for explicitly pedagogic purposes.

In this case study I examine the film's content and mode of exhibition to argue that *The Decision* contributes to the maintenance of the Party-state's unchallenged monopoly on power and its organizational involution. First, I consider how the film's content contributes to a wider state-directed discourse about corruption that deflects the supervisory gaze away from the system and toward individual consciousness. More particularly I show that one strategy for directing the gaze to the individual involves invoking common assumptions about gender in ways that naturalize a patriarchal and patrimonial form of rule: the Party-state educates each person just as the household head disciplines each family member. Next, I draw on ethnographic observation from Rivercounty to consider how the distribution and exhibition of the film affirms the top-down authority of the Party-state and its right to compel individuals to partake in its pedagogic activities. First, though, I review briefly the film's plot.

The Decision tells the story of Mayor Li Gaocheng who returns from one year studying at the Provincial Party School to find that over a thousand workers from a major state-owned factory, the Zhong Yang Textile Factory, are lodging a petition at the municipal government. The workers are angry that the factory is to be sold and that many are to lose their jobs or have not been paid wages or pensions. Mayor Li discovers that the leading cadres in the factory, whom he himself had promoted, are corrupt: they have channeled profits and state loans into subsidiary enterprises that they set up to augment their personal wealth and to employ relatives. A further revelation is that Li Gaocheng's wife, burdened by her parents' medical and funeral costs and tutor's fees for their mentally handicapped daughter, has accepted money from the directors of Zhong Yang. Most alarmingly, Li's mentor, the deputy secretary of the Provincial Party Committee, is revealed to be the main instigator in the network of corruption and his adopted son is one of the key strategists.

For much of the film, Li Gaocheng is unaware of the web of corruption that surrounds him. But Li becomes increasingly concerned as mounting circumstantial evidence suggests that he is protecting corrupt elements in the factory. When a colleague, Yangcheng, encourages him to initiate an investigation into the textile factory, Li mistakenly suspects him of being a political rival intent on ruining his career. But Mayor Li eventually recognizes that Yangcheng is upright and has only the integrity of the Party at heart. So against the wishes of his mentor and facing obstruction from the factory cadres, he orders an investigation into the factory by an external working group.

The shocking findings of the investigation force Li to decide: allow a whitewash and protect his wife and his mentor, or reveal the truth and save the Party and nation from corruption? After much agonizing, he decides on the latter and urges his wife to confess her crimes to the police. The deputy secretary of the Provincial Party Committee responds to the disclosure of corruption in Li Gaocheng's family by convening a meeting. Li is not invited to this meeting. But at the last minute, the Party secretary of the Provincial Party Committee, Mr. Wu, arrives from out of town accompanied by Yangcheng. They insist that Mayor Li be permitted to explain himself. In a rousing speech Li discloses the details of the whole sordid affair, including the involvement of the deputy secretary. The film ends with scenes of the key culprits being arrested and a ceremony that marks a new dawn for the factory.

Naturalizing Patrimonial Governance through Gender

The Decision exemplifies the ways in which Party-state propaganda portrays official corruption and official malfeasance not as an indictment of the system but as a justification for the Party-state's continued authority in coordinating the education and surveillance of individuals. This discursive innovation whereby the Chinese state is the source of the solution rather than the problem is articulated through increasingly sophisticated propaganda techniques. In the case of *The Decision* the producers use shared cultural values and everyday assumptions about gender to make their narrative amenable to a favored kind of interpretation,[30] namely, that all too often bad elements in society take advantage of domestic hardship or a weakness to compromise the wives of leading cadres. The social order naturalized in the film and accepted by many cadres is therefore one in which Party members must discipline family members just as a paternalistic state must educate the people. In Party newspaper editorials, *The Decision* is accordingly referred to as a "warning education film" (*jingshi jiaoyu pian*) that teaches "a person how to be a person" (*jiao ren zuo ren*).[31]

The theme that paternal authority must be exercised over individuals is stated explicitly in the film's climactic scene where Mayor Li addresses the Provincial Party Committee and admonishes himself for his neglect of family matters. The need for paternal authority is also reiterated in several Party newspaper editorials. For instance, a commentary on the film in the *JA Daily* says:

> At present an outstanding problem in the uprightness and discipline of cadres is that some irregular people use a time of hardship facing the spouses, relatives or dependents of leading cadres to bring the relatives and the cadres themselves down into the water. Party members should be alert to this kind of problem....Cadres must not only have high expectations of themselves. They must also strictly require that their dependents and others by their side are upright when dealing with power, money, leisure, and friends and relatives.[32]

In a similar vein, an editorial in a national publication, *Beijing Youth Daily* states:

> Life problems led Li Gaocheng's wife to crime....Many dishonest people use the hardships of some leaders' spouses, relatives and dependents to seduce them and drag them into the water. Outside a Nanchang cinema, the wife of one bureau level cadre explained: "*The Decision* has given us

all a wake-up call. As cadres' dependents we must learn the lesson from Wu Xiezhen and help individuals within the bounds of honesty, but definitely not within the bounds of corruption."[33]

The actions of the Publicity Department and other Party-state institutions in naturalizing a social order based on patrimonial authority is most particularly demonstrated in the ways that *The Decision* contributes to a wider media discourse about women precipitating the downfall of men. This discourse has gained ascendancy in Chinese society in the wake of several high-profile corruption cases involving officials' wives and girlfriends and following an avalanche of official and unofficial media representations of such women. One *Jiangxi Daily* article that appeared alongside a review of *The Decision* is titled "Beautiful Women and Corrupt Officials." It reads in part:

> The phenomenon of beautiful women accompanying corrupt officials is increasing by the day. Three high-level leaders sentenced by Provincial Peoples' Courts are Chen Xitong, Hu Changqing and Cheng Kejie. Chen Xitong's lover was He Ping, Cheng Kejie's lover was Li Ping and Hu Changqing had several extra marital affairs including with some prostitutes.... Corrupt officials hanker after "state power and beautiful women." But these beautiful women know their value and they demand fine clothes, apartments, villas, and cars. This means that corrupt cadres have to increase the extractions that they obtain through their posts, so they must accept bribes and move property to safe havens to keep their women in a luxurious lifestyle....As the grip of beautiful women over corrupt officials tightens they get ever bolder in their corruption.[34]

The theme of women compromising male officials also features in salacious sexual stories that appear in pop-trash magazines, most of them the publications of revenue-generating entities attached to Party newspaper agencies.[35] The perceived association between women and fallen men is so pervasive that cadres are relatively easily persuaded by the Party-state's perspective that corruption results from the inadequate paternal supervision of individuals. This is suggested by an opinion expressed by several Rivercounty officials following their viewing of *The Decision* — that wives should be instructed not to meddle in their husbands' work!

Another way that the producers naturalize a patrimonial focus on individual consciousness is through the use of gender in characterization. One aspect of this involves dramatizing the relationship between the protagonist and his wife to highlight the hero's personal qualities. Portraying Li's private life helps to give depth and substance to his public persona because the private domain is associated with authenticity and being one's self.[36] As an example, Li is always caring, steadfast, and decent in the home setting, even refusing his wife's offer of divorce, which would prevent him from being associated with her ruined name.

A second aspect of characterization pertains to the ways in which in political dramas in general, the primary role of the female protagonist is to elucidate the character of the male lead. For this reason, the producers of *The Decision* invested much attention to delineating the attributes of Mayor Li's wife. In the novel and the original screenplay, his wife was portrayed as a "mother tiger" (*mu laohu*), but the script editors decided that on reflection it would be inappropriate for a man of such sound Party character to have an unpleasant woman by his side.[37] The actress was therefore instructed to play the role as "a virtuous wife and honest mother" (*xianqi liangmu*), a quality that the actress You Ling notes corresponds with her own personality traits.[38] Various scenes depict her bringing soup to her husband, preparing a birthday dinner for him, and nursing their child. By his own emotional admission, it is Li Gaocheng's failure to supervise these domestic events that results in his wife's caring eventually extending to unwitting crimes.

A second theme of corruption — collective corruption (*jiti fubai*) — is also narrated in the film through gender, in particular through the construction of an opposition between domestic feminine purity and political male sordidness.[39] In political dramas, the protagonists in villainous networks are usually men who wheel and deal in public settings like boardrooms and restaurants where the motifs of suits, handshakes, and close-ups of faces with steely expressions are common. These characters use the language of reform to package plans that enable them to siphon off money whilst attributing losses to the harshness of market competition. Agency, plotting, and instrumentality characterize their interactions. This male collective corruption therefore differs fundamentally from the naive failings of Li Gaocheng's unvigilant wife.

The scenario of the individual male hero pitted against a coterie of plotting villains is an established component of political drama narratives and lends itself to the Party-state's agenda of encouraging attention to individual character rather than to systemic failings. In the case of *The Decision* it is the strong Party spirit (*dang xing*) and conscience of Mayor Li Gaocheng that cause him to thwart the clique of villains rather than protect his wife and prosper. Chinese newspaper commentaries about the film tie the qualities and fate of the individual protagonist to those of the nation.[40] One Chinese commentator on a law website writes:

> If the soul is polluted then a person is not a person and that would be the ultimate tragedy. In the life and death decision, the fundamental decision is not the value of the existence of the individual but whether or not the Chinese race will be glorious and grand on the world stage.[41]

Other commentaries recommend that cadres use the film as a mirror to reflect on their own actions because society needs more Li Gaochengs.[42] Yet others assert that like Li, each person will at some time face a life-and-death decision of whether to be a Han hero or a selfish cowardly devil.[43] Here, a symbolic excess is at work in the figure of the male political hero — a relationship between the individual and the nation whereby personal qualities do not just enhance but actually represent idealized political values and a national character.[44]

In official publications Party commentators proudly proclaim that in tackling topics such as corruption, *The Decision* demonstrates the increasing openness and democratic progress of Chinese society. At best though, this is only a partial truth. As this section shows, such self-congratulation is largely undeserved because increasingly sophisticated propaganda devices naturalize a patrimonial and paternal form of authority. And it is exactly this form of patrimonial and paternal authority that needs to be challenged if the systemic norms and incentives that underpin organizational involution are to be thwarted.

The Exhibition of a Pedagogic Text

Even though a textual analysis of *The Decision* reveals that propagandists are using ever more subtle production techniques, attention to how the film is exhibited suggests that the Party-state nevertheless wishes its pedagogic role to remain explicit. The Party makes its pedagogic activities explicit because it is only through the public display of pedagogy that it is able to dramatize itself as the crusader against corruption. The exhibition and consumption of the film therefore reinforces the Party-state monopoly on power because it incorporates the cadres by requiring that they publicly affirm their loyalty to the Party-state and its ideology.

Following the first few months of its release, *The Decision* attracted considerable attention in the national and international media for its box office success. It was hailed as the largest grossing domestic film in the history of ticket sales in China with both domestic and international commentators noting that the film had taken in more than 1.6 billion yuan during the first month of its release in August 2000.[45] These commentators explained the popularity of *The Decision* with reference to its glossy production values, claiming that its success challenged the conventional wisdom that only Hollywood blockbusters could make a stir in China's long-stagnant film market.

But in lauding the market competitiveness of *The Decision*, these observers overlooked that the pedagogic purpose of the film entailed an administratively directed mode of exhibition and the compulsory attendance of cadres. County-level organization departments and publicity departments supervised the screenings of the film, while county film companies, executive work units under the jurisdiction of county publicity departments, organized the logistical side of the distribution and marketing. The film companies' employees visited township and state work units in their counties, and all units were required to purchase a quota of tickets. Half the revenue from the ticket sales accrued to the provincial film companies, for reel hire. County film companies retained the remainder to cover wages, rent, equipment, and maintenance costs. In Hubei Province, in a move that reinforced the public association between gender and the need for patrimonial paternal authority, leaders even arranged special screenings of the film for the wives, secretaries, and drivers of cadres.[46]

When I saw the film in Rivercounty in October 2000 it was together with around three hundred village, township, and county cadres who had filed into the general hall of the People's Government Guesthouse. At the front of the hall that morning was a small stage, and above it a big red banner on which white characters proclaimed: "Rivercounty's Screening of the Anticorruption Film *The Decision*." The county government Party secretary opened the event with a short speech delivered in an official and staccato diction that echoed the content of Party newspaper editorials. He welcomed the audience and then proceeded to stress that only a minority of Party members have problems with corruption while the majority are honest. He urged the viewers to reflect on and implement the principles of Jiang Zemin's "three represents."[47] And he reminded them to teach their spouses, children, and relatives about what they had learned from watching *The Decision*. He also praised the film for its artistic, educational, and entertainment value.

The Decision in Rivercounty existed alongside numerous other pedagogic texts that included cadre handbooks, study session documents, Party newspapers, television programs, and wall slogans. Most particularly, the film was explicitly used as teaching material in a cadre education campaign called the three stresses" — study (*xuexi*), politics (*zhengzhi*), and a healthy atmosphere (*zhengqi*).[48] The three stresses campaign (*sanjiang*) collectively educated cadres in small study groups at the levels of the prefecture, county, and township. The cadres discussed theoretical documents such as Jiang Zemin's "three represents" and analyzed real life official corruption cases, including that of the former deputy governor of Jiangxi Province who on 3 August 2000 became the first provincial level cadre to be sentenced to death. They also wrote self-reflexive essays on their own morality, ability, industriousness, and enthusiasm (*de, neng, qin*, and *ji*) and solicited criticism from their peers. These groups were known as "democratic life groups" (*minzu shenghuo hui*). In Rivercounty, the role of the film in cadre education was featured on the local news. Cadres were shown entering the county guesthouse to watch *The Decision*, with the voice-over narrator iterating the official line that the vast majority of cadres are upright, but that in a complex society, individuals need to reflect on their character and remain vigilant.

The language used in *The Decision* necessarily reworked and reproduced concepts and words from the wider body of pedagogic texts. This flow of phrases across texts exemplifies Michael Schoenhal's argument that political language involves a kind of verbal condensation whereby phrases are impregnated with definite meaning and resonance, their rhythm and symmetry encouraging repetition, memorization, and acceptance.[49] One example is the phrase, "*yao che de che, yao zhua de zhua, yao sha de sha*" — "expel those who must be expelled, catch those who must be caught, and kill those who must be killed." This was stated by the provincial Party secretary in his address at the hearing of Li Gaocheng as well as by Li Gaocheng himself. The saying was featured in a popular soap opera screened in Rivercounty in 2004, *The Women behind Corrupt Officials,* and it was also used in a televised pronouncement by the then premier Zhu Rongji about a high-profile corruption case involving customs officers and the Yuanhua Export Company in Fujian Province. The phrase is often paired with another one — "the cadre mainstream is good" (*zhuliu de ganbu shi hao de*) — the overall warning being that the few bad apples that wreak such damage will be dealt with harshly.[50] The gravity of the threat posed by these corrupt elements is represented in yet another common phrase, "*hui dang, hui guo*" (destroy the Party, destroy the nation). This is frequently counterposed with statements about the need to maintain vigilance in order to *jiuguo jiumin* (save the nation and the people).[51]

All these phrases featured in a televised address by the then governor of Jiangxi Province, Shu Huiguo, which was subsequently published on the front page of the *Jiangxi Daily*.[52] Invoking state nationalism, an ideology whereby the interests of the nation are defined in terms of those of the Party-state,[53] Shu argued that corruption was just one kind of long historical struggle fought by the Chinese Communist Party, others being the fight against Western imperialism and corrupt lifestyles, and feudalism. In this political discourse far from conceding that the Party-state system has generated official malfeasance on account of its involutionary characteristics, the Party-state instead champions itself as the defender in the crusade against failed individual ethics.

The theme of the Party coordinating the struggle against failed individual ethics is exemplified in the following excerpt from a *JA Daily* commentary about the film that urges people to exercise surveillance over individual cadres at all levels:

> The film lets people see the resolve of the Party to fight corruption and this has steadied their confidence and caused them to self-consciously throw themselves into the fight against corruption, forming a solid anticorruption base among the masses, a huge social network of surveillance.[54]

This discourse about the need for the masses to exercise surveillance over local cadres is accompanied by media reports of cases in various townships and counties where, emboldened by *The Decision*, people lodged complaints against officials. In one county in Guangdong Province, for example, a cadre apparently levied tens of thousands of yuan to build a big cemetery but inspired by the film, the people rallied to stop him.

When I returned to Rivercounty in 2004, *The Decision* had been formally honored as a national pedagogic text. The Organization Department, the Publicity Department, the national ministries of Education and Culture, the Central State Office of Civilization, the State Administration of Radio, Film and Television, and the Communist Youth League had included it in their list of one hundred patriotic films suitable for the moral education of China's youth. Practically this has meant that schools and other youth organizations have purchased DVD copies of the film. The status of *The Decision* as a patriotic film also means more screening opportunities: there is an official guideline from the Publicity Department that when county film companies organize village screenings, a patriotic film must precede an entertaining one.

Patriotic education films such as *The Decision* are evidently important in top-down anticorruption campaigns. By viewing these media in orchestrated settings, the cadres visibly act out their compliance with Party ideals and authority. They are willing to do this because the campaigns provide an easy opportunity for them to showcase their loyalty and their enthusiasm for fighting corruption. For resource-poor agricultural localities, participating in such campaigns is also an inexpensive way to demonstrate political achievements to superiors. The entire pedagogic mode of governing therefore entails compulsion, dissimulation, performance, and obsequiousness, all practices that underpin organizational involution. So, ironically, rather than supervising the Party-state and its exercise of monopoly power — the true source of corruption — multiple facets of the distribution and exhibition of the Party-state's pedagogic products fortify the system's involutionary norms and practices.

Pedagogic Media and Cadres

Cadres are highly conflicted in their responses to propaganda materials. On the one hand, they are loyal to the Party-state and accepting of its messages. For example, the cadres I met in Rivercounty believed that the Party-state needed to oversee economic development and that individuals' failed ethics were responsible for poor governance. They also believed that the intentions of the central authorities in conducting pedagogy were good. In this respect they accepted the common view encouraged by the media's focus on local-level institutions and individuals that it is wayward organizations and lower-quality persons rather than the system itself that is to blame for governing anomalies. On the other hand, the cadres were cynical about the state and criticized its messages. For example, they observed the gap between the Party's claimed achievements and the situation on the ground.[55] And they doubted that pedagogy was sufficient to stop corruption. This conflict in their responses to the propaganda produced a mind-set of simultaneous compliance and disillusionment: a kind of tension that reinforces tendencies toward involutionary behaviors.

Why is it that cadres were loyal to the system and accepting of the propaganda? One reason was that they felt that the performance of their loyalty to the state was necessary for the accomplishment of their personal, professional, and political goals. Cadres accepted the state's right to compel them to participate because choosing to be excluded would mean losing their foothold in the system that confers status and a livelihood. To take the example of the *JA Daily*, even though local cadres did not relish reading the newspaper, they all strived to express the correct political attitude (*biaoxian*) by producing their own showcasing projects, courting journalists to report on successes, and performing diligently in their political study classes and journal writing. Similarly, in the anticorruption campaigns, the cadres were all anxious to show that they deplored corrupt actions.

But it would be too cynical to suggest that the cadres were simply duplicitous in performing their belonging to the Party-state. Like all forms of ritual, campaign activities involve bracketing out time and space so that codified actions and language that would seem out of place or false in everyday life become meaningful and acceptable.[56] The faithful participation of cadres in study groups and campaigns meant that such activities had become part of the regular work of their institutions. As any scholar who visits China frequently will attest, some form of official study is often underway. When I was in Rivercounty in 2000 the cadres were studying *The Decision* while on my return in 2004 the cadres were studying, watching, and writing about *Hello, Little Xiaoping* (an affectionate name for Deng Xiaoping), a documentary produced by the Jiangxi Party Research Office, the Jiangxi Party Committee, and the Jiangxi television station to commemorate one hundred years since the great leader's birth. Cadres have come to accept that these campaigns are an integral component of their work.

In the process of participating and affirming their belonging to the Chinese state, cadres inevitably internalize many of its perspectives. This is in part because the campaigns encourage people to make a connection between their own experiences and the political worlds represented in the propaganda. One example of an activity in Rivercounty that encouraged people to make such a connection concerned the use of *The Decision* to mobilize people to submit complaints anonymously against their superiors for the attention of an external *sanjiang* working team. In one township I visited, much to the delight of township employees and village cadres, a large number of petitions forced a township head to publicly account for his gambling habit. Such discursive and performative strategies not only enable people to vent their grievances but also direct their attention to the individual failings of a few bad apples rather than to any systemic failing.

The increasingly sophisticated content of the propaganda media also makes the cadres more receptive to the Party messages. This sophistication is manifest in two respects. First, as can be seen in the case of *The Decision*, the producers use ever more nuanced narratives and glossy production techniques: in fact many cadres in Rivercounty said that they had enjoyed watching *The Decision* because it was entertaining, suspenseful, and moving. Second, propagandists use a diverse range of media channels that traverse the official and market divide, thereby making their messages ubiquitous. For instance, in popular soap operas such as *Absolute Power* (*Juedui quanli*) handsome actors portray cadres who attend study meetings and write reflective essays in ways that naturalize patrimonial authority. In the film *Hello, Little Xiaoping*, the glamorous songstress Dong Wenhua[57] sings the soundtrack *Springtime Story,* which is featured in karaoke bars and television variety concerts, so listeners are reminded in multiple locations of the national leader's contribution to their growing prosperity. Finally, in patriotic films, stars from China's celebrity culture play lead parts and give interviews in both official publications and glamour magazines about their roles. In these interviews the actors often draw explicit parallels between their own virtues and those of their hero characters in ways that reinforce the Party line that people imbued with the Party spirit and Han Chinese virtue (one and the same) pursue a selfless and righteous path. This has strong appeal to audiences because it encourages them to make associations between the values espoused in the film and the individual celebrities who they know to be real people and who they trust and admire. In Rivercounty, I even heard cadres praise one of the leading actors in *The Decision*, noting that he had spent much of his youth in rural Jiangxi. This is an example of the kind of connection that viewers make between characters in the film and real celebrities with whom they feel an affinity.

Despite widespread acceptance of the Party-state perspective, however, there is considerable cynicism about the system and criticism of propaganda messages. The cynicism and criticism arise because although cadres in Rivercounty accept aspects of increasingly sophisticated media messages, like the interpreters of media texts everywhere,[58] they are far from being the passive recipients of propaganda: they use the propaganda texts to criticize the efficacy of a pedagogic approach to governance and to highlight aspects of the system that do not live up to the ideals in the media representations.

The ways in which cadres criticize the system and key propaganda messages can be seen in their comments following the viewing of *The Decision*. Most of their critical comments in relation to the film pertained to the characterization, the storyline, and the representation of the system. To begin with characterization, cadres questioned the personal qualities of the hero and by extension the dispositions of leading cadres. They noted that Li Gaocheng could not have been so naive. He surely must have realized the value of the bonsai pot plants that his wife was collecting. He must have been aware of the costs involved in hiring a home tutor and a nanny. He must have had some inkling of his wife's actions because husband and wife do not divide their affairs so clearly. He must have realized that the hostesses in the nightclub were prostitutes. As mayor of the city, he must have known the extent to which a major contributor to the municipal tax coffers, the Zhong Yang Textile Factory, was struggling financially. His absence for a year at the Party school was no excuse for this ignorance because the financial situation of the factory could not have changed so dramatically within the space of a year. And finally, to survive in politics, a person cannot be so innocent and good.

Cadres also used aspects of the film's storyline to question the efficacy of state pedagogy in reforming governance in the absence of systemic changes. They argued that despite all the newspaper and television talk of people needing to uphold a correct legal perspective, the law still did not address the problem of corruption. They explained that if a Party member has a corruption problem, the procedure is for the internal Party Discipline Inspection Commission or the Procuratorial Department to take charge of any investigation. Then when a decision is made about the presence or absence of wrongdoing, the Discipline Inspection Commission or the Procuratorial Department deliberates on whether or not to hand over the case to the judicial bodies. When a case involves a leader at a certain level, the investigators commonly proceed with extreme caution. The process involves extensive deliberation by individuals at various levels of the Party-state apparatus before a file can be sent to the peoples' procurate. In the few cases where it is decided that a corruption case requires an answer, the officials in the Procuratorial Department must first report to the leadership and ask the Party committee or the Discipline Inspection Commission if and how to proceed. The matter is then treated not as a crime to be assessed before the law, but as an internal Party matter to be investigated and dealt with by the Party Discipline Commission. It is usually only in cases where a high-ranking official has fallen foul of internal political maneuvering that s/he is likely to face severe penalties such as a long jail term or death sentence. Otherwise the penalties tend to be limited to criticisms, black marks in dossiers, being moved sideways, minor demotions, or fines.

The cadres also criticized the system of justice that was endorsed by the film. In this system, justice is obtained by individuals seeking the intercession of an upright official who holds a higher-level post.[59] This is a customary notion of justice, one that has recently been institutionalized in China through the creation of a Petitions Administration — though earlier in 2003 the showcase nature of this administration was exposed by the passing of a regulation forbidding petitioners from crossing administrative boundaries and therefore from ascending administrative levels until they had first had their complaint heard, processed, and ruled upon (a process that could be stalled indefinitely) within the administrative jurisdiction of their place of residence. The idea that social justice is guaranteed by good Party officials is implicit in the slogans on the billboards that advertise *The Decision*: "a battle between good and evil" and "the triumph of the Party character and conscience." Moreover, the importance that the state places on encouraging acceptance of the Party as a repository of justice is demonstrated by the producers' conscious manipulation of the storyline. In the original screenplay, Li was to be sentenced to prison but the film producers later changed this because they wanted to send out a clear message to viewers that goodness and uprightness triumph over evil. Yet as Rivercounty cadres noted with reference to *The Decision*, a foundation for seeking justice that depends on the intercession of honorable superiors affords too little protection to subordinates and whistleblowers. Indeed Mayor Li was only able to survive because the corrupt superior was the deputy of the Provincial Party Committee rather than the head. And if it had not been for the saving grace of an honest superior who had returned in time for the hearing, Li Gaocheng would have perished.

These criticisms resonated with criticisms that these same cadres made of the many gaps between propaganda and reality. Examples of these gaps are manifold. For instance, there is a big difference between the actual and the represented relationship between the cadres and the masses. On the one hand, newspaper articles praise exemplary townships in which the cadres and the masses work together to build socialism. On the other hand, cadres in Rivercounty are now so alienated from the masses that unless the cadres arrive at the gates of a village in a posh car the villagers are likely to doubt that the person is an official at all. The gap between ideals and reality has two kinds of effects. First, the purpose of the pedagogy can be said to mobilize individual agency to bridge the gap between ideals and reality and this reinforces the Party focus on individuals: that the cadres are to use their own work and vigilance to improve political and economic reality. Such an emphasis on individual agency resonates with a wider pervasive and persuasive neoliberal discourse whereby people must rely on themselves (*yi kao ziji*), find their own place (*zhao ziji de weizhi*), and realize their self-worth (*shixian ziwo*) by using hard work to bring forth achievements for themselves and their communities. Yet the gap is more forceful in fueling widespread cynicism. As Ann Anagnost observes: "The representation of the model makes reality look even more rotten by comparison."[60] The cynicism that arises contributes to a rotting of the system from within. This is because cadres think that as everything in their environment is false and manipulated, each person must look after her/his own interests, even if this involves using unchecked power over subordinates to pursue career advancement and money.

While it is potentially radical that the cadres find fault with the system and its pedagogy, the system itself remains relatively protected from scrutiny. This is because the cadres do not identify the system itself as the *cause* of official malfeasance. As discussed, the sophistication of the media products and their resonance with everyday life make the cadres more or less accepting of the view that the Party-state is trying to improve society. At the same time the cadres' own public involvement in the production and exhibition of the media texts makes them accept the power relations that belonging to the system embodies. Hence, in the medium term at least, the Party-state is likely to get away with responding to governance problems by continuing its practice of tweaking at the edges of the system,[61] sometimes increasing horizontal supervision, sometimes decentralizing, other times recentralizing, and oftentimes conducting pedagogic campaigns. But in the absence of a more open media and competitive local elections to increase independent supervision of officials and enhance their accountability to local people,[62] the simultaneous causes and effects of organizational involution such as political patronage, cadre cynicism and indiscipline, the diversion of resources to parochial projects and interests, and dissimulation in reaching top-down targets are likely to persist.

ACKNOWLEDGMENTS: The author is grateful to Tom Fenton, Vanessa L. Fong, Vivienne Shue, and participants in the conference on "Media, Struggle and Identity in Twenty-first-century China," Oxford, Institute for Chinese Studies, September 2004, for invaluable substantive and editorial feedback.

❑

4

QUERYING QUEER THEORY

Debating Male-Male Prostitution in the Chinese Media

Elaine Jeffreys

IN AN ARTICLE ENTITLED "TALKING SEX," Dennis Altman contends that the problem with queer theory is that it has failed to imagine itself outside of the "Iron Triangle of London, Paris and New York." The "development of genuinely new regimes of sexuality and gender," he continues, "seems more likely to emerge from Rio, Manila and Soweto than the hyper-academized hothouses of western theory."[1] Putting Altman's utopian gesture to some better and future sexuality aside, the point to note is that scholars have queried the queer tendency to mobilize an idealized image of "the West" as a yardstick by which to measure the perceived progress or failings of gay and lesbian cultures around the globe. As Grewal and Kaplan explain, metropolitan studies of sexuality in non-Western contexts have tended to reproduce the tradition/modernity divide by reifying Euramerica as the site of the modern, and hence progressive, social movements, while other parts of the world are presumed to be traditional and oppressive, especially with regards to sex and sexuality. Such studies have thus failed to consider how different nation-states, forms of government, economic formations, and consumer and media cultures, produce and uphold diverse sexual subjectivities and communities in an increasingly globalized world.[2]

The tendency of metropolitan studies of sexuality to reify Euramerica as a unified site of "modern freedoms" owes much to the apparent and perceived lack of sexual rights in many developing countries. The NGOization of social movements — in "the form of the emergence of global feminism as a policy and activist area"; struggles by gay, lesbian, and other activists; and the imperatives of HIV/AIDS prevention programs — has seen the extension of Western liberal conceptions of human rights to the rest of the world.[3] Although some postcolonial and queer theorists have criticized the neocolonialist implications of this particular form of globalization, for valorizing Western-style sexual liberation as the "the only possible progressive trajectory," and for constructing universal and potentially oppressive feminist and gay subjects, such criticisms tend ultimately to be rejected on the grounds that they sound too close to arguments against a universal respect for human rights and therefore offer support to traditional and repressive regimes.[4]

The People's Republic of China (PRC) is an oft-cited example of a country that is allegedly traditional and repressive vis-à-vis the governmental regulation of sexuality, especially homosexuality. Fran Martin, for instance, begins her discussion of the emergence of a queer counter-public in Taipei by stating that the "official treatment of 'homosexuality' (*tongxinglian*) in 1990s Taiwan presents a marked contrast to its representation in other states within the region," such as the PRC and Singapore. In contrast to Taiwan's "official" if still belated "embrace of liberal sexual politics," Martin suggests that mainland China is characterized by "official homophobia" and a failure to recognize what are construed as the natural rights of sexual minorities.[5] Wan Yanhai, a Chinese activist for gay rights, similarly maintains that the PRC is a Party-police-state that refuses to recognize the rights of gays and other sexual minorities, including their assumed right to consume and provide commercial sexual services.[6]

This article questions these claims with reference to mainstream media controversy surrounding the case of Li Ning — a 34-year-old native of Nanjing City, Jiangsu Province, who made legal history in the PRC on 17 October 2004 when he was sentenced to eight years jail and fined 60,000 yuan for organizing male-male prostitution services in a recreational business enterprise.[7] Reportedly the first conviction of its kind, the case attracted national and international media coverage and was nominated as one of "China's ten biggest legal cases in 2004."[8] The case attracted widespread controversy for three reasons. First, it prompted legal debate over the nature of China's recent shift to a "rule of law" and associated conceptions of due legal process, and individual and sexual rights. Second, it intimated that homosocial prostitution — male-male prostitution in which neither participant may self-identify as homosexual — is an integral but frequently neglected component of China's burgeoning, albeit banned, sex industry. Finally, it raised questions regarding the perceived appropriate parameters of same-sex sexual conduct in a country facing rapidly increasing rates of HIV/AIDS infection.[9] An examination of media coverage of these concerns suggests that accusations of official homophobia in the PRC are overstated. They elide the specificity of debates on homosexuality in present-day China due to their overarching concern with Western understandings of sexuality as constitutive of selfhood and (rightful) sociopolitical identity.

Contextualizing Media Coverage of China's First Same-Sex Prostitution Case

The act of organizing, inducing, introducing, facilitating, or forcing another person to engage in prostitution is a criminal offense in China, punishable by up to five or up to ten years imprisonment with the possible addition of a fine, according to the PRC's first criminal code, promulgated on 1 January 1980, and the revised 1997 *Criminal Law of the PRC*.[10] First-party participation in the prostitution transaction is not criminalized, but rather was banned as constituting a social harm and a violation of the rights of "woman-as-person," punishable by a maximum of fifteen days detention for investigation and the possible addition of a fine; and, in more serious cases, by between six months and two years detention for reform through education and/or labor with the possible addition of a fine, according to stipulations outlined in the former Chinese system of administrative sanctions.[11] The Chinese system of administrative sanctions came into being during the Maoist period (1949–76), when the legal system fell into disrepute as a tool of class-based oppression. Following the promulgation of the PRC's first criminal code in 1980, it was used, and not without criticism, alongside the formal legal system to police the activities of those who were deemed to have committed social offenses, but whose criminal liability was not deemed sufficient to bring them before the courts. This meant that the vast majority of prostitution-related offences, i.e., the processes of investigating, determining guilt, and suitably penalizing the activities of sellers and buyers of sex, were handled by the Chinese police, with only serious cases, such as those relating to the organization of prostitution, forced prostitution, and trafficking in women and children, being handled through the courts and criminal justice system.[12] The PRC's new *Security Administration Punishment Law* of 1 March 2006 continues to ban first-party engagement in the prostitution transaction as a social harm, but it significantly reduces previous penalties. It states that offenders may be punished by a maximum of five days administrative detention or a fine of five hundred yuan; and, in more serious cases, by ten to fifteen days administrative detention with the possible addition of a fine up to 5,000 yuan.[13] Hence, the emerging body of Chinese prostitution law can be technically described as abolitionist not prohibitionist in that it criminalizes third party involvement in the running of prostitution businesses, rather than first-party participation in the prostitution transaction per se.[14]

The PRC's legally articulated commitment to abolishing the prostitution industry owes much to the history of the Chinese revolution. Along with its assumption of political power in 1949, the Chinese Communist Party (CCP) embarked upon a series of campaigns that purportedly eradicated prostitution from the mainland by the late 1950s. The extraordinary nature of this feat, irrespective of its actual validity, meant that the eradication of prostitution was (and still is) vaunted as one of the major accomplishments of the new regime. Indeed, a Chinese government white paper describes it as effecting an "earth-shaking historic change in the social status and condition of women."[15] Following Marxist theory, the early CCP viewed the institution of prostitution as an expression of the exploited and denigrated position of women under capitalism-patriarchy, and therefore as incompatible with the desired goals of building socialism and establishing more equitable socio-sexual relations. Since the early 1980s, however, along with the shift from a planned to a market economy, governmental authorities in China have acknowledged that the phenomenon of prostitution has not only reappeared on the mainland, it also constitutes a widespread and growing problem. In fact, it is now considered that the introduction of new laws and regulatory measures has failed to curb the prostitution business, especially its proliferation in diverse forms throughout China's new and burgeoning hospitality and service industry.[16]

The Li Ning case, or the "Nanjing same-sex prostitution case" as it has become known, thus achieved notoriety as the first widely publicized conviction for organized male-male prostitution in the history of the PRC.[17] According to Chinese media reports, the details of this case are as follows. On 17 August 2003, the Qinhuai District police in Nanjing City detained Li Ning for investigation for organizing prostitution, in the form of recruiting young men to provide "companionship" and commercial sexual services to male clients of the Zhengqi Bar for an estimated profit of 124,700 yuan.[18] The Qinhuai police asserted that Li and his accomplices had advertised in local newspapers and on street posters for young men (approximately eighteen to nineteen years of age) to work in "marketing" or "public relations" during May 2003, and subsequently had opened a bar with facilities for small-scale musical and other entertainment in July 2003. It was alleged that most of the respondents to this advertising campaign self-identified as heterosexual and did not realize the actual nature of the work they were expected to perform. But having paid a 300 yuan nonrefundable deposit for the job and being expected to pay Li Ning a 200 yuan monthly "management fee," some had agreed either voluntarily or because of financial coercion to accompany male clients of the venue to eat, drink, and sing, in exchange for financial recompense; others had consented to provide commercial sexual services.[19] The Qinhuai police further asserted that Li Ning had opened a series of such bars in consecutive fashion since 1999; that is, Li had a documented history of conducting such business, and therefore should be handled according to the full weight of the criminal law. Moreover, in the case of the Zhengqi Bar, they could prove that he had organized young men to provide commercial sexual services to male patrons of the venue and that he had commanded a "commission" for doing so on at least seven occasions.[20]

Beginning on 6 February 2004, the courtroom hearing was closed, reportedly to ensure that the verdict would not be prejudiced by public opinion. Journalists and members of the public were precluded from attending due to the controversial nature of the case as relating to male-male prostitution and due to the fact that the Nanjing procurator originally had released Li Ning from police custody on 25 September 2003. Li was released because he had already spent thirty days in police custody and there was no legal case to be prosecuted, since the PRC has no written laws or regulations explicitly criminalizing the organization of same-sex as opposed to opposite-sex prostitution.[21] Unsatisfied with this decision, police officials in Nanjing City applied to the Jiangsu Province Political and Legal Committee for a review of the case between late September and early October 2003. Upon debating the case and concluding that the prostitution industry is banned in the PRC as constituting a social harm, that committee applied to the Chinese Supreme Court for further advice on how to proceed, a request that was presented, in turn, to China's top legislative body, the Standing Committee of the National People's Congress (NPC). In late October, the Legal Affairs Committee of the NPC made an oral reply to the effect that Li Ning should be prosecuted based on Article 358 of the Chinese criminal code, which suggests that the organization and facilitation of all commercial sex acts, irrespective of whether those acts occur between members of the opposite or same sex, is unlawful. Following this response, the Nanjing procurator filed a suit with the Qinhuai District People's Court on 2 January 2004 charging Li Ning with organizing prostitution. The case opened on 6 February and concluded with his sentencing on 17 February for seven counts of organizing prostitution.

Li Ning's lawyer, Chen Yi, requested that the charges against the defendant be dismissed on four grounds. First, Chen argued that there were no relevant laws and regulations to convict Li Ning, since the Chinese criminal code contains no explicit reference to the issue of same-sex prostitution.[22] The PRC's ban on prostitution, he continued, was designed historically to oppose the exploitation of women by men and that understanding constitutes the basis of social condemnation of the prostitution industry in China today. Contemporary Chinese-language dictionaries, for example, define prostitution as characterized by the commodified exchange of transient sexual relations for money, with the providers of such services being gendered as female and those who demand such services as male. In addition, Article 3 of the 1997 *Criminal Law of the PRC*, in Chapter 1, "Tasks, Scope of Application and Basic Principles," states: "Any act deemed by explicit stipulations of law as a crime is to be convicted and given punishment by law and any act that no explicit stipulations of law deems a crime is not be to be convicted or given punishment." Chen therefore concluded that the charges against Li Ning should be dismissed since it was *legally* impossible to say that he had committed a crime.[23]

Second, Chen Yi drew on the popular (liberal) argument that the prostitution transaction is a private transaction that occurs between consenting adults and therefore should not be subjected to criminal sanctions because it constitutes a *mala prohibita* or victimless crime.[24] Arguing that the PRC's historical and Marxist-based objection to prostitution as an example of the feudal-patriarchal-capitalist-exploitation of women is outdated if well-intentioned, Chen maintained that no individual had been harmed by Li's business activities, hence criminal charges were unnecessary. Adding to this point, Chen maintained that Li Ning may have facilitated actions that contravened social morality, but he had not committed a criminal offense. Chen consequently concluded that Li Ning should be tried according to the more lenient provisions outlined in the former Chinese system of administrative sanctions, rather than on the basis of the criminal code.[25]

Third, Chen Yi contended that Li Ning should not be prosecuted for organizing prostitution per se, since he could only be held responsible for the management of activities that occurred within the Zhengqi Bar, not those that occurred outside of the premises.[26] In modern Chinese, this distinction is referred to as the difference between activities known as *zuotai* and those known as *chutai*. *Zuotai* (literally, at the "business" counter) refers to the fact that the services of female or male service personnel may be available within a given entertainment or recreational business enterprise for the purpose of providing "companionship" to the venue's clientele. Service personnel may provide companionship in the form of eating, drinking, singing, and dancing with the patrons of a given venue in exchange for financial recompense in the form of "tips" and/or a commission on the monies forwarded for the consumption of food and beverages, and the use of a semi-privatized space to participate in karaoke and so forth. Technically speaking, the exchange of money for companionship in recreational venues is banned according to the PRC's 1999 "Regulations concerning the Management of Public Places of Entertainment."[27] However, such services are widely available in practice within the confines of recreational venues. In contrast, *chutai* (literally, away from the "business" counter) refers to the fact that service personnel may make individual arrangements to engage in other activities, including commercial sexual activities, outside of the recreational venue where they are theoretically employed.[28] Chen's defense of Li Ning thus turned on the suggestion that "employers" cannot be held responsible for what occurs outside of their business premises and responsible supervision.

Finally, Chen Yi concluded that there was insufficient evidence to tie Li Ning to the seven counts of organizing prostitution that had been laid against him.[29] According to Chen, the charges were based on oral testimonies and insubstantial evidence. The Qinghuai police had built their case around the testimonies provided by several young men who had "worked" in the Zhengqi Bar and who were thus keen to displace legal attention away from their own activities and toward Li Ning. Concomitantly, Chen maintained that the charges and associated profits that were laid against Li could neither be proved to be the direct product of his actions nor his sole responsibility. Given that Li's alleged "accomplices" had absconded, he claimed that Li Ning was being held responsible in an exclusive fashion for the criminal actions of other people. Chen therefore concluded that there was insufficient evidence to tie Li Ning to the seven counts of organizing prostitution that had been laid against him.

In sentencing Li Ning to eight years jail and a fine of 60,000 yuan for organizing male-male prostitution services in a recreational business enterprise, the court clearly disagreed with Chen's defense. This sentence was decided on the grounds that the Chinese criminal code may not contain any explicit regulations regarding the handling of same-sex prostitution, but it proscribes the act of organizing, introducing, facilitating, or forcing another person to engage in prostitution.[30] In other words, Li Ning's conviction turned on the contention that the body of Chinese prostitution law is non–gender specific and hence covers the facilitation of prostitution practices between members of the opposite or same sex, irrespective of historical and legal precedent. The court further determined that the case should not be handled in a lenient manner, i.e., according to the former Chinese system of administrative sanctions as opposed to the penal code, because Li Ning's refusal to admit his guilt, in keeping with the fault-based orientation of Chinese law, indicated that he felt no remorse and refused to admit any responsibility for the consequences of his actions.

Despite the closed nature of Li Ning's trial, the handing down of this sentence generated widespread public debate. Lawyers and legal scholars, in particular, entered into a media-induced debate about Li's conviction, one that raised questions about the PRC's proclaimed shift to a rule of law and associated conceptions of due legal process and individual and sexual rights. Accordingly, the next section of this article examines the broader legal debate conducted in the PRC media that was generated by Li's conviction.

Media Debate of the Legal Implications of China's First Same-Sex Prostitution Case

According to Chinese media reports, legal commentators who dispute Li Ning's conviction insist that it was both unlawful and unconstitutional to try him; hence, the court proceedings demonstrate the PRC's lack of regard vis-à-vis the protection and promotion of individual rights, particularly those of participants in same-sex sexual behaviors. The basic contention here, in keeping with Chen Yi's defense, is that the Chinese criminal code may adopt gender-neutral language in stating that the organization and facilitation of prostitution is a crime, but it makes no explicit reference to the subject of same-sex prostitution. This consideration, taken in conjunction with the elimination of the use of precedent as stipulated in Article 3 of the penal code, indicates that the act of providing same-sex commercial sexual services cannot be construed as a criminal offense, because there is no explicit reference to this offense in Chinese law.[31] Critics further aver that, if the use of precedent is considered to be acceptable legal practice, then the case should have been dismissed outright. This is because, in November 1998, a case relating to the organization of homosocial prostitution in a teahouse in Chengdu City, Sichuan Province, was dismissed on the grounds that there was no legal basis to deal with the phenomenon of same-sex prostitution in Chinese law.[32]

Critics of Li Ning's conviction also maintain that the case proceedings underscore the PRC's failure to adopt a rule of law by demonstrating that individuals are denied the right to a fair trial. Accusations of unfair proceedings relate to the practice of law enforcement agencies appealing to higher authorities for instructions on individual cases, thereby allegedly compromising both the defendant's right of appeal and the impartiality and independence of the different levels that make up China's legal system.[33] In Li Ning's case, critics contend that his conviction resulted from the NPC's oral response to requests for advice on how to proceed with the case from lower-level law enforcement agencies. As they argue, the oral nature of that response, combined with the fact that the NPC is a legislative and not a judiciary body, suggests that Li Ning's conviction was based on the non-verifiable and subjective opinions of an unspecified body of the NPC rather than on the basis of the implicitly impartial and objective letter of the law. In short, critics maintain that the NPC's reply not only effectively rendered Li Ning's defense null and void, but also compromised the desired independence of the lower levels of China's legal system by giving "higher authorities" the power to determine how a specific case, as opposed to generalized legal norms, should be handled.

Critics of Li Ning's conviction further claim that the severity of his sentence demonstrates that the Chinese legal system, akin to the general public, is homophobic.[34] The basic argument here is that eight years imprisonment is a harsh punishment for the act of facilitating and organizing prostitution, especially when those acts are viewed as consensual. Hence, Li was sentenced on the basis of social distaste for homosexual behavior, that is, for failing to conform to heterosexual norms. According to critics of Li Ning's conviction, the Chinese public and Chinese law enforcement agencies are uninformed about the subject of homosexuality, and not only look upon same-sex sexual acts with repugnance, but also blame participants in same-sex sexual practices for the spread of HIVS/AIDS in China today. The severity of Li's sentence is thus taken as evidence of the perceived failure of the Chinese government to protect and promote both individual rights and the rights of sexual minorities.

Conversely, media reports indicate that other legal commentators proved keen not only to establish the legality of Li Ning's conviction, but also to demonstrate that arguments alleging that he was sentenced for being a "homosexual" were untenable.[35] According to upholders of Li's conviction, the court neither ruled against the right of individuals to engage in same-sex sexual practices nor against their right to define themselves as homosexuals: it merely ruled against third party profiteering from the organization of the prostitution of others. Contrary to accusations of official homophobia, supporters of Li Ning's conviction maintain that there are no legal prohibitions against same-sex sexual behaviors in the Chinese criminal code. Likewise, there are no legal prohibitions against same-sex sexual behaviors in the Chinese system of administrative and Party disciplinary sanctions. The revised *Criminal Law of 1997* eliminated previous references to the crime of sodomy (*jijianzui*) and to the problematic category of "hooliganism" (*liumangzui*), which was formerly often used to police the activities of participants in same-sex sexual behaviors. Hence, the only laws against same-sex sexual behaviors in China today are designed to prohibit sex with minors, and therefore to protect the rights of children; to prohibit nonconsensual sex, and therefore to penalize rape; and to ban practices that are likely to cause public offense, such as committing sex acts in public and engaging in group sex in places patronized by members of the public. As supporters of Li Ning's conviction continue, the existence of these laws, and laws against the organization of same-sex prostitution, are supported by members of China's homosexual community, as evidenced by the fact that commentators on the Aibai gay website agreed with Li's sentencing, even as they called for greater tolerance of same-sex love.[36]

Supporters of Li Ning's conviction further emphasize that Chinese law may be opposed to the organization of prostitution, but it is certainly not "antigay," by arguing that the conviction flowed from adherence to correct legal procedure. As they argue, the use of precedent in Li Ning's case was entirely appropriate. The Chinese criminal code may not make any explicit reference to the subject of same-sex prostitution; it may also be the case that common law and common sense are gendered, in that a prostitute is assumed to be a *woman* who exchanges sex with men for money or financial recompense. However, the spirit of the law clearly opposes the organization of prostitution in any form since chapter 6 of the penal code bans the organization and facilitation of "others" (*taren*) to engage in prostitution as a crime that obstructs the correct administration of public order, and hence as something that constitutes a social harm.[37] Furthermore, the clearest existing instruction on same-sex prostitution in the Chinese legal system to date, namely, the 2001 "Reply from the Ministry of

Public Security on How to Define and Handle the Exchange of Same-sex Sexual Conduct for Money or Property," explicitly states that those who offer and/or buy transient sexual relations, whether between members of the opposite and/or same sex, for money or property as the medium of exchange, including the provision of oral sex, hand jobs, anal sex, and so forth, should be treated as engaging in prostitution and handled according to the law.[38] In short, this instruction suggests that the organization of same-sex prostitution should be handled in precisely the same manner as heterosexual prostitution. Consequently, upholders of Li Ning's conviction maintain that he was sentenced in keeping with correct legal procedure, since the case does not concern a new type of crime that requires specific legislation. Moreover, the fact that the case was referred to the NPC may highlight the failure of lower-level courts to understand and apply the law, but it cannot be used to exculpate Li Ning from criminal responsibility.[39]

Despite this ongoing legal debate, media reports indicate that the NPC's reply on the Li Ning case effectively gave the Chinese police the green light with regard to law enforcement, with coverage of Li Ning's conviction being soon followed by media discussions of similar cases. On 18 May 2004, in what was described as the first case of organized male-male prostitution in China's northeastern province of Jilin, the Nanguan District People's Court in Changchun City sentenced Ren Guohui, Song Shuang, and Na Yan, respectively, to thirteen years imprisonment and a fine of 20,000 yuan, six and a half years imprisonment and a fine of 10,000 yuan, and six years imprisonment and a fine of 10,000 yuan, for recruiting young men to provide commercial male-male sexual services in recreational venues such as hotels, saunas, and bathhouses. Ren received a harsher sentence for the additional crime of drugging and robbing a person whom he had met during the course of these activities.[40]

Then, on 11 June 2004, in what was described as the first case of organized same-sex prostitution in China's southeastern coastal city of Guangdong, the Yuexiu District People's Court sentenced Liu Xianzhi and Zhou Deming to a fine of 1,000 yuan and five and six years imprisonment, respectively, for organizing prostitution.[41] Liu was sentenced for organizing commercial sexual services in the twenty-four-hour "Man's Dream Bar" and commanding a commission of thirty yuan out of a minimum fee of one hundred yuan from five young men whom he had retained for the purpose of providing hand jobs and/or blow jobs to patrons of the venue. Zhou was sentenced for keeping ten young men in rental residential premises for the purpose of providing male-male prostitution services, for restricting the personal movement of his "employees" (in one instance keeping an individual locked in a separate room), and for commanding a weekly fee of sixty yuan for food and accommodation, and a commission of thirty to fifty yuan from a maximum fee of three hundred yuan for facilitating the prostitution transaction.

Finally, on 2 March 2005, in what the media described as the first conviction for organized same-sex prostitution in China's southwestern province of Sichuan, the Jinniu District People's Court in Chengdu City sentenced Tang Fajun to six years imprisonment and a fine of 5,000 yuan for organizing male-male prostitution services and violating an individual's human rights.[42] Unlike the preceding cases, which came to court following public reports of suspected offenses to local police stations, this case came to light through a statement provided by a young male rural migrant, Chen Minghui. In April 2004, Chen came to Chengdu from a remote township to find work and had been deceived by Tang, who had offered him employment as a waiter in a teahouse for a monthly wage of six hundred to eight hundred yuan plus food and accommodation. However, Tang had then taken Chen to a residential home and forced him to have sex with ten or more men over the course of a month; other reports suggest that he was forced to service up to twenty and even sixty clients. Chen claimed that he was initially beaten into compliance and then acquiesced to repeated acts of rape in an attempt to convince his "employer" of his submission and thus enhance his opportunity to escape. Conversely, Tang's defense was premised on the understanding that the other young men he had organized to sell sexual services not only did so on a voluntary basis, but also received high sums of money in recompense, thereby impugning the veracity of Chen's testimony.

The topical nature of these cases, combined with the fact that their incidence could be observed throughout the PRC, prompted Chinese media commentators to conclude that same-sex prostitution was an integral if overlooked component of China's burgeoning, albeit banned, sex industry. Indeed, many commentators argued that the Li Ning case simply exposed the tip of the iceberg with regard to the extent of male-male commercial sexual services in China today.[43] Not surprisingly, media coverage of such cases often served as the springboard for a more extended discussion of issues pertaining to male-male prostitution and homosexuality in China more generally, and it is to an examination of these issues that we now turn.

Debating the Social Implications of Male-Male Prostitution in the PRC Media

As with most discussions of prostitution in Western societies, media coverage of China's "first same-sex prostitution case" generated broader debate based on the standard anthropological-cum-sociological questions: namely, who provides male-male prostitution services? what are their motivations for doing so? and, in what kinds of spaces do they provide such services? According to media commentators, a quick search of the internet, some candid talks with anonymous informants, and a series of interviews with some of China's growing number of "sexperts," soon reveal that "money boys" are a common feature of bar life in present-day China.[44] It bears noting here that the English phrase "money boy" is often used in Chinese-language discussions rather than the Chinese equivalent of "*tongxingmaiyin*" (same-sex sex seller), on the grounds that this is the terminology used by members of China's homosexual community themselves. Concomitantly, members of China's homosexual community describe themselves interchangeably with reference to the English term "gay," the Chinese term *tongxinglian* (same-sex love), and the Hong Kong-derived appropriation of the politically correct appellative for all Chinese citizens during the

Maoist era, *tongzhi* or comrade.[45] Also in line with most discussions of prostitution in Western societies, Chinese media commentators tend to avoid related anthropological-cum-sociological questions such as these: who demands male-male prostitution services; what kinds of venues do they frequent; and what are their motivations for doing so, even though they posit as the presumed side of demand a generic community of people who are erotically inclined toward members of the same sex.

Media commentaries suggest that the majority of money boys in present-day China are young unmarried men (approximately eighteen to twenty-four years of age), from poor communities in the rural hinterland who have moved to urban and more developed parts of the PRC to look for work, and/or are university students with limited means of financial support. On this issue, Zhang Beichuan, a noted medical scholar on the subject of men who have sex with men in China, estimates that there are between four and ten thousand male rural migrants who offer same-sex sexual services in the city of Beijing alone. Most of these young men reportedly self-identify as heterosexual, but are willing to provide commercial homosocial sexual services in exchange for relatively high sums of financial recompense and flexible working hours.[46]

The prices commanded for the provision of male-male commercial sexual services vary depending on the nature of those services, the involvement of third parties, and the kinds of venues in which the prostitution transaction takes place. Quick transactions negotiated and conducted on the street command between ten and thirty yuan, whereas sexual services that are arranged at or provided in recreational venues such as hotels, bars, karaoke/dance venues, saunas, health centers, fitness clubs, bathhouses, and teahouses command between fifty and three hundred yuan. Money boys earn three hundred to four hundred yuan per month for providing hospitality and companionship services in such venues, with their income deriving from "tips" and commissions charged on the consumption of food and beverages. They command a further one hundred to three hundred yuan for the prostitution transaction in instances when they either utilize the facilities of a given venue, or else depart from that venue with a patron, in order to provide sexual services. Media reports suggest that the owners or managers of such entertainment venues routinely extract a commission or "management fee" from money boys for providing the space in which they can ply their trade, introducing them to prospective clients, and generally facilitating the prostitution transaction.[47] To date, the available literature does not address the question of who precisely demands the services of male sex sellers in present-day China, other than gesturing toward an unspecified group of usually married men.[48]

Given the rapid proliferation of venues for homosocial activities throughout the PRC, media and academic commentators in China often suggest that a gay subculture is emerging in the PRC; and, this development illustrates both the tolerant nature of traditional Chinese sexual culture and the progressive nature of China's continued opening up to the rest of the world. Such commentators usually characterize the history of sexuality in China as follows: A traditional period of openness and toleration with regard to all forms of sexual practices was followed by a gradual but increasing series of governmental prohibitions on sex that culminated in the repression of the Maoist era, when the topic of sex allegedly became taboo and people were punished for a wide range of sexual "transgressions." Now, with economic reform and the abandonment of "puritanical socialism," it is claimed that China is slowly reclaiming its former tradition of sexual tolerance and eclecticism, whilst simultaneously embracing the kinds of sexual behaviors that are associated with "the more advanced and sexually liberated 'West.'"[49]

Extrapolating from this conventional account of the history of Chinese sexuality, concerned commentators tend to describe the history of homosexuality in China in terms of a shift from a culture of toleration and acceptance to one of repression and, more recently, back to a culture of acceptance.[50] As they argue, homosexuality has a long and venerable history in (Confucian) Chinese culture, as evidenced by the documented love of certain emperors for their young male companions, and as depicted in eighteenth-century novels such as the *Dream of the Red Chamber*. That tradition was overturned during the Maoist period, when homosexuality was classified as a disease and homosexuals became subject to political attack. This new culture of condemnation continued throughout the 1980s and early 1990s, during which "gay males were routinely harassed, detained, interrogated, and often arrested and jailed each time a political or social movement of virtually any kind was announced." But, recent social and legal changes indicate that homosexuality in the PRC is finally being accepted as a legitimate and natural expression of human sexuality once again.

Subsequently, contrary to Western accounts of China as characterized by "official homophobia," some Chinese commentators describe the PRC as a "half-heaven for homosexuals," based on the ambiguous status of homosexuality in contemporary Chinese society and law.[51] Although homosexual identity is problematized in China as reflecting an aberrant choice of lifestyle, Chinese academics and media commentators similarly suggest that the act of engaging in same-sex sexual conduct per se carries little or no social stigma. Instead, they maintain that "Chinese society" views engagement in same-sex sexual behaviors as acceptable so long as such conduct occurs in private and does not interfere with the traditional social obligation for members of both sexes to marry and produce an heir.[52] The standard argument here is that, unlike "the West," homosexuals in China are not forced into "the closet" by morally based religious proscriptions on same-sex sexual behaviors, and hence by social and self-internalized conceptions of guilt. Rather, they are constrained by the traditional Chinese expectation that everyone ultimately will enter into a monogamous heterosexual marital arrangement for the purposes of reproduction.

This perceived absence of moral taint arguably is reflected in the ambiguous status of homosexuality in Chinese law. As many commentators note, the increasingly tolerant legal attitude to homosexuality in China today is indicated by the fact that reference to "hooliganism," an umbrella term that formerly was applied to men arrested while cruising for sex in public toilet blocks and parks, was removed from the 1997 criminal code; and, in March-April 2001, the Chinese Psychiatry Association removed homosexuality from its list of mental illnesses.[53] These shifts are viewed as confirming a step taken by the Chinese Ministry of Public Security, which effectively declared homosexuality a private, not legal, concern in 1992, when it denied a father's request that the police arrest his daughter and her lesbian lover for cohabitation, arguing that the police had no cause to intervene, since China has no laws on homosexuality.[54] Adding to these perceived signs of growing toleration and progressive "civilizational" advancement, many commentators contend that the so-called former taboo on public discussions of sex and sexuality in China has been abandoned in favor of informed academic debate and the open provision of courses on gay and gender studies in Chinese universities.[55] Hence, media commentators often draw on the work of recognized academics to imply that the provision of information about male-male prostitution is not about acquiring a voyeuristic readership or selling sex in a different form; rather, it is about guiding the public in terms of promoting increased tolerance through understanding of same-sex sexual behaviors.[56]

The subject of homosocial prostitution, however, occupies a problematic position in this generalized rendition of the PRC as a country that is joining an idealized conception of Euramerica in terms of viewing homosexuality as a legitimate and natural expression of human sexuality. On the one hand, media commentators draw on recent studies to indicate that the majority of self-identified homosexuals in China still enter into heterosexual marital arrangements in order to fulfill their filial obligations, i.e., to produce an heir.[57] And, given the general understanding in China that sex is a natural desire that requires an outlet, the existence of male-male prostitution is implicitly posited as an inevitable consequence of China's continued adherence to a traditional family system. Viewed in this context, the existence of male-male prostitution is presented as inevitable but still undesirable, with the most pressing problem being construed as the form in which male-male commercial sexual services occur. Put simply, the provision of public and promiscuous commercial sex in bathhouses, saunas, health centers, and so forth is looked upon with moral disapproval, whereas the recent shift to more discreet forms of male-male commercial sexual services, in the form of using the internet and mobile phone technology to advertise services and arrange meetings with clients, is viewed as less public and therefore potentially more acceptable.[58]

On the other hand, it appears that members of China's homosexual community and concerned academics alike view sellers of male-male commercial sexual services as problematic in various ways. In "Qualities of Desire: Imagining Gay Identities in China," Lisa Rofel draws on interviews with self-identified gay men in Beijing to argue that members of China's emerging gay community view the existence of money boys with considerable anxiety. As Rofel notes, Beijing gays look down on money boys, describing them as uneducated and "poor quality" rural youth, who contaminate the advancement of urban "homosexual culture," and destroy the perceived purity of homosexual love, by bringing "money or materiality" into the equation.[59] This way of categorizing money boys, she concludes, not only divides gay men, but also establishes hierarchical distinctions between "proper and improper expressions of gay identity." Following talks with self-identified members of China's gay community in Nanjing and Shenzhen, Fu Jianfeng similarly notes that many gay men view money boys as criminal lowlifes who bring the homosexual community into disrepute, and whose activities need to be curbed via the implementation of stricter governmental controls.[60] This apparent rejection of male-male prostitution as an acceptable component of homosexual life in China raises the question of who precisely demands the services of money boys, whilst simultaneously pointing to the existence of an emerging consensus regarding the question of what is considered to be the appropriate range of same-sex sexual behaviors.

Most notably, Chinese academics, policing scholars, and self-identified members of China's homosexual community similarly contend that male-male prostitution needs to be made subject to governmental constraints in order to curb the PRC's rapidly increasing rate of HIV/AIDS infection.[61] As in many other countries, adherence to World Health Organization (WHO) directives has ensured that homosexual and prostitutional sex have been problematized as high-risk sexual practices and potential vectors for the spread of HIV/AIDS in China. Hence, on 1 December 2004, China's Department of Health and Hygiene issued the first official estimate of the male homosexual population in the PRC to the world — an estimated 5 to 10 million people.[62] This figure is highly conservative when compared to those provided by media and scholarly commentators. Extrapolating from Alfred C. Kinsey's contention that 3 to 4 percent of a given population is homosexual, they suggest that there are between 36 and 48 million adult gays and lesbians in China today.[63]

Numerical discrepancies aside, recent discussions of homosexuality in China share a common concern. As many commentators argue, male homosexuals comprise a substantial yet overlooked proportion of the Chinese population; moreover, surveys indicate that homosexual men constitute the second major risk group for the spread of HIV/AIDS in the PRC after intravenous drug users, with an estimated 70 to 80 percent of that group being married, and 50 percent engaging in sexual intercourse with their female partners. In consequence, understanding the sexual behaviors of China's male homosexual population and making that population aware of safer sex practices and the goals of HIV/AIDS prevention are construed as vital for safeguarding China's future.[64]

While drawing on concerns over high-risk sexual behaviors to advocate stricter legal controls over homosocial prostitution, media commentators note that China's law enforcement authorities insist that they are not opposed to homosexuality; they are simply against the organization of commercial sexual services. Unlike Western media commentators, who often use cases such as Li Ning's to suggest that "gayness" is treated as equivalent to vice in the PRC, Chinese media commentators maintain that Li Ning's conviction does not signify that China is antigay. Rather, it highlights the PRC's continued commitment to the abolition of prostitution, and, insofar as it sends a warning to the homosexual community, that warning is not to engage in what are considered to be new and inappropriate same-sex sexual practices, i.e., homosocial prostitution.[65]

The suggestion that homosexuality is acceptable — but commercial sex is not

— is reiterated in media discussions of the implications of China's entry to the World Trade Organization for homosexuality and the law. Media commentators often cite Gong Guojiang, who completed an MA at Beijing University Law School on precisely this subject, to argue that Chinese law needs to be expanded in order to protect the rights of homosexuals as Chinese citizens.[66] The general contention here is that the rights of homosexuals as citizens will be guaranteed by legalizing same-sex marriage, by legislating against the existence of money boys, and by specifying in law that the rape of men by men and the forced prostitution of men are criminal offenses. These arguments received a recent airing in the Chinese media following a statement made in June 2005 by Liu Baiju, a member of the Chinese People's Political Consultative Conference, on the subject of nonconsensual same-sex sexual violence. According to Liu, sex-related legislation in China to date has concentrated on the task of protecting women's rights and interests and has failed to extend the same protections to members of the male population. He therefore recommends that China move toward protecting and promoting men's sexual rights by acknowledging in criminal law that men too can be victims of sexual violence.[67]

Conversely, other media commentators point out that noted Chinese academics such as Li Yinhe and Pan Suiming have variously argued that China must relax its opposition to the prostitution industry, both in order to protect the human rights of sellers of commercial sex and to comply with WHO directives regarding the promotion of HIV/AIDS education and safer sex practices.[68] The question of exactly how China should revise its prostitution laws remains a matter of dispute: some commentators favor decriminalizing the prostitution transaction, i.e., removing the prostitution transaction from the purview of the Chinese system of administrative sanctions,[69] whereas others argue for stricter controls over the organization of prostitution and an increased focus on the historically neglected side of demand.[70] However, outreach work that targets providers of commercial sexual services is becoming more common in China, and, in accordance with the funding obligations of organizations such as the Ford Foundation, that work not only emphasizes the provision of free condoms and safer sex education in public entertainment venues, but also constructs providers of commercial sexual services as disadvantaged workers who require labor and health protections.[71]

At the same time, growing HIV/AIDS awareness among Chinese officials and the general public has generated contradictory outcomes for providers of both heterosexual and homosocial commercial sexual services. Governmental recognition of the economic and social implications of the spread of HIV has resulted in the implementation of much-needed HIV/AIDS education programs. But this same recognition has prompted the implementation of stricter regulations over workers in certain sectors of China's hospitality and service industry. For example, in February 2005, the Departments of Health and Hygiene, Industry and Commerce, and Culture, in Henan Province, jointly issued new regulations that require all workers in the hospitality and service industry to undertake testing and training vis-à-vis sexually transmissible infections (STIs), including HIV/AIDS, as a condition of legitimate employment.[72] The same regulations stipulate that owners of recreational enterprises must ensure that all their employees undergo the requisite testing and training, and that employees are registered under their proper (i.e., legally verifiable) names with the Department of Disease Control, as a condition of conducting business. The stated rationale for introducing these regulations is to prevent the spread of STIs and HIV/AIDS from those categorized as "high-risk" members of the population to those categorized as "ordinary" members of the population. Insofar as recreational venues that are known sites for the provision of commercial sexual services are cited as potential sites of disease transmission, i.e., karaoke/dance venues, hairdressing salons, saunas, bathhouses, and venues offering foot washing and other forms of massage, these regulations clearly target providers of commercial sexual services, even though the regulations do not explicitly state this. In China, as in the West, therefore, the imperatives of HIV/AIDS prevention work has encouraged a paradoxical pathologization of participants in prostitutional and same-sex sexual behaviors as vectors of disease; whilst simultaneously constructing participants in commercial sexual practices as sexual minorities who possess identifiable needs and rights that require improved social awareness and new legal protections.

Conclusion

An examination of the media coverage surrounding Li Ning's conviction for organizing male-male prostitution demonstrates that the relationship between sex and government in contemporary China is not characterized by straightforward repression, official homophobia, and a corollary refusal to embrace the rights and accompanying legal strategies that are associated with progressive, liberal sexual politics. There are numerous impediments to self-identifying and living openly as a "gay" in present-day China, and there are clear restrictions on the public display and consumption of what some might term an open and transgressive "gay lifestyle." But, contrary to the claims of many Western commentators, these impediments do not offer straightforward evidence of a traditional and repressive ethos on the part of the Chinese Party-state with respect to the governance of sex-related issues in general.

Although more localized struggles for improvements in the status of China's homosexual community are required, an examination of the media publicity surrounding Li Ning's conviction suggests that discussions of homosexuality in the PRC turn on what Rofel describes as "an economy of sex and sociality that is distinct from an economy of the closet." In Rofel's words, "the visions of many Chinese gay men in China about what it means to be gay are certainly connected to the knowledge that gay people exist all over the world," but "these men do not simply imagine a global community of horizontal comradeship."[73] Imaginings of gay identity in the PRC are both constrained and enabled by the fact that being homosexual is not understood in terms of an inherent yet repressed identity, or "the existence within the self of a separate sexual domain that is a constitutive principle of the self." Instead, homosexual identification is negotiated within conceptions of "face" and "status" that continue to invoke both the family and the nation as forces that are constitutive of one's social being. To the extent that this characterization is apposite, the queer rendition of promiscuous and commercial homosocial sex as rightful expressions of a transgressive consumer lifestyle is unlikely to receive much support in China.

❑

5

THE INTERNET AND THE FRAGMENTATION OF CHINESE SOCIETY

Jens Damm

THIS ARTICLE EXAMINES THE USAGE AND CONTENT of the Chinese internet, with its focus on consumerism and lifestyle, to argue that dominant discourses, both Western and Chinese, are wrong in their assessment of the impact of the internet on Chinese society because they pay inadequate attention to a consumerist postmodernity that emerged in China during the early 1990s. The first part of the article reviews the dominant Western and Chinese approaches to the study of the internet in China. The second part draws on evidence from some influential Chinese Bulletin Board Systems (BBSs) to demonstrate how and why Chinese internet users consider social and commercial uses of the internet much more important than political uses.

Western Mainstream Discourses on the Internet

The Liberation Discourse: "Spamming for Freedom"

The internet boom at the end of the 1990s and during the first years of this millennium increased speculation about the degree of change that could be expected in Chinese society:[2] media commentators, politicians, and political scientists in the West, the so-called "China-watchers," have all focused on the great changes that might be wrought in China by the introduction of the internet. In much of this research, a deterministic view of technology prevails: users, in pursuit of "objective" information, are expected to be highly IT-savvy and able to employ the newest technologies to circumvent the censorship measures of the Chinese government. Technologies such as P2P (peer-to-peer), which are used in the West for downloading various kinds of allegedly "illegal" content such as copyright-protected films and music, are expected to be used in China for downloading Falun Gong-related material and the *Tiananmen Papers*.[3] That is to say, the specific features and characteristics of the media shape our society and politics, or in the words of Marshall McLuhan "we shape our tools and they in turn shape us."[4] In the case of the internet, "The biggest of big brothers is increasingly helpless against communications technology. Information is the oxygen of the modern age," as former U.S. president Ronald Reagan once said.[5] Such predictions are based on the structure of the flow of information. In contrast to "traditional" media, including TV and radio, which have a "one-to-many" structure with a one-sided flow of communication, the internet covers all possible means of communication: one-to-one, one-to-many, many-to-many, and many-to-one; it also allows an interactive dialogue.[6] In addition, the internet is said to offer the opportunity for everybody to become his/her own publisher with only marginal costs.[7]

Thus, the first discourse on the internet in China could be entitled the "liberation discourse," where, in addition to the involvement of Chinese users, the role of the West is emphasized: "How the U.S. can free China's internet"[8] is a typical heading in this kind of discourse. The China watchers have often also expressed great enthusiasm for the supposedly liberating effects of this technology. They not only see the internet as an uncontrollable form of technology, they also refer to the wealth of information available on the internet that subverts attempts at silencing voices. Former U.S. president Bill Clinton pointed out that "attempting to control the internet in China was like trying to nail Jell-O to a wall."[9] The U.S. Embassy in Beijing has remarked that "the Internet will almost certainly become a more important, positive force in facilitating the rights of Chinese users to be informed, and to be heard" and has concluded that "as the number of Internet users grows,…the medium will become an increasingly important tool in fostering the development of civil society in China."[10] The internet is thus regarded as a "technology of freedom."[11] Even mass mailings — usually named "spam" in the West — are considered to be valuable for the dissemination of information; Chinese dissident groups in the United States, including Falun Gong, are notorious for sending hundred of thousands of pieces of unwanted mail to Chinese email accounts.[12]

Research carried out on the role of the internet in China also reflects the dominance of one particular concern of the West: the question of freedom versus state controls. Western research has focused, for the most part, on the controls implemented by the Chinese government, an approach that is clearly visible in two prestigious internet research projects on China: "Internet Filtering in China," by Jonathan Zittrain and Benjamin G. Edelman, and "Berkeley China Internet Project," headed by Xiao Qiang.[13] Xiao Qiang wrote in 2004: "Ever since the Communist Party took power in 1949, the Chinese media have been tightly controlled by the government. On-line publishing is a real threat to that control, and the government is clearly worried. A crackdown in 2003 closed websites and Internet cafes and saw the arrest of dozens of online commentators."[14] The problem lies not in the facts as they are presented by Xiao Qiang, but rather in his mono-causal interpretation. He also fails to take into account the thousands of other websites, forums, and blogs left untouched. These are not focused specifically on political issues, but nevertheless discuss essential societal developments in China. This narrow approach to research, focusing only on censorship and crackdowns, disregards the much wider societal implications of the internet; only recently have some scholars started to extend the scope of their work beyond the previously limited field to gain a more comprehensive picture of the impact of the internet in China.[15]

So what then is the reason for the current Western interest in the internet and on control? It could be argued that the emphasis on the internet's purported role in the creation of a civil society and criticism of all state interference in its functioning can be traced back to a very early phase of the internet in the West. In the 1980s, most users of the internet were students and academics in prestigious U.S. universities.[16] During those years, it was not the World Wide Web, which we today often equate with the internet, but Usenet and other forms of newsgroups that shaped the Net. The role of the noncommercial Usenet was celebrated in academic publications. Many observers regarded the internet as a tool to overcome geographical borders and to establish new kinds of communities. There was, therefore, an emphasis on the democratizing and equalizing effects of the internet, not with regard to "authoritarian" states, but with regard to the United States itself: there was a widely held belief that the internet would lead to the much wider participation of U.S. citizens in the democratic processes and to the revival of civil society. Today, however, the commercialization of the internet in the West is loudly lamented and the power and influence of the big media companies is indisputable.[17]

Howard Rheingold, one of the early pioneers in the field of virtual communities, commented: "Civil society, a web of informal relationships that exist independently of government institutions or business organizations, is the social adhesive necessary to hold divergent communities of interest together into democratic societies. The future of civil society in America and elsewhere is uncertain, even gloomy."[18] He then posed the question: "Can virtual communities help revitalize civil society or are online debates nothing more than distracting simulations of authentic discourse? Enthusiasts like myself point to examples of many-to-many communication that appear to leverage power in the real world of politics."[19] Rheingold seemed to be fascinated by the infinite possibilities of many-to-many communication. Unlike direct, one-to-one communication via the telephone or one-to-many communication such as television and radio (where one station can send one message to millions of people, but viewers/listeners cannot communicate back), the various forms of communication combined in the term "internet" mean that any user is able to communicate with another person or millions of people at the same time. And they are able to communicate in the same way or with one another. In 1995, Fernback and Thompson wrote, "Ideologically, community within cyberspace appears to emphasize a shared belief in the principles of free speech, individualism, equality, and open access to the same symbolic interests that define the character of American democracy."[20]

This early discourse on the democratizing and participatory role of the internet — with regard to the West — has gradually declined and today's discussion emphasizes the influence of government and multinational corporations on the internet:

Picture, if you will, an information infrastructure that encourages censorship, surveillance and suppression of the creative impulse. Where anonymity is outlawed and every penny spent is accounted for. Where the powers that be can smother subversive (or economically competitive) ideas in the cradle, and no one can publish even a laundry list without the imprimatur of Big Brother. Some prognosticators are saying that such a construct is nearly inevitable. And this infrastructure is none other than the former paradise of rebels and free-speechers: the Internet.[21]

In summary, owing to political considerations and a "feeling of superiority" in the West, images of internet subversives dominate in Western narratives about the internet in China. Although the "China's response to the West" paradigm has not been part of mainstream academic research for more than a decade, it still shapes journalistic and political descriptions of China's recent developments.[22] These portrayals of the internet as a liberating and democratizing force that can only be held back by strict governmental control is different from the kinds of narratives that are used to describe the effects of the internet on Western society. In these discussions, Western observers neglect to mention the role played by the major Chinese companies and innovators in shaping the internet; they deliberately reduce the numbers of agents to two, the state and the user, and both are described as being involved in an antagonistic relationship.

The Control Discourse: "Big Mama Is Watching You"

It seems that the growth of the internet in China together with the country's unexpected political and economic stability has led Western observers to change their views regarding the "liberating potential" of the internet. Instead of examining the inherent features of the internet that might possibly counteract or simply neutralize the liberalizing effects, the focus of Western observers has now shifted toward the role of the government: every single action taken by the Chinese authorities is immediately interpreted as a "crackdown" and as censorship: a "control discourse" has emerged or, to use the description of Lokman Tsui, "Big Mama is watching you."[23] Michael S. Chase and James C. Mulvenon at the RAND Institute in Santa Monica, California, for example, formulate the key questions for their research as follows:

> Does the Internet provide dissidents with potent new tools that they can use to promote their causes, break through the barriers of censorship, and perhaps ultimately undermine the power and authority of non-democratic regimes? Or, on the contrary, is it more likely that those authoritarian governments will use the Internet as another instrument to repress dissent, silence their critics, and strengthen their own power?[24]

One particular incident, the closing down of cybercafes in 2002, highlights the differing perceptions of the Chinese government and Western observers over the role of the internet in Chinese society: When reported in the West, the event was immediately pounced on by commentators to draw attention to the strict control measures employed by the Chinese government; the reason for this action, as given by the Chinese media, was not taken seriously and viewed only as a pretext. For their part, the Chinese press/media explained that many cybercafes were unlicensed and they quoted worried parents who had tried to prevent their children from visiting internet cafes where all they did was play games all night and where they also had easy access to porn sites.[25] U.S. press reports focused solely on the closing down of the cafes as the latest form of repression. CNN reported: "China: Cyber cafes closed in new clampdown....Anonymous cybercafes are popular because they allow people to evade tough content laws, whose infringement on a personal homepage or message board authorities are likely to track to its source."[26] CNN ignored the fact that over the same time period, legislators in the United States were demanding stricter control for cybercafes in the United States:

> Earlier this year, Los Angeles council members passed an ordinance that required the presence of security guards at cyber cafes that stay open to the public at night....Pending results from the citywide investigation into cyber cafe violence, Zine and fellow city council members are proposing that cyber cafes be more closely regulated and that in addition to the steady presence of security guards, that they carry age restrictions.[27]

Regulations, such as libraries being forced to use filtering software for underage youth in the United States are not seen in connection with control and censorship but in terms of the protection of youth.[28] The explanations offered by the Chinese in defense of their actions are simply disregarded, for example, that certain measures were necessary for the "protection of youth," or that "unlicensed cybercafes" without adequate fire and safety precautions represented a hazard. The content of the narratives related to the closing down of cybercafes thus depends on location and on the political stance of the reporter.[29]

The Chinese "Leap-Frogging Discourse"

In sharp contrast to Western discourses, Chinese discourses have focused on the internet's role as a tool for China's economic development with frequent reference being made to Western analysts. Technology-oriented modernization and the leap frogging of industrial development has remained at the heart of Chinese research and the official news agency Xinhua sees a rosy future for China in its internet development: "Technological leap frogging supports the tomorrow of the Republic."[30] Another indicator for the dominance of the Chinese teleological discourse on modernity and the role played by ICTs is the popularity of the American "futurologist" Alvin Toffler. His work *The Third Wave* was translated into Chinese in the early 1980s; all his works are said to have become bestsellers in China and many of his phrases have been widely used in China's social, economic and cultural lives.[31] The term "technological leap frogging" (*jishu kuayue*) is used in this context to refer to the idea of omitting a stage in economic development with the help of information and communication technologies, that is, of leap frogging the industrial phase and achieving, through informatization (the third wave), the foundations of the second wave (industrialization).[32] Agents ranging from the government,[33] the mass media, companies, and average internet users participate in a public discourse that is shaped by these ideas. This kind of discourse can also be found in the works of Chinese mainstream academics: Xie Kang, for example, believes that "informatization is one of the most efficient means by which a country can achieve industrialization, gain economic benefits and increase production efficiency…the Internet is a critical multiplier in China's drive toward achieving an advanced level of economic development."[34] There is also an astonishing emphasis on the development of the infrastructure and new technology, such as, the introduction of the third generation of mobile phones and the Internet Protocol Version 6, which will make the — still highly controlled — Chinese internet one of the fastest in the world.[35]

In China, in addition to these mainstream developments, a few research projects have dealt with internet use in the hinterland or with the impact of the internet on "especially vulnerable groups" such as children, women, peasants, migrants, and minorities.[36] This research is based on empirical studies and focuses on the self-image of the groups interviewed. A fairly optimistic attitude about the modernizing potential of the internet also prevails in these studies. The internet is portrayed as the technological tool for incorporating backward regions and groups into the modernizing mainstream by providing them with modern information, ideas, and experiences of using equipment.

Limits of the Discourses and Diffusion of the Internet in China

Discourses dealing with the impact of the internet on Chinese society capture only a few aspects of the ways in which this technology is promoting change; the arguments remain at best incomplete because insufficient empirical attention is paid to who uses the internet and how s/he uses it. The reasons for this lack of empirical attention are various. One reason is that Western research on the internet in China is often influenced by Chinese dissidents, now working in various departments of U.S. universities. And these dissidents are well aware of the high priority given to questions of censorship by the U.S. mainstream media. Another reason is that anyone seeking to carry out a content analysis of the internet in China faces the problem of how to deal with the sheer mass of available content. Finally, internet providers in China are reluctant to provide researchers, whether Westerners or Chinese, with data on internet usage, such as information about the exact numbers of accesses. In the case of research into BBSs, for example, it is possible to calculate the number of registered users at any particular time, but it is impossible to estimate how many users have only an inactive "observer status."

Much of the research on the internet in China is now being carried out by commercial institutes (such as CCID Saidi-consultant[37]), which have strong interests in promoting e-business and e-commerce. Although these institutes are concerned with lifestyle and consumerist attitudes, they generally do not focus attention on aspects of identity politics and societal changes, concentrating instead on matters of brand-name building and on how to increase the efficiency of the internet in selling products.

In order to assess whether Western discourses of censorship and liberation or Chinese discourses of modernization provide an accurate picture of the influence and impact of the internet in China today, it is necessary to examine some of the specific features of local Internet usage and content. In the subsequent sections I examine the demographic user profiles as presented in the statistical reports published since 1997 by the Chinese Internet Network Information Center (CNNIC), which include information on user demographics, access locations, and average online behavior.[38] Next, I present interviews with users that were carried out in 2002 and 2003 in Fuzhou and Xiamen cities in Fujian Province and in Nanhai City in Guangzhou Province.[39] Finally, I consider the example of one the BBSs/Internet forums that have become an essential part of all big Chinese Internet portals to consider what a qualitative content analysis of a site can tell us about the local usage and local content of the Internet in China and its focus on consumerism and lifestyle.

Who Is Using the Net?

Internet use in the People's Republic of China (PRC) has grown at a tremendous pace: CNNIC statistics show that 130 million Chinese had on-line access in mid 2006.[40] The internet arrived at a time when the nonprofit and academic Net had already undergone commercialization worldwide, as reflected in the hype surrounding the "New Economy." It is therefore hardly surprising that three of the five most popular websites in China today are stock-listed portals: Sina, Sohu, and Netease — the other two being focused search machines, www.3721.com-search and www.baidu.com-search.

Some conclusions about who is using the Net can be drawn from the data in the CNNIC reports. Although a variety of different groups of Chinese internet users can be identified, they share some common characteristics. The average user is male (60 percent), young (80 percent under thirty-five), and highly educated (more than 75 percent have a senior high school degree or higher qualification), belongs to the new urban middle class, and is a beneficiary of the economic, and to some extent, political reforms of the late 1990s and the new millennium.[41]

The typical internet user has a highly pragmatic approach toward the government and the Chinese Communist Party (CCP): for example, English-speaking Western visitors to China, whether business people, students, or tourists, will invariably note after their first stop at a cybercafe that the technology is highly developed, but will complain that the big news portals such as CNN and the *New York Times* are blocked.[42] For the Chinese, however, this is not astonishing: they expect the government to censor all media. Yet even taking this censorship into account, the internet, unlike TV and the newspapers, still offers hundreds of thousands of informative and unblocked sites. Even interviewees with an academic background expressed strong support for the filtering of websites; their arguments usually followed the official line that pornography or "evil cults" (that is, Falun Gong) pose a threat to the masses of not-so-well-educated Chinese people. "Many people in China are still very backward, and they could easily be persuaded to believe in the Falun Gong propaganda, but you know, many people have killed themselves because they were told to do so by this evil cult [*xiejiao*], and it is the duty of our government to protect the people."[43] This interviewee, however, regarded himself as sufficiently well educated to recognize "good" and "evil" without the help of the government.

These users support the regime's efforts to establish the internet as part of a modern economy and society and to control "sensitive political issues." In their view, a political discourse aimed at overthrowing the current regime would probably lead to political instability ("chaos" or *luan*). Russia and Taiwan were frequently depicted during the interviews as examples of emerging "chaos." The democratization processes in Russia were believed to have led to increasing corruption and economic problems, developments that compared unfavorably with China's rapid economic growth. Taiwan's democracy, praised in the West, was described in terms of chaos; the interviewees mentioned newspaper pictures and TV reports of members of parliament indulging in fistfights, economic growth well below the rate in the People's Republic, and many social problems such as pornography, gambling, and corruption. It is remarkable that people in Xiamen who had better opportunities to access various Taiwanese media, including the internet (only the bigger portals were blocked),[44] were nevertheless highly critical of democratic developments. This was perhaps because the extensive reports in the Taiwanese media on corruption ("black gold politics") were not interpreted in terms of Taiwan being more open, but in terms of Taiwan being more corrupt. In addition, the interviewees were firmly against any move toward independence by the Taiwanese, and stressed that only a strong CCP would be able to prevent Taiwan from becoming a "renegade province."[45]

Students at Xiamen University also showed a very ambiguous attitude toward the closing of "illegal" cybercafes in the university neighborhood: on the one hand, they were aware of the problems that could arise from alcohol consumption and smoking in the cafes and could understand parents' worries; on the other hand, some of the students had also used these cafes because the opening times were very user friendly and these places offered all-night facilities for playing games. In my interviews, nobody mentioned that these internet cafes might offer easy access to "illegal political sites."[46] With regard to societal changes and identity politics, the general opinion seemed to be that the internet offered new space for personal development: the internet was used to contact people living outside China, and various marginalized groups used the internet as a virtual meeting place.[47] To mention only one example, gays and lesbians have started to use the internet as a virtual meeting place. The website http://www.gaychina.com, for example, is such a forum, with links offered in both Chinese and English. People of different nationalities, along with Chinese who reside in mainland China and elsewhere, use these forums.[48]

To sum up, China's internet users are for the most part the winners of political reform: they are highly educated and live in the well-developed urban regions in China. Even though controls by parents and society are stricter than in the West, internet users have begun to develop their own private space. Even in poorer regions, though, where one could be expect to find more dissatisfaction with the government, internet usage appears to be following the same trend.

Research carried out by Bu Wei and Guo Liang of the Chinese Academy of Social Sciences (CASS), for example, has revealed that many internet users reside in small cities where there is a high density of legal and illegal internet cafes. They showed that more than half of the users in small cities in 2004 were young people aged seventeen to twenty-four (58 percent) who care more about playing online games and chatting than politics.[49] This is not to say that they ignore politics; they are quick to respond when government action threatens to disrupt their seemingly apoliticized lifestyles. As an example, the case of Du Daobin involved a user who had not engaged in any activities that other users would consider unacceptable. He had only lobbied for the release of a fellow cyber-dissident Liu Di (aka Stainless Steel Mouse). It was obvious that the authorities had singled him out to serve as an example, and this led to massive protests by netizens.[50] That is to say that a community of netizens emerged that was willing to act in the event of fellow netizens being arrested. I would argue, however, that on the whole internet users do not demand the democratization of China or the adoption of a multiparty system but express a high degree of trust in the government as has been shown by opinion polls carried out during recent years.[51] It is simply a matter of their being prepared to protest when the government tries to interfere in the special "zone of freedom" that the internet has created.

Other politically motivated users include Chinese hackers and nationalist students who also do not use the internet in accordance with Western expectations. That is, they do not simply use the internet to fight for "democracy" against the Chinese state. Rather, many of them support the Communist Party regime against "Western neo-imperialism."[52] This concurs with de Kloet's argument that hackers' actions are not usually directed against their own government, as the West usually assumes, but against Western imperialism, as in the case of the plane that was shot down off the coast of China in 2001.[53] A strict dichotomy between the government, seen as the oppressor, and a free, global-hacker initiative is nonexistent. "The Internet does not seem to eliminate national borders and geographical distance," de Kloet concludes.[54] The Chinese internet user is, therefore, not necessarily interested in subversive activities against the government, he/she often has a positive stance toward the government and a critical stance toward Western governments and multinational companies; he/she represents the typical "winner" of the economic reforms and sees a positive value in the internet itself.

Bulletin Board Systems — Symbols for the Chinese Netizen?

If we accept the convincing premise that Chinese internet users belong to a postmodern consumerist society and that this has led to a nonpolitical kind of "cultural" and "do-it-yourself" citizenship that includes adherence to identity politics, then it is reasonable to expect a more extensive use of certain internet applications such as chats and BBSs, the latter also being known as (internet) forums.[55] All these applications are characterized by many-to-many communication and thus provide an ideal place not only for discussion but also for building virtual on-line communities.[56]

The great importance of BBSs and chats in the Chinese internet is confirmed by Giese,[57] who reports that although the internet in China offers "virtually all services in Chinese that are available on the World Wide Web around the globe," 34 to 39 percent of Chinese users in later surveys when asked for their favorite web activity stated that they favored on-line chat most; another 18 to 19 percent stated that they favored BBSs.[58] Giese concluded that this "seems to reflect a particularly strong affinity of Chinese internet users toward interpersonal communication via the Internet that is not at all consistent with the familiar usage patterns of Western countries."[59] Guobin Yang and Giese also described these discussions as "insider discussions," assuming that the users had a high degree of familiarity with the Chinese language, e.g., the use of homonyms and Chinese tradition and culture, as well as with the more recent past, that is, expressions derived from the Cultural Revolution.[60]

In China, these BBSs are not only provided by the big portals,[61] but by numerous public, private, and semiprivate websites as well.[62] A typical BBS as presented on the big portals is divided into several topics: culture and art, lifestyle (e.g., film gossip, pop stars, love and emotion, including a *tongzhi*, queer section, and "night life") health, women, cars,[63] real estate, finance, and the stock market.[64] For example, Sohu's BBS start page offers discussion sections entitled "culture and art" (*wenhua yishu*), "lifestyle" (*shenghuo shishang*), and "camp of love" (*qinggan zhenying*), among many others.[65] Clearly, the emphasis is on lifestyle and private life, and also reflects the dominance of the urban middle class.

Going into one of the sub-sites, we see how virtual groups are constructed by the big portals. As an example, I have chosen "Sohu's women's club" (http://club.women.sohu.com/), which is structured as follows: at the top, there are links to the general BBS topics offered by Sohu; directly below are links to the sub-groups of the "women's club" such as fashion, makeup, hairstyles, body shaping, gossip, men and women, brides, marriage, men, women's views, babies, pregnancy, horoscopes, and dating — all in all, a very traditional spread of women's interests is presented, with women's roles represented only in terms of motherhood and heterosexual partnerships. Below this, several currently popular threads are highlighted, including [Mid-life people] "Such a strong woman," [Women are afraid of ghosts] "Love can sometimes embody sinister intentions," and [Women's society] "Do women go for money? Or for love?"[66] In addition to text, pictures of young, attractive, fashionably dressed women, mostly Chinese, appear. Amateur photos of Sohu users are also placed on-line; the women in these photos, however, show a remarkable resemblance to those appearing in the professional shots.

On the left-hand side of the web page, the user is informed about the number of "clicks," that is, the number of visitors to the respective subgroups. But these figures do not indicate when the visits were made, or how long users stayed within a group. Nonmainstream topics only appear at the bottom of the page, for example, the community forum (*shequ luntan*) that covers threads such as "lesbian love," "what women are afraid of," and "singles." A socially conservative stance is prevalent, but the variety of threads offered by mainstream portals reflects a heterogenization of Chinese society that gives some space to nonmainstream topics such as "queer passion" (*tongzhi qingshen*) and "nights in the city."

Another feature of the BBSs in China is the localization of virtual communities. It could be assumed, as the term "virtual" indicates, that these communities are borderless, but the popularity of geographically restricted virtual groups and analyses of site content show that users of these groups often eventually make personal contact. Sohu, for example, lists thirty to forty BBSs topics for Beijing alone, including "hotel for all and everybody," "on-line love," "single men and women," and "*tongzhi* love."[67] Indeed, for Guangxi, the province with the lowest rate of internet usage, we found that forums were established only on the basis of geographical locations: "Guangxi families," "Nanning City forum," "forum for Guilin City," "forum for Baise City," and "forum for Yulin City."

This brief overview of the characteristics of the internet BBS sites in China reveals that they are for the most part concerned not with politics and subversion but with identity politics, in particular, lifestyle identities and regional identities. Lifestyle identities are for the most part oriented around consumerism, as exemplified by discussions of fashionable brands of jeans, though they also include less mainstream concerns such as sexuality (*tongzhi* love, male city, women's club). Regional identities are reflected in the geographically localized content of the sites and the role of the internet in building virtual communities that are geographically limited in their reach (see the examples of Beijing and Guangxi).

Conclusion

Three points need be mentioned: first, the diametrically opposed discourses found in the West and in China on the role of China's internet; second, the fragmentation and localization of the internet, which in many aspects mirrors contemporary Chinese society; third, the interest-focus of Chinese internet users on consumerism and lifestyle issues, including identity politics.

Fundamental differences can be found between the discourses of Western analysts and the discourses of Chinese analysts regarding the social and political impact of the internet in China. Western discourses have focused on democratization and political change, paying little attention to broader social changes. During the 1990s, a prevalent view in Western publications, described earlier in this article, was that the introduction of the internet would result in Western models of democracy and democratic participation taking root in Chinese society. In recent years, however, a new assumption has emerged — one that presents the Chinese Party-state as being successful in controlling the internet. But this discourse is only an "inverted" version of the discourse focused on democratization and political change. The Chinese discourse, on the other hand, is very technology-deterministic, focused entirely on the potential economic and modernizing benefits of the new communication technologies, while politely ignoring the internet's increasingly significant role as a playground for socializing and sexuality. The Chinese discourse has thus to be seen in terms of an uncritical modernization paradigm that not only has shaped the Chinese Party-state and academic discourse, but has also become part of a seldom-questioned general societal discourse.[68]

When writing about the West, commentators today do not assume an essential role for the internet in fostering democracy and citizen participation, but they do assume such a role to be vitally important for China and for other "authoritarian third world states." So, an "early political discourse," long abandoned in the West, is now being used as the dominant paradigm for research into China's internet. The civil society approach, which could be used effectively to describe the role of the internet in China, is more frequently used in a very narrow sense within the Western discourse, with a dominant focus on political discussions that are largely restricted to topics seen as crucial in the West, such as Taiwan or human rights.

Despite these dominant discourses the current use of the internet in China is shaped by fragmentation and localization. The fragmentation of the Chinese internet mirrors the societal developments that Sheldon Lu has convincingly described as emerging "consumerist postmodernity" characterized by "the superimposition of multiple temporalities; the pre-modern, the modern, and the postmodern, which coexist in the same space and at the same moment."[69] This fragmentation and plurality stand in contrast to cultural, religious, and ideological grand narratives.[70] The internet, or to be more precise, the Chinese specific forms of the internet such as forums and interactive, communicative localized features, foster such fragmentation.

This fragmentation can be found in the form of a digital divide between developed and undeveloped regions, urban areas and the hinterland, and within the urban postmodernist society itself. The digital and economic divide in China shapes the different uses of the internet and these differences in use are much broader than those found in the West. Some more recent Chinese field research carried out in the hinterland came to the conclusion that the internet was seldom seen as offering an opportunity and as bringing change to China's rural economy; the dominant view was that information and communication technologies (ICTs) are "toys for the middle class."[71]

The Chinese middle class, which makes up the most important group of internet users, is part of a postmodern society, with a strong interest in personalized and individual lifestyles; this group is now much less politicized than it was in the 1980s, when the reforms had just taken off:

> Cultural discussion in China has turned away from politically engaged and intellectually oppositional topics: historical and cultural reasons of despotism and tyranny; the urgency of political reform and democracy; the need of social enlightenment and its humanistic values of tolerance, civil liberty, and intellectual freedom; deliberation on the rule of law versus the rule of man; and debate on new authoritarianism versus democracy. Cultural discussion of the 1990s has considerably reshaped its orientation. Most new currents of cultural discussion, by choice or circumstance, have

shown either a reconciliation of intellectual inquiry with the prevailing political order or a deliberate avoidance of sensitive sociopolitical issues.[72]

It is no wonder, then, that the Chinese internet is more a playground for leisure, socializing, and commerce than a hotbed of political activism. The fragmentation within urban postmodernist society is most clearly demonstrated by the popularity of the BBSs. In these BBSs, conservative elements such as the emphasis on traditional gender roles and "family values" are dominant, but other elements also point to a new openness including sexual liberation. While the greater openness does not offset the prevailing conservatism it does illustrate the fragmentation of society. In some ways, this fragmentation has led to more diversity, but since the internet does not actively encourage communication between different groups, a society has emerged that is shaped by many isolated niches. It has been argued that in contemporary societies "public participation is much higher and more enthusiastic in 'commercial democracy' than in the formal mechanics of representative politics."[73] The citizens of the People's Republic of China do not have any experience of a representative democracy, but consumerism and economic opportunities in times of globalization and commercialization mean that people develop their very own public spheres: a "'civil society' of a nation without borders, without state institutions, and without citizens."[74] In this context, we should take into consideration that, from the very beginning, the internet in China was driven mainly by commercial interests that were exploited by private companies such as Sohu, Sina, and Netease and also by state ministries.[75] This commercialization of the internet is significant because it has underpinned much of the trivialization and depoliticization of internet content and usage in China. And in many ways, it is precisely this depoliticization that has helped to create social spaces in which marginal groups such as gays and lesbians can claim a voice.[76] Discussions on the emergence of a "Chinese citizen" (*shimin,* or *gongmin*) have stressed that a very specific form of "cultural" and "do-it-yourself"[77] citizenship is being created that is not defined by conventional politics so much as by a strong adherence to identity politics (including regional, youth, gender, religious, and minority identities).[78]

❑

6

SMS, COMMUNICATION, AND CITIZENSHIP IN CHINA'S INFORMATION SOCIETY

Kevin Latham

AT THE BEGINNING OF THE TWENTY-FIRST CENTURY China is a complex whirl of contradictory social, political, and economic practices, some of which are new and some of which bear the marks of the pre-reform period. Moreover, China has entered a new information age,[1] and this calls for a reconsideration of some key presuppositions about the relationship between Chinese media, communication, society, and culture. It is time to question some of the stereotypes that dominate representations and understandings of China such as the appealing, though too simple, model of propaganda versus free speech and political repression versus democracy or those anticipating the emergence of a more or less Habermasian "public sphere."[2]

Less than three decades ago, China was a black hole regarding information — viewed from afar by academics who craved the slightest morsels of information that could be wrenched from Mao Zedong's enormous gravitational pull. Meanwhile, within China there was a stern, forbidding, and sometimes sinister political economy of information characterized, among other things, by personal dossiers, self-criticisms, restricted "internal" (*neibu*) publications and sections of bookshops, along with power-supporting hierarchies of access to information.[3]

China's media and communications landscape has undergone a root and branch transformation over the intervening decades.[4] Now, China is suddenly awash with information and driven by an economy of information desire. People crave national and international news and business and economic headlines; they have tens of television channels as well as hundreds and thousands of newspapers, websites, radio stations, magazines, and other media products to choose from. According to the Ministry of Information Industries (MII) at the end of September 2006 there were more than 77 million broadband internet users and more than 812 million telephone subscribers in China including more than 443 million mobile phone subscribers and 369 million fixed-line subscribers.[5] However, media and communications have played a fundamental part in the construction of Chinese political subjectivity, and hence citizenship, since the foundation of the People's Republic of China (PRC) in 1949 and to some degree before that.[6] Indeed, the Chinese Communist Party (CCP) and Chinese government structures were founded upon notions of communications systems.[7] They are themselves media of fundamental importance in contemporary China and many of these conceptualizations of the Party, the media, and communications still affect China's media today.

It has been widely documented that Chinese media production is now largely commercially driven, producing competing pressures on editors, journalists, and media executives to meet the demands of the market while also fulfilling their political responsibilities.[8] Indeed, one of the recurring generic problems facing media reform in different sectors in China in recent years has been the persistence of contradictions and disjunctures between media organized along the lines of political subject formation and the new demands for media to operate in reaction to the volition of independently minded consumer citizens.[9] In this way the Party voices rhetoric from the past, while many people, particularly in metropolitan centers, are driving their own alternative visions of the future.

At the same time the combination of a commercializing and liberalizing media landscape along with a new China largely opened up to the rest of the world has to some degree undermined the media's role as the "throat and tongue" (*houshe*), that is, the mouthpiece of the CCP, and its accompanying assumptions of a hermetically sealed Chinese populace.[10] However, these arguments have been made largely in relation to mainstream mass media, predominantly television and newspapers. In this article, by contrast, I will explore this changing media landscape using the less commonly considered example of telecommunications, and the recent explosion in popularity of short messaging service (SMS) text messaging in particular.

SMS now constitutes an important new set of communication practices in China. It is far more widely used than the internet and by a far more diverse section of the population. More than one in four Chinese people nationally now have mobile phones whereas fewer than one in twelve use the internet. In early 2005, fifteen times more SMS messages than emails were being sent per person in China.[11] Yet, the received frames of reference for understanding Chinese media and communications do not offer a model appropriate to the ways that it is used. I will argue that consideration of what I call "orderly" and "disorderly" media reveals areas where we need to question received models of analysis in relation to Chinese media and their relationship to power, political subjectivity, and citizenship.

Media and Citizenship in China

China's media has long been centered on the notion of citizenship, given its key role in the political education of the populace, the maintenance of political consciousness, and the mobilization of Chinese people in the national project of modernization whether under Mao Zedong, Deng Xiaoping, or more recent leaders. The fundamental and in theory unquestionable operating principle of Chinese media is its role as the mouthpiece of the CCP. Given the CCP's understanding of people as malleable, "blank sheets" to be reeducated according to a socialist understanding of society,[12] the mouthpiece principle alone defines Chinese media in terms of its capacity and duty ideologically to produce good Chinese citizens.

Under Mao's principle of the mass line, the Party and its media and communications apparatuses were the crucial links between the national leadership and the people.[13] Indeed, with the widespread organization of regular political meetings in the past, it is almost possible to argue that Chinese society itself became a communications system.[14] The media had a key role to play in mobilizing the people into political and social action through mass mobilization campaigns[15] and maintaining a level of both participation and ideologically driven understanding.

It is this model of the relationship between the media, society, and citizenship that still officially underpins, and practically constrains, many aspects of contemporary media production. The mouthpiece principle undergirds the work of China's media industries,[16] even if questioned occasionally inside the media industries;[17] party organ newspapers are still defined in terms of their specific propaganda roles and other publications also have propaganda responsibilities.[18] However, recent developments in Chinese media and communications have problematized this model.

Telecommunications in particular fall outside of this mass media-centered model. This was most dramatically demonstrated in May and June 1989 when telephones and fax machines were used extensively by people outside China — particularly in Hong Kong — to tell people in Beijing and other Chinese cities what was going on in the capital once martial law had been imposed.[19] However, the development of telecommunications in China in the intervening period has taken the significance of this "fax effect" far beyond its very visible manifestation in the summer of 1989. Telecommunications have introduced a whole new set of communicational and social possibilities into Chinese people's lives. This can be viewed structurally as the diminution of the effects of the established vertical model of political communication through the introduction of more horizontal possibilities. As Daniel Lynch points out, telecommunications have been crucial to the formation of transorganizational and transregional social networks and groups in China.[20] By contrast, the development of China's "multi-centric" telecommunications network

> is shattering this decades-old (even centuries old) pattern of local isolation and establishing conditions for the development of cross-hatching "societal *xitong* [system]," linking individuals, organisations, and groups throughout the country with each other and with people abroad.[21]

The growth of the internet has drawn particular attention in relation to debates about the emergence of new forms and modes of communication[22] while other areas of telecommunications have been relatively neglected.[23] Although there are common issues clearly arising between the internet, SMS, and telecommunications more generally — and we will discuss some of these below — this article will focus on the way that recent developments in telecommunications have affected the mediated relationship between the state and its citizens. In particular, I will consider the emergence of SMS text messaging in the early 2000s.

SMS in China

In the late 1990s and early 2000s SMS text messaging grew rapidly in popularity[24] to become the latest in a series of new telecommunications technologies (following fax machines, pagers, fixed-line phones, mobile phones, and the internet and e-mail) to be used as new sources of information, enabling new forms of communication. SMS is popularly used in two ways: either for self-written messages or for subscription information services, often through websites. SMS messages can also be sent from a PC to a mobile phone.

According to the MII, just under 19 billion SMS messages were sent in China in 2001. In the following year this rose to 95 billion messages between the two mobile phone operators China Mobile and China Unicom. By 2003 the number had more than doubled again to 220 billion messages. With a more than eleven-fold increase over just a three-year period, this is remarkable growth by any standards. In 2004 the growth rate slowed quite sharply but in the first four months of 2005 alone there were 90.25 billion messages sent, still representing growth of around 39 percent year-on-year. In all, 304.65 billion SMS messages were sent in 2005, representing 40 percent growth on 2004. This has made SMS a multibillion yuan industry, with an estimated market value of around Rmb30 billion per year in 2005. Economically, SMS has also played a key role in making China's previously loss-making internet portals, such as the country's top three, Nasdaq-listed Sina.com, Sohu.com, and Netease.com, all turn profits for the first time in 2002 and 2003.

The importance of SMS is not just a matter of economics, however. SMS has also transformed daily interactions and even traditional celebrations. Over the one-week holiday for Chinese New Year in 2005 more than 11 billion SMS messages were sent in China. Indeed, the New Year's holiday has become a high point in the SMS calendar as hundreds of millions of mobile users exchange New Year's greetings. Going back only as far as the early 1990s it was relatively uncommon for Chinese people, even in the large, wealthier cities like Beijing, Shanghai, and Guangzhou, to have either fixed-line phones in their own homes or to have mobiles. Passing Chinese New Year in Guangzhou in 1989 entailed a week of cycling from the home of one friend or relation to another, largely unannounced, though not necessarily unexpected. Just fifteen years later the bike has for many been replaced by a motorbike, taxi, or even a private car, complex meeting arrangements are worked out in advance and on the hoof using mobile phones, and many people receive more New Year's greetings by SMS text message than in person. SMS is, of course, not solely responsible for these changes in modes of socializing and social interaction. Clearly the mobile phone used for SMS itself has had a fundamentally important role, but the SMS New Year's greeting message offers a succinct metonymic indicator of how much social interaction, in Chinese cities in particular, has changed in a relatively short period of time.

As well as transforming the way that many mobile phone users in China communicate with each other, SMS has also given them new ways to keep up to date with current affairs, financial news, sports, entertainment, travel, and other kinds of information. Chinese internet portals all offer an extensive range of SMS news and information services to cater to almost any interest. A survey carried out by the *People's Daily* in April 2004 found that among SMS services, news provision was still the most popular, accounting for 45.9 percent of responses.[25] This was followed by 30.7 percent saying they used SMS for practical information, 28.3 percent for greetings and salutation, 28 percent for images and ring tones, 27.2 percent for jokes, 17.3 percent for entertainment, and 9.2 percent for chatting. However, the survey also found a clear trend away from traditional news and information services toward entertainment and social interaction. For instance, when asked about services that they hoped to subscribe to in the future 41.7 percent said entertainment information, 32.6 percent said humor services, and 26.2 percent said they would use SMS for chatting. By contrast those expecting to subscribe to news services was down to just 26.4 percent.

The diversifying use of SMS is perhaps most clearly illustrated by the technology's input into the world of literature. In 2004, China's first text message novel was published and sent to tens of thousands of paying mobile phone users. Written by a businessman called Qian Fuzhang, *Out of the Fortress* was forty-two hundred characters long and was sent in twice daily installments of some seventy characters. In return, Qian was paid around US$20,000 by the text message distribution company. Some literary critics have hailed the concise, poetic style of the SMS novel as a new form of writing reminiscent of classical Chinese.[26]

SMS has also transformed media consumption by opening up new ways to engage with other mainstream mass media such as radio and television. By 2004, SMS had become regularly integrated into other media, sports, and entertainment activities, offering novel forms of media interactivity. Television and radio programs, for instance, increasingly encourage audience participation through SMS messaging. This may range from participation in a competition to expressing views on issues discussed in a program. At the same time additional information services and competitions or games operated via SMS have become increasingly regular features of sports and cultural and entertainment events. During the 2004 Athens Olympics, television stations, radio stations, internet portals, newspapers, and other media all ran SMS competitions, offered results services, sports updates, and the opportunity to express opinions on events at the games. In this way, SMS has played a crucial role in enhancing media interactivity. Prior to SMS key forms of media interactivity included radio phone-ins,[27] news hotlines, letter writing, and emails. Sun has argued that online journalism also opens up new forms of interactivity in news consumption.[28] Bulletin boards, on-line forums, email, and, more recently, blogging all offer opportunities to open a dialogue with journalists, to comment upon or supply further information about news stories.[29] However, the speed, flexibility, and possibilities for automation offered by SMS have made it a preferred form of media audience interaction for many program producers in other media. Thousands of people can feel directly involved in a television program through SMS in a way that only a small handful could using a traditional phone-in.

SMS is also becoming increasingly used in other areas of social activity apart from news or information services and chatting with friends. Commercial use of SMS is increasing and spreading, including adventurous steps into banking and stock trading. At the same time, **regional governments in a number of** areas, including Shanghai, have adopted SMS both as a means of internal communication within government departments and operations as well as for communicating government messages to the general populace. In all of these ways, SMS is transforming Chinese social interaction, cultural production, media consumption, and communication practices.

Orderly and Disorderly Media

SMS has become a significant mode of communication, straddling the line between what I call "orderly" and "disorderly" media. The notion of order and disorder used here is intended to draw together several concepts related to government attitudes and practices toward the media. In short, the notions refer to the degree to which the government and the Party feel they can or need to influence the output and production of media messages with orderly media being more and disorderly media less able to be influenced.

Hence, the traditional mass media, like radio, television, and newspapers, are relatively orderly. In the current Chinese media environment, most media output is politically cautious, uncontroversial, and unlikely to incur any kind of severe direct intervention on the part of the authorities. At the same time, however, the media are ultimately controllable. They can, if necessary, be closed down, taken off the air, taken over, run directly, monitored more closely, or guided in some other way.[30] These more orderly media are predictable and knowable. The complex mechanisms of self-censorship, a sense of responsibility, professionalism, and hegemonic notions such as the fear of chaos[31] or the "quality" of the population[32] combined with relatively light-touch supervision, with potentially serious consequences, by propaganda bureau officials, means that the authorities can generally rely on both written and unspoken rules and guidelines being adhered to. Journalists and media producers ascertain which lines not to cross. In this sense orderly media are predictable. They are knowable in the sense of being able to know what they have produced in the past, what they are producing at present, and what they are likely to produce in the future. The authorities know who is producing what for whom and they know how to influence outcomes should the need arise. They also know that if need be they can be made "safe."

By contrast, disorderly media are more individualized or small-group focused. The "content" of telecommunications is unregulated, contingent, unpredictable, and largely unknowable (without individual targeted interception or tapping). It is impossible to know when they will be used, what will be said, by whom, to whom, and for what purposes, and they cannot easily be switched off, controlled, or made safe by centralized supervisory authorities. Telecommunications, whether fixed-line phones, faxes, mobiles, or some aspects of the internet, fit clearly into the notion of disorderly media.

However, the notions of orderly and disorderly media can also have more specific connotations in the Chinese context, particularly in relation to China's political definition and organization of the media. For instance, the organization and commercial operation of radio, television, and newspapers, that is, China's orderly media, are also largely incorporated into the structures of Party and government administration and supervision. In China's telecommunications system, by contrast, "even the Ministry of Information Industries itself has little influence over telecommunications development at the provincial level and below, with what lingering influence it does have continuing to decline."[33] In this sense it is also interesting to note that disorderly media in China have been left to develop much more under the influence of market forces and competition although not necessarily with greater private sector involvement. Yet at the same time, in the absence of regulation of use and content, there has nonetheless often been a strong emphasis on maintaining order in the market through the regulation of the MII.[34] This was achieved, for instance, by limiting the number of companies involved[35] and introducing regulations that favored large corporations rather than smaller, more independent enterprises.[36]

In China the ideas of order and chaos also have strong social and political connotations. Chaos is widely associated with the disruption and suffering of wars in the first half of the twentieth century as well as the Cultural Revolution a little later. More recently, the control of chaos and the reintroduction of order were repeated day in and day out in the Chinese mass media in the months following June 1989 as the justification for sending troops into Beijing's Tiananmen Square and also into other Chinese cities, notably Shanghai. Hence, the notion of "order" already has connotations in official discourse of necessary and justified political control. Orderly media therefore are not only orderly in themselves but they play a crucial role in maintaining order in China's social polity.

Disorderly media are not seen as having this role. Although they are disorderly, their disorderliness has not been perceived by the Chinese authorities to be a problem. Whereas orderly mass media are believed to have effects — positive in the right hands, negative in the wrong ones — disorderly media have been conceived more in terms of their utility rather than their effects. Telephones, faxes, mobiles, and pagers are seen to facilitate interpersonal communication, to enhance the operation and development of business and government, and generally to make life easier and run more smoothly. At least until the advent of the internet, and the silent organization of the Falun Gong spiritual movement in the late 1990s, disorderly media in China have not, on the whole, been associated with being a threat to the regime or to political education and thought work. In short, disorderly media have been assumed to be sufficiently benign whereas orderly media are seen to be potentially dangerous.

To be sure, the distinction between orderly and disorderly media is not in reality clear-cut and simple. Some media cross over divisions and may be seen in different ways as both orderly and disorderly. It may be that their degree of orderliness has changed over time — the Internet for example.[37] Indeed, the Chinese authorities have regularly found ways of trying to bring order to disorderly media that come to be seen as less benign than they once were. In some cases, the authorities have also tried to appropriate disorderly media for their own more orderly purposes. In 2005, for instance, Chinese newspapers were also reporting undercover government officials who were being trained to infiltrate on-line chat rooms and on-line bulletin boards in order to put forward the government position on topics arising in discussion.[38] Hence, there are orderly aspects of disorderly media, as we will see with SMS below, and disorderly aspects of orderly media.[39]

SMS exhibits both disorderly and orderly characteristics. At first it appears to be distinctly disorderly. Used as a means of interpersonal communication to send messages to friends, family and colleagues on an individual or small-group basis, SMS is as disorderly as other forms of telecommunications such as voice calls, fax messages, and so on. However, used as a source of news and information people's use of any of the thousands of subscription services available on-line draws SMS back further into the realm of orderly media. SMS news services are not exactly in the realm of mass media like television or radio, but the news they carry is overseen by mechanisms of self-censorship and supervision similar to other news media and the messages are sourced from official news organizations.

This kind of interrelationship and interpenetration of orderly and disorderly media means that these notions of orderly and disorderly media should not be oversimplified, or for that matter applied too rigidly. However, the concepts are useful for highlighting trends in the development of China's media landscape and revealing some of the problems of previous models of communication applied in the Chinese context. Below I shall elaborate how the distinction between orderly and disorderly media reveals the shortcomings of some of the standard conceptualizations of media and politics in China, including those assumed by the government, as well as those employed by external analysts such as journalists, academics, and governments. I shall argue that these are still dominated by understandings formulated in relation to the orderly propaganda model of Chinese media inherited from the past and fail to account for either disorderly media or disorderly aspects and developments in orderly media. In the end, we shall also see how these relate directly to notions and understandings of Chinese citizenship.

Rethinking Assumptions and Presuppositions of Chinese Media

A cluster of interrelated assumptions about media, communication, political control, and subject formation has dominated understandings of Chinese media for at least the last fifty years. These assumptions relate to the propaganda nature of Chinese media as discussed above. For reasons of space, I shall focus on two core, interrelated assumptions in this cluster: first, that media have effects, and second, that information has durable value. I suggest that we need to reconsider these assumptions in the light of new emerging media technologies and practices such as those related to SMS and other disorderly media. In short,

I shall argue that in the past, the relationship between media and citizenship has been over-determined by ideological models of information transfer and communication and that these models are inadequate to the task of conceptualizing the relationship between media and citizenship in contemporary China.

Media Have Effects

The media studies field has long wrestled with the question of whether, and if so to what extent and in what way, media have effects.[40] Whatever the outcome of such academic debates, the Chinese government (and its critics) have insisted for decades that media have effects. This core assumption is exemplified by the fundamental role given to mass media in disseminating government policy, in mobilizing the population, in thought-work, and in political education. It also underpins the Chinese government's cautious and sensitive attitude toward private and foreign involvement in media sectors and it explains why the Chinese authorities, even while accepting a swathe of market-oriented reforms and commercial media operations, nonetheless insist on state ownership of media organizations and vehemently protect their right to control news output and why they have ended up in recent years with what in many other contexts would be seen as rather convoluted media policies such as the separation of production and broadcasting in television or the separation of commercial and editorial aspects of media businesses and the use of shell companies in order that media companies may list on the stock market or seek private finance.

The assumption that media have effects was also historically behind the strict exclusion of foreign media representations in China under Mao, in the early post-Mao period, and even to some degree to the present day with the blocking of websites and the effective absence of foreign broadcasters or newspapers in China. The assumption that Chinese people needed, and to some degree still need, to be sealed off from the outside world of alternative media representations is premised on the dangerous effects that media can have.[41]

Associated with this assumption of effects comes a strong understanding of communication — or at least significant communication — as vertical. The educational, informational, and propaganda role of Chinese media entails a hierarchy between those who teach, disseminate the information, or formulate the propaganda at the higher levels of the political hierarchy and those lower down who are its recipients. Orderly, propaganda-oriented mass media operate on the model of sending messages down the communication hierarchy.[42] The CCP assumes that messages (good or bad) are sent vertically (from central government to the people) and received without consideration of contexts of "decoding"[43] or personal, contextualized interpretations of the messages.[44]

This is an assumption also made by those who associate Chinese state-controlled and propagandistic media with indoctrination, ideological domination, and thought control. Recent academic debates and understandings of contemporary China are based upon this assumption. For instance, debates since the late 1980s about the emergence of a "public sphere" in China have often centered on the existence or otherwise of non–state-controlled messages[45] that work to counteract the effects of state-controlled messages, despite the widespread acknowledgment of various forms of media cynicism since the late 1970s.[46]

Hence, the search for the roots of democracy in different social practices, and complaints about the lack of freedom of the press in China and the authoritarian control of the media, all make the same assumption. There is, of course, justification for this in that it provides a model of understanding that highlights undesirable and repressive power relations, for instance. Given the rapid growth of more and more forms of disorderly media in China, however, this model also restricts and constrains the parameters of the debates about and how we understand mechanisms of change in Chinese media. For example, Daniel Lynch's work[47] on telecommunications in China, is launched from the observation that

> [i]ronically and mistakenly, most specialists on Chinese "thought work" (*sixiang gongzuo*), or propaganda, have focused their research on the *mass* media (television, radio, film and print) not considering *tele*-communications (telephone, fax, e-mail, and the Internet) as constituting significant components of the thought-work enterprise.[48]

Lynch rightly draws our attention to telecommunications, yet he forces us to see it precisely in relation to the orderly, mass media frame of reference that I suggest telecommunications makes us question.

Durable Information Value

The second related assumption that underpins common understandings of Chinese media is that media messages have durable value as information. The orderly, propaganda model of media and communication assumes that messages continue to have value as information, continue to inform people's actions, and therefore also continue to have effects. The notion of propaganda assumes that citizens absorb, digest, and hold on to messages for a significant period of time. If "misinformation" were instantly forgotten, there would be no need to protect against it and if the educative effects of media output were not assumed to last then their perceived importance would be greatly diminished.

In relation to SMS, however, this assumption proves to be inappropriate. With many SMS messages and with disorderly media more generally, just as important, if not more so, as the notion of information value is the notion of the *disposability* of information. For instance, if we consider an SMS news headline subscription service, although the information sent in the message must ideally be useful and have some value to the subscriber when it arrives, it is nonetheless important that the message has limited durability. One of the key principles underpinning such headline services is that they should become out of date fairly rapidly. In fact the arrival of the next headline message ensures that the service has its own built-in redundancy mechanism. If the headlines do not change and do not get updated every few hours, people will not subscribe to the service. In fact the driving mechanism of such services is the need to make messages expire and become irrelevant as quickly as possible. In this case, and with other subscription information services, importance must be attached to disposability and expiration as much as durability.

With SMS we also have to think outside the frame of reference of news, propaganda, and information. Billions of SMS messages are sent every year in China that are personal communications and that may or may not contain information sourced from the Chinese authorities. Many of these will also have very limited durability. What, for instance, happened to the billions of messages sent over the Chinese New Year period? For sure billions have been deleted and forgotten about. However, the notion of disposability does not fit into the contemporary, dominant, ideology-centered model of communication. When information value is limited and transient, the standard questions and assumptions that surround the orderly propaganda model of media start to have little relevance. The notion of disposability introduces a new ephemerality of information that we have to come to terms with in our understandings of China.

SMS, Media, and Citizenship

In April 2005, a Beijing resident well known to me, Mr. Wang, received a text message on his mobile phone. It was an anonymous mass-mailing message urging the reader to be patriotic, to stand up to Japanese imperialist history, and to boycott Japanese companies. He received the message at the height of the diplomatic rift between the two countries over the portrayal (or lack of it) in Japanese school textbooks of Japanese war crimes perpetrated in China in the early twentieth century. Mr. Wang forwarded the message to a friend adding the phrase: "Now revolution comes by mobile phone."[49] He deleted the message and read the next one from his daughter. The simplicity of this everyday scene — a man in a Beijing street looking at his mobile phone, pressing a few buttons, and canceling an SMS message — betrays the complexity of the issues it raises in relation to Chinese media and citizenship.

Mr. Wang's message embroiled him, momentarily, in a discourse of citizenship attempting to appeal to his sense of presumed patriotism. The origin of the message was unclear, but Mr. Wang assumed it came from nationalist protesters who had organized anti-Japanese demonstrations around China in previous days and weeks. For Mr. Wang, this political message had nothing to do with the Chinese authorities and nothing to do with ideology, although it did offer the opportunity to make a quick joke and, hopefully, cause a friend to smile. Hence, if we consider that this media encounter seems to have little to do with vertical ideological communication or political control it would appear to fall well outside the frame of reference that has dominated discourses on Chinese media. Nonetheless, this kind of mediated interaction is becoming increasingly prominent in Chinese people's everyday lives and we are obliged to find alternative ways of looking at them.

Taking these issues seriously, however, requires not simply contriving another adaptation of or appendage to the propaganda model. It is not sufficient simply to suggest that the old model is fine for orderly media, but we need to formulate something different to account for disorderly media. On the contrary, what we learn from disorderly media needs to be incorporated into understandings of orderly media also. For example, the issue of the "disposability" or ephemerality of information does not end with SMS but could be equally applied to television, newspapers, emails, websites, and so on. In fact, the majority of media output in China in the early twenty-first century is not political news but rather relates to lifestyle, consumption, entertainment, leisure, sport, food, and other issues considered nonpolitical in China. Attention to issues of disposability, entertainment, leisure, interpersonal interaction, and commentary are likely to offer far greater insights for understanding a deliberately apolitical lighthearted entertainment drama than is the propaganda model of media. Everyday consumption of orderly media involves a swathe of disorderly media practices.

Chinese citizens are now subject not only to the political structures — or "orderly" aspects — of the mass media, but also increasingly the "disorderly" aspects of the mass media and the complex, shifting combination of orderly and disorderly aspects of new media such as telecommunications, the internet, SMS, and broadband. We have seen in relation to SMS various ways in which media and citizenship have developed an alternative relationship. The SMS citizen is not simply a target of political education and centrally directed subject formation. Rather s/he is first and foremost a consumer, a customer, and an independent decision-maker. The primary relationship between media and citizen, in fact, is a commercial one in which a state-owned enterprise takes money from the consumer for a service provided. However, beyond the economic aspect of the relationship various other official conceptualizations of this relation also come into play.

For instance, in April 2004, the *People's Daily* reported an interview with Yu Zhicheng, a senior mobile telecom markets researcher at the MII. Asked what problems had to be dealt with in order to ensure the long-term healthy growth and development of SMS in China, Yu listed a range of issues to be addressed, including market supervision and regulation, the scope of practice of SMS providers, the problem of junk messages, the technical side of SMS security, the application of SMS in the commercial sector, and the regulation and management of SMS content.[50] Some of these issues relate to regulatory supervision of business, but the problems of junk messages, SMS security, and the regulation of content refer principally to consumer-protection measures. The issue of content inevitably touches upon politics, but of greater concern to the authorities and most consumers in 2006 is not political subversion but pornography, unsolicited publicity and marketing, and SMS financial scams.[51] The 2004 *People's Daily* survey, in fact, found that nearly 80 percent of those surveyed had received either pornographic (33.4 percent) or other kinds of unsavory SMS messages (45.7 percent). This was in addition to 85.8 percent receiving unsolicited advertising messages, 69.8 percent receiving "tedious information," and 39.9 percent saying that they had received harassing messages of one kind or another.[52] The relationship between media and citizen in this context is one centered on the notions of vulnerability and harassment rather than political consciousness.

When SMS is being used for interpersonal communication, like other telephony, it acts as an extension of the range of individual communication. Chinese people send messages locally, nationally, and internationally often without any real consequences for citizenship. Indeed, one of the lessons to be learned from SMS and consideration of disorderly media is that citizen and media, which have been mutually constitutive in the past, are now often dislocated.

So let us return briefly to Mr. Wang and his text message encounter. First, we see clearly that a propaganda model of media focusing on ideological effects and government control tells us little about the incident. Rather what we see is the need to deal with new issues such as contingency (the email appeared to be received somewhat at random), disposability (the message was fairly quickly deleted), transformation (that the received message was entirely transformed when it became the forwarded message), and a combination of group (mass mailing) and individualized (reception and forwarding) media practices. We might consider, for instance, how this incident involved not a single, fixed relationship between media and citizen, but rather a chain of transforming media practices. A randomly received politicized but non-state, call-to-arms became in an instant just another junk message among others before being transformed with a sense of humor into a lighthearted, but politically satirical message sent to a friend. Within seconds, the message was then deleted without a second thought. This is a far more complex chain of media practices than any that the ideological model is able to cope with.

Conclusion

Within the space of this article it has only been possible to indicate in fairly broad brushstrokes a set of issues arising out of the emerging popularity of what I have called disorderly media practices. Even from these broad strokes, however, we can identify key areas in the SMS text messaging practices that call for new conceptualizations of Chinese media and their relation to society and citizenship. I have further suggested that such reconceptualizations also need to be extended to other areas of China's media and communications landscape that includes the more traditional, orderly mass media.

SMS practices, for instance, are often more about socializing, entertainment, having fun, and practical interpersonal communication than they are about the transmission of political messages. At the same time, however, SMS can be used for highly political purposes. Subscription news services draw SMS back toward the issues raised by conventional propaganda models of the media. Yet the use of SMS to organize grassroots political movements — whether it be the Falun Gong meditation cult or a nationalistic anti-Japanese protest — calls for quite different understandings of the relation between citizenship and media. Assumptions about verticality, durable media effects, and propaganda models of communication need to be replaced by a wider range of concepts that better suit the new kinds of media that we are dealing with in contemporary China. In this article I have briefly introduced, for instance, the notions of disposability and ephemerality in relation to people's engagement with information and media output as well as introducing the notion of "disorderly" media more generally. This is not to impose a new conceptual straitjacket on our understandings of Chinese media. Rather it is intended to indicate ways in which we might start to loosen the straps of the old understanding. In fact one of the key points of this article is to ask how "we" — analysts, academics, journalists, and other writers on contemporary China, both Chinese and foreign — are so often drawn into the same paradigm of "orderly" thinking as that which has, in recent years, made assumptions at the heart of the Chinese government's conceptualization of media anachronistic.

❑

7

THE NEW CHINESE CITIZEN AND CETV

Yingchi Chu

IN 1986, THE CHINESE MINISTRY OF EDUCATION launched the China Education Television network (CETV) to speed up the retraining of the population on a mass scale in order to accelerate China's transition from a planned economy to its new "socialist market economy." Through its network of more than seventy television stations at provincial and city levels, CETV provides a rich offering of training services. At the same time, it also broadcasts to 82 percent of China's population infotainment programs that include education news, educational documentaries, preparation for tertiary entrance examinations, and dialogue and lifestyle programs. Given its reach and influence, it is no exaggeration to say that the main task of CETV is the training of a new type of Chinese citizen.

Since the CETV network is a government institution, one could be excused for assuming that we are dealing here with a fairly straightforward case of propaganda (*xuanchuan*), although in the Chinese ideological discourse, the term has positive connotations of education absent from the pejorative meaning in English. Indeed, the Ministry of Education hardly misses a beat in making its parameters clear to the CETV management. However, the use of the term "propaganda" has two serious disadvantages: it melds what is happening now in China with the dogmatic straightjacket that characterized the media in the Mao period and homogenizes what on closer scrutiny turns out to be a highly diverse and heterogeneous field of directives and television programs. The task of this article is to provide some evidence that makes such simplifications unattractive. It does so by first attending to questions of policy and reform before introducing a number of typical CETV programs at the heart of which is the creation of "the new Chinese citizen." What does this citizen look like? In sum, a person who is hardworking, technically competent, self-reliant, cooperative, dependable, optimistic, forward-looking, creative, and participatory: above all, a citizen able to survive in the new market economy.

This article analyzes a major television documentary, *My Sun* (*Wode taiyang*), the CETV flagship in 2005 and 2006, and a representative example of its other didactic programs. In doing so it contends that the program reforms the CETV management has been encouraged to initiate in order to meet both the demands of official, top-down directives and the pressures of the market, especially those of the media industry and a radically new horizon of audience expectations, contribute to the production of a new kind of participatory market citizen. In late 2003 CETV introduced policies and program reforms aimed at improving its ratings in an increasingly competitive Chinese media market. I argue that in this process, citizenship education in the media appears to be gradually moving from an authoritarian style of political indoctrination to the provision of technical training on a broad scale and an acknowledgment of the principles of consumption. An essential part of this transformation, the article also claims, is a significant increase in audience participation in media programs, as well as the inclusion of production specialists from outside the network.

The CETV Citizen

Approaching the question of what constitutes the new Chinese citizen from the narrow angle of program content and programming style alone could be misleading. Clearly, we also need to consider the different ways CETV mediates government directives, program reform and program policy, commercial pressures, program content and mode of presentation, public feedback, and audience participation. As a consequence, we note a change in the construction of TV audiences and citizens, from Foucauldian "docile bodies" and bodies as "effects" of power to critical participants in public debate. As to content, what is now being emphasized is a modern, internationally oriented lifestyle (fashion, new technologies, consumption, modest wealth) and the know-how likely to make such a style affordable (marketable skills, ways of increasing employability, fostering talent in a broad range of fields, acquisition of information and knowledge) for "consumer citizens" training.[1] As far as the presentational style of today's programs is concerned, the stress is also on encouraging debating competence, the expression and negotiation of differing views, the interaction between individuals and groups, the recognition of different perspectives and their significance, criticism of public institutions and local and provincial officialdom, within the boundaries of shared but tacit constraints. Given this reshaping of the conception of the Chinese citizen on the mass scale of CETV's audiences, the question arises whether or not we should speak here of the birth of a genuine "public sphere" beyond the bourgeois sense in which Habermas introduced the term in his paper of 1964 and that he elaborated in *The Structural Transformation of the Public Sphere*.

The Need to Reform

CETV was established on 1 July 1986 to broadcast teaching programs of the Central Television University (CTU) via satellite. Founded in 1978, CTU was a response to an instruction by Deng Xiaoping to develop a strategy for raising the nation's education standard after the Cultural Revolution, which, he had the courage to observe, had left a vast educational vacuum in its wake. Subsequently, twenty-eight provinces in China founded their own television universities to alleviate the shortfall of qualified employers and places in tertiary education. As the demand for televised education increased rapidly by the mid 1980s, the Ministry of Education decided to establish a centrally controlled television station in Beijing for production and broadcast of education news and teaching programs via satellite: CETV. Inevitably, new and not entirely predictable citizenship qualities were to emerge from this government initiative, which suddenly legitimized the pursuit of new skills, new technologies, wealth creation, market orientation, employability, upward mobility, electronic and computing expertise, and a certain freedom in striving for personal goals.

CETV has clearly had a major educational and informational impact on Chinese society since 1986: it boasts millions of graduates at all levels, as well as millions of qualifications in accounting, agriculture, and a range of other technical disciplines. It has also contributed greatly to training primary and secondary teachers and technicians, and to providing the peasantry with agricultural programs and students with general knowledge in science, history, arts, society, literature, and moral education. As Professor Yin Hong at Qinghua University observes, education has once more received the recognition it deserves and CTU has played an important role in getting the best results from a limited national budget.[2] CETV's significance lies in the expansion of its narrow subject offerings to a broad transmission of general knowledge. As a consequence of this shift, the conduit of knowledge was no longer just the traditional teaching expert from various technical and professional fields; informed members of the general public were able to offer new perspectives on a wide range of topics. The democratizing effects of such televised education programs cannot be overestimated. In principle at least, a broad spectrum of Chinese TV viewers now had the means to improve their personal levels of knowledge and skills and, if they chose to do so, acquire a new conception of what it meant to be a Chinese citizen.

However, the idealized notion of a better informed, more highly trained, and more broadly educated citizen leaves out a major raison d'être of television in China today: public approval. Like most television stations in China, CETV faces stiff market competition — perhaps more severely so than most other networks. After all, CETV is regarded as a specialist television channel for broadcasting educational programs; it is not mandated to broadcast commercially viable programs such as popular dramas and soaps. Furthermore, the emergence of competing specialist channels, especially in science and technology and in documentary programming, does not bode well for CETV. At the same time, the trend to compact large conglomerates of stations into powerful regional media groups further challenges CETV's leading role. In particular, educational television providers at the provincial level are now in the process of forming their own local television groups, such as Sichuan Television and Jiangsu Television. In addition, foreign media groups are beginning to offer educational programs, in the wake of relaxed media regulations following China's entry into the World Trade Organization (WTO) in 2001. Minister of Education Chen Zhili has warned that as a result it is now "difficult to maintain national sovereignty in education; there is increasing competition in the educational market; an increasing imbalance in education; an increase in conflict in the employment structures; and the emergence of new problems for the mobility of human resources and talents."[3] By "imbalance" Chen means the gap between privileged and underprivileged educational access, while her comment concerning conflictual "employment structures" draws attention to discrepancies, especially between rural and urban employment practices.

In this atmosphere of competing demands, CETV faces a serious "identity" problem, hesitant as it is about its role and its service as educator, its function and pedagogical methods, and how its traditional conception of education fits into the new market economy. As much as some would like to believe that CETV "should not sacrifice its role as educator to screen those vulgar programs that attract audiences and increase ratings,"[4] this belief fails to address the key issue of how to make the station commercially viable. As You Chun argues, the problem lies in a muddled conception of CETV in the market economy: (1) teaching via television and Education Television are contradictory concepts; (2) students and the general public are incompatible audiences; (3) the market demand for a multiple interactive system cannot be reconciled with the tradition of authoritarian styles of teaching; (4) what makes media appealing differs from what makes education successful; and (5) there is a profound difference between income via ratings and achieving high rates of education.[5]

Accepting this kind of critique, Kang Ning, CETV's president, believes that the station needs to reform: "We have been overstressing our function of classroom teaching," she explains, "an outdated pedagogic style in a changing society, where the traditional relationship between campus, teachers and students is no longer relevant. As a result, CETV's reputation is now marginal; in particular, it has a reputation of wasting resources."[6] The demand for media reform by both government and the market has been widely accepted in China well beyond CETV. Since China entered the WTO in 2001 media institutions have been instructed by the government to change from being "policy directed" to being "guided by law"; from being "limited open" to "fully open"; from "individual opening" to "a mutual opening amongst the WTO members." So it would be wrong to assume that media reform is in some way in opposition to government policy. The reform impetus is clearly a two-directional process: a bottom-up, market-driven evolution and a top-down process driven by official policy. The Party's 16th Congress of August 2003, for example, proposed the creation of "a learning society" (*xuexi xing de shehui*). At the National Broadcasting Conference in 2004, Xu Guangcun, deputy minister for publicity and head of the State Administration of Radio, Film and Television, suggested that media reform should

> create a new system: face the masses, face the market, using the "mouthpiece" function of the media to promote business, and using its business function to support its "mouthpiece" function, and separate those functions which could be operated in the market economy apart from the

institution to allow them to develop their own business, according to market economic principles.[7]

In December 2003 the government issued several documents urging institutional media reforms, including these two: "The Ministry of the Publicity, The Ministry of Culture, The State Administration of Radio, Film and Television, the Central News Publisher on the Reforming of the System of Cultural Institution" and "Two Policies Addressing the Reform of the System of Cultural Institutions: In Support of the Transformation of Cultural Institutions into Cultural Enterprises." In "Encouraging the Development of Broadcasting Enterprises," issued by the State Administration of Radio, Film and Television, we read,

> Channels which show a potential for profitable business such as sports, transportation, film and television, arts, music, lifestyle, finance, science and technology, should be allowed to become independent from the center to establish individual production companies outside the system, as long as the state's resources and equipment are not regarded as saleable commodities, and the final broadcasting rights are controlled by and belong to the stations," [and] "we should also explore possibilities of operating television channels on business terms."[8]

The state here is actively promoting a new citizen, one that is technically qualified and self-motivated. Yet as the media, especially media such as CETV, are forced to survive in an increasingly publicly challenged market, they cannot help but produce a kind of citizen who is not only a survivor in a new commercial world but one who will gradually wish to have his or her concerns heard publicly. This, I predict, points to the emergence in China of the media-produced participatory citizen.

Policy Reform in CETV

It has fallen to CETV as the major provider of nationwide TV education to lead the way in the thaw in media politics and assist in making this type of learning environment a social reality. CETV president Kang Ning believes that media policy reforms should first address some fundamental changes in CETV as to its "position, identity, attitudes, and perspectives."[9] In order to improve its public image, reforms should balance top-down regulative directives with public ratings. CETV attitudes need to change from "educating" to "learning," from "training talents" to "discovering and exploring human resources and abilities," and from supervisory "teaching" to the "three principles of closeness": close to life (less government policy), close to reality (less ideology), and close to the masses (close to the market). These statements impact directly on the production of a new kind of citizen, one who is able to exert an influence on the media by voicing approval or disapproval on a broad range of issues, except basic Party dogma. What is new is that a type of citizen is likely to emerge whose personal concerns, problems, failures, and difficulties begin to be recognized publicly as legitimate concerns and matters of public debate.

In her February 2004 reform proposal to the Ministry of Education and the Ministry of Publicity, Kang highlighted a series of fundamental principles, which can be summed up as follows:

- To create the biggest platform of "learning via television in the world." "The selling point of CETV," she stated, "lies in all areas of study and training for employability."
- **The principle of the bridging** of school and lifelong education, of formal and informal education. Learning, as she believes, must become fashionable.
- The reform of the CETV infrastructure must involve the separation of news from the "mouthpiece" function of the official media. CETV as part of the newly established "China Education Media Group" must acknowledge the principles of the market economy.
- In accordance with this change, all employees are to be placed on two-year, renewable contracts within an award system.[10]

In spite of the difficulties CETV is facing in trying to adjust to the new Chinese market economy, its president remains confident. After all, China's market for education is immense. The government explicitly supports CETV's role in the creation of a "learning" society by funding 10 million educators to be employed by CETV catering for 300 million students. In addition, CETV has been mandated to play a significant role in re-skilling the labor force on a large scale, providing primary, secondary, and distance education in rural areas.

Post-Reform Programming: *My Sun (Wode taiyang)*

Given the dual pressure of top-down directives issued by the Chinese government and the demands of the media market, how has the CETV blueprint for reform affected its programming? And what kind of citizenship pedagogy becomes visible in its actual programs? In other words, what kind of a new citizen is being trained by CETV nationwide? In the second part of this article I analyze a number of prominent recent TV programs that, I suggest, offer answers to these questions.

I single out one particular program, a documentary series, *My Sun (Wode taiyang)*, in some detail, to give an impression of its scope and didactic ambition. What is striking about this series is a certain tension in its episodes in terms of filmed subjects, presentational styles, a degree of didactic idealization, and the images of citizens projected. It is this tension and its sources that I wish to address in order to better understand the kind of citizenship training CETV aims to achieve. *My Sun* is the brand documentary of CETV, having been awarded several prizes, including best documentary series in China, and an international award from Spain. The series was a collective effort by the state-controlled media, film scholars, and more than a hundred unit producers, writers, and directors, the majority of whom are semi-independent and freelance filmmakers from outside CETV. Furthermore, the series consciously aimed to lift the profile of CETV to increase ratings. It first screened during China's two long public holidays, Labor Day in May and National Day in October 2005.

In light of government's call for the creation of a "harmonious" (*hexie shehui*) and "creative society" (*chuangxin shehui*), *My Sun* offers a representation of society in post–economic reform China from the perspectives of government, film scholars, and independent filmmakers. The producer of *My Sun*, Kang Ning, uses the metaphor of the "sun" to describe the social life of the subjects, creators, victims, and beneficiaries of economic reform, the sun symbolizing people's hopes and goals, as well as suggesting a new beginning in the face of yesterday's disappointments. Selection of the filmed subjects is on a large scale. About 196 episodes in four series focus on the middle and lower middle class. With an emphasis on the theme of a "harmonious society," the first part of the 2005 series records a day each in the lives of fifty-six individuals, while the second part depicts thirty teams under the overarching theme of the principle of cooperation. The 2006 series illustrates the idea of a "creative society." Again, the first set of episodes deals with the ingenuity of seventy-two individuals, as they try to invent new ways of guaranteeing progress in their professional fields. The second celebrates the initiatives of collectives, demonstrating entrepreneurial teamwork in small business. The filmed subjects range from architects and cooks to pilots and restaurant singers.[11]

One thing these individuals in *My Sun* have in common is that they are all good citizens in a new sense of citizenship. They work hard without complaint. Generally, they are optimistic in spite of difficulties, an impression underlined by the theme music and the warm colors of golden yellow and red in the opening sequence. In the first series we see fifty-six individuals with busy daily schedules, struggling in a harsh commercial environment: a self-employed puppet maker and single mother bringing up three children on her own; a young reporter hunting for news in Beijing, unable to fulfill her wish to visit her parents; an insurance saleswoman experiencing social discrimination. These documentaries capture immediate social actuality by focusing on the strength of individuals facing and overcoming difficulties on their own. Having cooked and served dinner for her guests on the eve of her puppet exhibition, the single mother is captured on camera as she quietly leaves the room, shedding tears of exhaustion. Her struggle, however, has not been in vain; the next day she is rewarded by the success of her exhibition. Another touching portrait is the documentation of a day in the life of the 23-year-old reporter who has spent long hours in the rain chasing news while facing indifference and hostility from the people she is trying to interview. She looks forward to surprising her parents at dinnertime, but only ten minutes before she reaches their home she is called back to the news agency for further chores. She bravely fights back her tears and knuckles down once more to do her job. The *My Sun* camera also captures the disappointment of a glamorous former television hostess, now a freelance insurance broker, when her former colleagues snub her. Once more we see tears being shed, followed by images of the woman regaining her composure and resolutely pursuing her new occupation. But not all the episodes border on the sentimental; most of them address the daily routines and new business practices of quiet achievers.

Cooperation and team effort are the spirit in the series portraying thirty teams performing their professional tasks mainly in state-owned organizations.

Some of these are well-known villages, as for instance, Dazhai, once called by Mao Zedong "the model" in Chinese agriculture; Xiaogang in Fengyang, the village that had pioneered the "household responsibility" initiative in 1978, launching China's economic reforms; and Sanyuanzhu village, which spearheaded hothouse horticulture in Shangdong, making vegetables available in winter. In the industrial area, the series features railway workers of the "Mao Zedong," China's leading train model, a wharf team in Qingdao port, and aircraft engineers in Shaanxi. The viewers are also treated to episodes selected from the Chinese border: a border security team in China's most remote northwest region, marine customs officers in Zhuhai searching for illegal goods, and a drug control unit in Yunnan. We see the daily routines of police officers at Beijing airport, 110 emergency police teams, and a fire brigade in Hunan. Entertainment and sport are represented by a troupe on horseback in Inner Mongolia, musicians from the Beijing Music Academy collecting folk songs in Inner Mongolia, the leading football team in Beijing, and a school for blind football players in Qingdao. The effort of hospital teams is illustrated by an in-vitro fertility clinic in Beijing, while education and research are showcased by a professorial and postdoctoral study group from Northeast Agricultural University and a rocket research team. An assembly of social workers from Shenyang and a student-run cafeteria at Qinghua University flesh out the theme of community service, while the depiction of workers in the Beijing Zoo and a nature protection team in Tibet broadcasts new standards in animal management.

What makes these documentaries interesting is their emphasis on the teamwork required to solve conflicts by negotiation. For instance, an entertainment ensemble in Inner Mongolia is under pressure to win the top award in a competition. Their leader, a Han Chinese party secretary who has little knowledge of Mongol singing and dancing, is told that if they win the host city will be able to get their sponsorship back and all his employees will have the opportunity to change their contract status to tenure. Throughout the show, we see conflict, drama, and frustration in the rehearsals amongst Mongol producer, directors, and performers. In another episode we encounter the desperation of staff in an in-vitro fertility clinic that is losing its only male doctor. Frustration is also a theme in an entertaining documentary about a field trip to a remote forest where a professor and his postgraduate student conduct research in a less than competent fashion.

Many of the documentaries are not merely entertaining, but often highly informative as to the details of specific and new professions. This is the case with the special care provided for a blind football team, during military parade instruction, and in an episode showing customs officers performing their duties as border control agents. We are informed about professional schedules, details to attend to, and the time limits within which the work has to be undertaken. In the third series, produced in 2006, we encounter seventy-two individuals who have either created a new professional specialization for themselves or upgraded a traditional skill. One episode shows a TV producer running a business making fiction films for families who want to see their relatives on screen. In another documentary a man who has lost his job creates a new "profession" by discovering news for journalists. Another man is shown inventing the nonexisting profession of freelance building inspector, an occupation that is now flourishing all over China. A Tianjin craftsman has turned a ten-cent feather duster into art work, each costing some ten thousand yuan. While this series deals with individuals inventing their own market niches, the final series showcases small business entrepreneurs and their teams trying to capture a share of a fast-growing market. In both series intelligence and dedication are the source and hallmark of success. But even where success proves evasive, the episodes of *My Sun* drive home the message that energy and effort will ultimately be rewarded. The documentary also leaves no doubt that it is the collective achievements of people — such as we see in the various episodes — that are responsible for China's economic miracle. In this sense, the breadth and diversity of *My Sun* can be read as a "textbook" illustrating the lower middle class of contemporary Chinese society, their lifestyles, living environments, working conditions, professional routines, collegiate behavior, and family relations — their desires, achievements, and concerns.

No doubt, *My Sun* has inherited some of the stylistic features of the Chinese dogmatic documentaries prominent during the period of the planned economy. Though much toned down in *My Sun*, we still encounter some heroic music, especially when tragedy is presented, redundant narration, and embedded instructions to the viewers as to how to read the moral of an episode. Political and ideological didacticism sometimes still spoils the realist impact of some of the presented actuality, of real persons, places, and events. What we should not overlook, however, is the fact that in many of the episodes of *My Sun* the immediacy of events, human activity, and conflict are felt through location sound, with voices being heard that are clearly distinct from the drone of government guidelines. For instance, in an episode showing the good deeds of social workers in a neighborhood community in Shenyang, clearly oppositional voices can be heard. When the camera follows workers collecting hygiene fees, a woman asks: "Why collect fees? Have you done anything about people keeping ducks as pets in the building?" Another person refuses to pay, saying, "I will pay the fees after you have removed the filth." A man questions the demolishing of a pagoda, "Why demolish it? It is a waste. Why don't you leaders use the money for the poor, the unemployed, and the disabled? Why don't you leaders think in this direction?" Another man asks, "Do the voices of ordinary people [*laobaixing*] count at all?" One of the main reasons for this break with the dogmatic tradition is the fact that as the series evolved, about a hundred key filmmakers from inside and outside the government media system began to exert their heterogeneous influence. As a result, we can now observe the emergence of a polyphony of voices, even in the mainstream of the government media.

For all its diversity at the level of detail of choice of subject, presentational documentary mode, and competing voices, there is no escaping the fact that the broadcasting of *My Sun* is putting into practice a well-orchestrated, government-directed, didactic agenda: the creation of a new kind of citizen. What sort of citizen then is being produced here? In sum, we could say, a kind of formula citizen capable of realizing her/his full educational and economic potential, resilient and inventive, a citizen full of verve and optimism, self-reliant as well as dependable in a team, driven by clear goals, such as the achievable prospect of a better life and even the possibility of fulfilling personal dreams. Perhaps this is reminiscent of the definition of the American Dream; certainly, it is a conception of a Chinese citizen far removed from the ideal of the heroic, but docile, body of the Mao period.

My Sun is by no means an isolated case in this kind of citizenship training. Another important aspect of the new Chinese citizen is public participation in media events. This applies as much to CETV programs as it does to hundreds of other stations around China. Particularly popular are the new debating programs. CETV for instance offers a number of dialogue and debating programs concerned with such hot topics as China's education system, university students with psychological problems, tuition fees, professional competency and ethics, the real estate market, food hygiene, waste disposal, environment, health issues, consumer affairs, relations with Japan, the auction market, and many more, with the exception of such obviously political issues as national sovereignty or the one-party system. These explicitly participatory programs make full use of debates, advice from experts, and audience feedback, both in the studio and through remote response via phone and the internet. Like other television stations, CETV has a program devoted to amateur digital-video-makers, including students and local residents. In addition, CETV also broadcasts invitations to the public to contribute ideas to the production process by internet feedback. Perhaps it is important to note in this context that the president of CETV makes a special point of reading every weekly report on audience feedback. CETV reportedly used a significant portion of this feedback in the making of *My Sun*.

In all these programs, the goal of training a new kind of citizen clearly emerges. This new citizen is reassured that the government is maintaining responsible control of the nation's education system, recognizes that self-advancement is a legitimate goal and that self-discipline and self-reliance are good qualities to achieve success in the new market economy, and is encouraged to actively participate in national debate on a broad range of topics, including criticism of corruption of lower-level administration, though not of official government policy. Given the specific structure of these programs, it is unhelpful to write off the Chinese media today as mere mouthpieces of government dogma. They are neither mere mouthpieces nor oppositional in any democratic sense. The matter is entirely more complicated. This is why the broadly accepted claim that the media are no longer mere channels of official doctrine, though not false, is in need of qualification. For it conceals the sobering fact that much of what we tend to regard as progressive media initiatives is actually in line with general government guidelines. So while CETV is not confined to the direct proclamation of government dogma, as would have been the case between 1950 and 1980, its very strategies of citizen education fall squarely within government parameters.

How precisely, then, do CETV programs achieve the formation of citizens who see themselves as participants in public debate rather than mere recipients of official dogma? Here I cite one small example that demonstrates the kind of media discourse conducive to the new citizenship training. *Today I Am at Home (Jintian wo zai jia)* was initiated during the SARS period when many children were not allowed to leave their homes. The program uses interactive methods, inviting children to email a TV host about their views, their studies, and their concerns. Here the TV host takes on the role of a virtual television babysitter whom the students can call and talk to. The program employs many different games. For instance, in the "yes or no" game the children call two hosts live to ask them questions about general common knowledge. Each of the two hosts links with one child over the phone, to create a competition between two teams. Another version presents the hosts taking children outside to play. The whole process is recorded without editing, employing long-take filming. In yet another format the producer invites children to organize a reporting club, or a television host competition. Children are invited to submit their applications to the station, the only restriction being an age limit. After only a few hours of training, each young reporter, on different campuses, uses a camera to report whatever they think is worth reporting. The children establish a reading club, presenting their views, reviews, and comments on books. There is also a talent show, with an open invitation to all children to participate, as long as the talents displayed are not harmful to health and their talents have not otherwise already been formally recognized. In line with the aim of the program, the show's emphasis is not only on "participation" but also on inviting "as many children as possible to become themselves the host of the program."

In *Today I Am at Home* audience participation is maximized. Without it the program would not exist. Both education and entertainment mingle to produce an effective TV performance. The program's interactive character depends on the dynamic relationship and negotiatory practice among the hosts, CETV studio personnel, and the children, without the formal channels of school, teachers, or parents. The children learn from their own actions, discoveries, research, and above all, debate. In addition, what is being learned is knowledge relevant to society — something rarely formally taught in school. This approach is particularly useful in a society in transit to an increasingly competitive market economy in which skills of analysis, negotiation, the assertion of needs and wants, self-reliance, and initiative are in high demand. The optimization of participatory activities CETV's producers aim for certainly announces an entirely new style of social interaction, one that encourages the emergence of a new kind of citizen and that could be viewed as a necessary prerequisite of an evolving "public media sphere."

Conclusion

There can be little doubt that the media reforms initiated by the Chinese government and implemented in specific ways by CETV and its rival stations have ushered in profound changes to the design, production, distribution, and consumption of television programs in today's China. Nor should there be much doubt that these changes have had significant effects on the conception of what it means to be a good and successful Chinese citizen. It would be a mistake, however, to describe the new style of the media's citizenship training as no more than propaganda. To do so would miss important differences between the use of the media in Mao's China and media's role in contemporary Chinese society. Nor should we reduce these differences to simple distinctions between citizenship criteria in a planned economy versus those that are proving useful in the new Chinese market. To do so would be to miss the detail and staggering diversity of today's media portrayals of a broad spectrum of Chinese citizens struggling to improve their daily lives. Most importantly, to shrink the new media citizenship education to no more than yet another form of propaganda would certainly miss the significance of the popularity of participation in media programs and increasingly critical debate.

ACKNOWLEDGMENTS: The author would like to thank the Asia Research Centre, Murdoch University, for its generous support. The author is also grateful to Professor Beverley Hooper for her comments on the paper, Dr. Kang Ning for her valuable time in interviews, and Rachel Murphy and Tom Fenton for their editorial assistance.

❑

NOTES

Introduction
1. Abbott 2001; Geoffry 1998; Yan and Pitt 2002.
2. Link, et al. 1989; Link, et al. 2002; Zha 1995; Zhao 2000.
3. Chan 1994; Fong 2004a; Sun 2002.
4. Yang 1997.
5. Bakken 2000; Fong 2004b; Fong and Murphy 2006; Greenhalgh 2005; Murphy 2004; Yan 2003.
6. Anagnost 1997.
7. Dickie 2007.
8. Bray 2006.
9. Kahn 2007; Smith 2006.
10. Magnier 2006, Williamson 2007.
11. Scott 1990.

Chapter 1 – Zheng
1. Wang 1995, 149–73.
2. Ibid., 156.
3. Jian 2001.
4. Wang 1995, 149–73.
5. Zheng 2003; Zheng 2004.
6. I conducted my fieldwork in karaoke bars in Dalian during four periods in 1999, 2000, 2001, and 2002. This research would not have been possible without the supportive funding provided by the Yale Center for International and Area Studies, and the Council on East Asian Studies of Yale University.
7. See Christiansen 1990; Solinger 1999.
8. First appearing in its modern form during the New Culture movement (1905–1923), the figure of the peasant came to embody the old, "totally objectionable" regime that avowedly had been overthrown by the Communist revolutionary ascendance to power and replaced by the new socialist order. See Cohen 1993.
9. Ibid.; Brownell 1995.
10. This term is borrowed from Solinger 1995b.
11. Solinger 1995a, 155–83.
12. Lu 2000.
13. In the late 1980s, counties in the provinces of Anhui, Hubei, Henan, and Jiangsu sold local urban household registration papers, known as blue cards or blue seals,

Notes

to migrant workers. These local governments employed this scheme to raise their own development funds at the time of the "national austerity drive." Wong and Huen 1998.
14. See ibid.; Woon 1999.
15. Bai 2001.
16. Khan et al. argue that the "regressivity" of rural fiscal policy hinders the effort to alleviate rural poverty and hastens income polarization and inequality. Khan and Riskin 1998.
17. Li and O'Brien 1996.
18. See Honig 1992; Zhang 2001.
19. Honig 1992; Siu 1990b.
20. Chan points out that the threat to the CCP and political stability derives from the peasantry, workers, and dissidents. Peasant migrants in the city constitute a "periphery flexible workforce," held in "forced and bonded labor." They suffer an abuse of labor rights in the "sweatshop socialism," receiving control of bodily functions, huge deduction of payments, physical abuse, and so on. Yet there have been no measures taken to limit their working hours or prohibit their corporal punishment. Chan 1993, 31–61.
21. Tan 1996.
22. Foucault 1972, 49.
23. Bourdieu 1991.
24. Moore 1994, 92.
25. Huang 1988.
26. Ibid.
27. See Xu 2001, 20. Shen 1999, 6.
28. Liu Dalin 1995.
29. Tong 1995, 103–4.
30. Wen and Ma 1991, 221–26.
31. Huang 1990.
32. Huang 1988, 3.
33. McClintock 1992, 111–31, at 114.
34. Li 2000a.
35. Chen, Hui 2001; Chen, Ming 2001a; Dong et al. 1995, 65–67.
36. Chen, Ming 2001b.
37. Ibid., 57.
38. Zhang and Xiao 1998.
39. Liu 1998, 33–35.
40. He 2001, 18; Yang 2001, 7.
41. Liu 2000, 27.
42. Ma and Qu 2001, 14.
43. Huang 1999, 3.
44. Bian 2001, 10–11.
45. Anonymous 1999; Wang 2001, 2.
46. Li Yu 1999, 43–45.
47. Berger 1972.
48. Chen, Ming 2001b, 49–56; Li 2000b, 70–75.
49. Stories of this type not only offer male readers an alternative fantasy outside the real world, but also excite their sexual desires. See Marcus 1966.
50. Liu 2001, 8; Yu 2001, 10.
51. Jiang 2001, 11; Sun 2001, 11.
52. Wu 2001, 2.
53. This information comes from my interview with political officials.
54. Hostesses are portrayed as seducing and infecting men with STDs and HIV/AIDS. Li Yaling 1999, 2; Liu 1999, 3; Xiao 2001, 18.
55. Guan et al. 2001, 50–52, at 51.
56. Zhao and Liu 2001, 19.

57. Helen Siu (1989) points out that the state's cultural control penetrates the daily life so effectively and powerfully that it has been taken for granted by local agents whose self-interested activities only legitimize state control.
58. Moore 1994.
59. Edwards 2000, 115–47; Wakeman 1995, 19–42; Wang 1999.
60. Helen Siu (1990a) points out that the historical sources of literacy in China explain why intellectuals feel compelled to attach themselves to moral and political authority.
61. Ibid., 288.
62. Ibid., 26.
63. Feuerwerker 1998.
64. Ibid., 245, 256.
65. Barlow 1997, 506–13, at 509.
66. Ibid., 536.
67. Ibid., 530.
68. Liu, Lydia 1995, 198.
69. Xu 1993, 87–107, at 102.
70. Sociologists Wang Jinling and Xu Sisun (1997, 276–97) argue that sex workers share an early maturation of sexual biology, distorted sexual psychology, high masculine vigor, and aberrant abnormal personalities.
71. Foucault 1978, 201.
72. Ibid.
73. Ibid.
74. Ibid., 202.
75. Evans 1997.
76. Alcoff 1988, 405–36, at 415.
77. Butler 1993, 3.
78. Dworkin 1980, 153.
79. MacKinnon 1987; Vance 1997, 440–52 at 447.
80. Segal 1992b. Sweet sorrows, painful pleasures: Pornography and the perils of heterosexual desire. In Segal and McIntosh, eds., 1992a. 65–91, at 72.
81. Ibid., 77.
82. Foucault 1978, 24–26.
83. For the antivice political campaign, see Hershatter 1997.
84. Chatterjee 1989.
85. Cook 1996, 65–97; Finnane 1996, 99–131.
86. Brownell 1995.
87. The government seems to regard migrants as a necessary evil: it tolerates migrants' presence in the city because of their important economic functions, but only reluctantly and with many stipulations. The main condition imposed on migrants is that they eventually (i.e., after contributing their labor power) return to their homes in the countryside. Media reports invoke the rhetoric of traditional family values and native place sentiment to construct an emotionally evocative, moral argument for the migrants' duty to return home. See Lu 1998, 11.
88. Moore 1994, 82.
89. Ibid.
90. Ibid.
91. Butler 1993, 3.
92. Manalansan 2003.
93. Ruhlen 2003, 117–39.
94. Schein 2000.
95. Manalansan 2003, 144.
96. Chapkis 1997.
97. A hostess who had lost her clients' phone numbers exclaimed, "Shit! I lost my clients' phone numbers. Do you know what those numbers mean? They mean money! Clients are renminbi [Chinese currency]!"

Notes

98. Chinese version of poem: jin men xiaoxixi / zuoxia xiang fuqi / xiaofei yi daoshou / qu ni ma le ge bi.
99. Ong 1999.

Chapter 2 – Florence

1. Dean 1999, 32.
2. The word *dagong* connotes discipline and submission to extremely harsh regimes of work and involves a plurality of meanings ranging from fierce exploitation, loss of control of one's time and space, an intense feeling of precariousness and severe injuries to one's dignity to symbols of modernity and prosperity.
3. Scott 1990, 102–3. I also draw on Scott's argument that since the "hidden transcript" (i.e., discourse, practices, gestures, etc. that are outside the direct gaze of the ruling elite) is by definition virtually out of reach of the researcher, it is through forms of popular expressions such as songs, poems, tales, and jokes that we may hope to come across elements that stand at the border between the hidden transcript and the public transcript. Ibid., 19.
4. On the nature of these classifications and the fact that these were not only economic but also political, see Billeter 1985, 127–69; Dirlik 1983, 182–211.
5. Apter and Saich 1994, 13–15.
6. Rofel 1999, 27.
7. Chen et al. 2001, 12–13; Schein 2001, 225–26.
8. Dutton 1998, 9–10.
9. See Barmé 1999, 115–16, 252. See also Zhao 1998.
10. Anagnost 1997, 88.
11. Yan 2003, 92.
12. Murphy 2004, 5.
13. Ibid., 78.
14. This goes together with processes of disciplining and individualization of workers.
15. Hoffman 2001, 46–47.
16. Lin 2001, 4–5.
17. Guldin 2001, 127.
18. Thireau and Hua 2001b, 38. In 1980, 90 percent of the population of Shenzhen held permanent household registration, while in 1993, only 40 percent was registered permanently in Shenzhen. For further details, see Scharping and Schultze 1997, 177.
19. Woon 1993, 588.
20. Shi 1999, 119. Anita Chan noted that while the Chinese economy was going through a period of rapid expansion, the minimal salary kept unchanged in real terms. See Chan 2003, 44–45; see also Chan 2005, 23–32.
21. Chan and Zhu 2003, 563. I am grateful to Rachel Murphy for helping me to frame this argument more clearly.
22. See Lee 1995; Lee 1998; Chan 1998.
23. See, for instance, Beijing daxue, Dongguan mingong keti zu. 1995, 81–87; Lee 1998, 88.
24. Pun 2004, 6. Pun Ngai also makes a strong argument about the "dormitory labour regime," which "generates hidden costs which are borne by women workers." Ibid., 2.
25. I am grateful to Rachel Murphy for helping me to frame this argument.
26. Jacka 2000.
27. Anita Chan points to a similar feature in her analysis of letters of female migrant workers: Chan 2002, 173. One should not however generalize and apply this feature to all cities of the Delta. Most migrants I interviewed told me that the intensity of police controls varied both in time and space. Some explained, for instance, that after the death of Sun Zhigang in March 2003, control checks were somewhat fewer; I have also been told that controls tend to be tighter in Dongguan and Shenzhen than in smaller cities.

28. Chan 2003, 49.
29. Fieldwork notes, Guangzhou, January 2004.
30. Let us consider the important bureaucratic machinery designed to collect data, manage, and control the migrant population. Scharping 1997, 28.
31. Chen et al. 2001, 7. This idea that a "virtual layering of citizenship" is taking place against a background of market forces and socialist institutions is one of Solinger's main arguments in her benchmark volume (1999).
32. See Solinger 1997, 98–118.
33. According to a study in 2000, between one-third and one-fourth of rural migrants in Beijing had had some of their belongings confiscated and had been forced to pay fines to get them back. This proportion reaches nine out of ten of those rural migrants who are more exposed in their work and whose jobs are low in prestige. Li 2003, 126–37.
34. Zhang Li notes that one of the distinctions between migrants and urban residents is the degree of state intervention in people's private and public spaces. For instance, she highlights the fact that migrant housing may be the object of unwarranted inspections, while this seldom happens for urban residents. Zhang 2001, 37–38.
35. By "externalizing" I mean that through such mechanisms migrant workers are turned into immigrants in their own country in the sense that their stay in Chinese cities is conditioned on their obtaining residency and work permits, and they are not provided the social entitlements permanent residents usually get. Their pay is also on the whole much lower than that of permanent residents.
36. The newspapers investigated here are the *Shenzhen Special Zone Daily* (*Shenzhen Tequbao*, hereafter *STQB*), the *Shenzhen Evening* (*Shenzhen Wanbao*, hereafter *SWB*), and the *Shenzhen Legal Daily* (*Shenzhen Fazhibao*, hereafter *SFB*). The papers are all linked institutionally to the Shenzhen authorities and all are under the supervision of the Party propaganda department. The two periods considered here are January to March 1994 and 1998. For further details, see Florence 2004, 42–63.
37. See Zhao 1998.
38. Latham 2000, 638.
39. He 2000, 134.
40. Zhao 2002, 130.
41. Barmé, 1999, 235–36.
42. Although in this text I write "migrant magazines" or "migrant workers' magazines," it should be noted that these magazines are usually not published *by* migrant workers, but *for* them, even though some of the articles are written by them. Most of the journalists working for these magazines are not of working class background. Thanks to Zhao Yuezhi for highlighting this point.
43. In January 2004, I found nine different titles of such magazines in a small bookshop in Guangzhou.
44. Migrant workers in their letters to the editor did stress this tension very much.
45. Letter 25, see also letters 8, 9, 11, 15, and 28. In author's possession.
46. In this article, I have chosen to analyze a body of forty-one letters written by migrant workers and sent to the editor of one of the several migrant workers' magazines. Altogether, I obtained seventy-four unpublished letters, which were given to me by journalist friends working on the magazines.
47. I cannot account for the fact that most of the letters were written by males. This may be the result of a bias linked to the selection process by journalists.
48. The proportion of female migrant labor is usually even higher among people between the ages of fifteen and nineteen, as in Shenzhen and Foshan where female migrants account for around 75 percent of the total migrant population. This reversed sex ratio has to do with the strong demand for female labor in labor-intensive factories in the electronics, textile, and toys industries. Scharping 1999, 79; Tan 2000, 296.
49. Among the letters collected, about one-fifth had not been opened, hence not read.

Notes

50. I have highlighted the main topics of the letters and recorded them in a table with codes representing each topic. This allowed me to isolate the key topics in the stories told in these letters.
51. Similar elements stand out also in the analysis by Anita Chan of letters written to and by female migrant workers and found after a blaze in a Shenzhen factory. See Chan 2002, 180–82.
52. In one such letter (letter 33) the author refers to the fact that he and his fellow workers did not complain to the labor bureau because the factory boss was a member of the village party committee and was getting on well with the director of the labor bureau. On such issues, see Tan 2000; Lee 1998; and Chan 1995.
53. According to a survey conducted in a rural county of Hubei Province, 40 to 50 percent of rural households' net incomes goes into education when all of the children are enrolled in school. See Unger 2002, 184.
54. Anita Chan makes a similar argument in her analysis of women migrant workers private letters with their families. She states: "The overall impression made by the letters is that the young people would not have gone to the factories had their families not been under such financial strain....Their apparent freedom of choice needs to be set against the poverty trap they were in at home." Chan 2002, 181–82.
55. In this respect I follow James C. Scott's suggestion to be cautious about any interpretation of the supposed effects of the dominant ideology since it is extremely difficult to distinguish between strategic moves and ethical submission. This is what Scott calls "radical indeterminacy." See Scott 1990, 92. It may be argued tentatively that some authors "frame" their stories, drawing from a repertoire of specific categories, arguments, or plots that they think are likely to concur with either the editorial line or narrative structure favored by the magazine they are writing to. The editors of migrant magazines I interviewed actually confirmed this argument to me.
56. Letter 15. See letter 8 for a strikingly similar line of argumentation.
57. Lee Ching-Kwan 1995, 15–23; Jacka 2000; Tan 2000, 303–5. A similar paradox of being faced with new forms of domination and experiencing emancipation through migration has been highlighted by the sociology of international migration. See, for example, Sayad 1991.
58. Fieldwork recording, interview no. 3, summer 2001, Guangdong Province.
59. For a detailed analysis of the Shenzhen mainstream press representation of migrant workers, see Florence 2004, 42–63.
60. *SWB*, 23 March 1994, 3.
61. *STQB*, 15 February 1998, 6.
62. From February to March 1998, six special pages out of nine devoted to migrant workers contained articles on model migrant workers, while other articles presented model factories.
63. Xu Feng, documenting the mobilization of model workers within the Party ideological work in a State-owned factory in Jiangsu Province, argued that "model workers are used as examples that one can achieve personal development at any job position." See Xu 2000, 175.
64. Bayart 2004, 262, 272–94.
65. Bakken 2000, 60–62.
66. On these policies and their consequences on Chinese society and development, see Cheng and Selden 1994, 644–68; Cheng 1991; Guo and Liu 1991.
67. Schein 2001, 225, 228.
68. Hoffman 2001, 45.
69. Lee 1998, 74, 84.
70. Rofel 1999, 29, 98, 101, 129. Rofel also notes the heterogeneity of imaginings of economic reform because of great social inequalities and because their eradication was one of the central tenets of Maoist discourse.
71. See letters 8, 13, and 16, for instance.

72. I do not mean to deny the fact that some rural migrants do learn a lot or are trying as much as they can to learn things that may help them in their social mobility process. On this point, see Murphy 2002; Thireau and Hua 2001b.
73. Fieldwork recordings, Pearl River Delta, summer 2001.
74. I am grateful to Guy Massart for highlighting this point.
75. Crane 1994, 76, 83, 89; see also Clark 1998, 103–25.
76. Shenzhen is often called the city of "immigrants" (*yimin chengshi*). Interestingly, the term "immigrant" (*yimin*) is usually not used for temporary rural migrants but for state-sponsored migration or for international migrants. Shenzhen, according to Jiang Zemin's talk in 1993, "could continue as model for the Inland in the strengthening both of the market system, the building of the 'socialist spiritual civilization,' and also to find a new role for the Party in this brand new China." Quoted in Kjellgren 2002, 148.
77. Lee 1995.
78. By "naturalization of power" I mean that the reduction of social stratification to issues of individual psychology is part of a process that aims at turning such stratification into legitimate ones or natural ones.
79. Lee 2002, 70–71.
80. James C. Scott identifies "euphemisation" and "concealment" as two of the four major manifestations of the public transcript, along with "affirmation" and "unanimity." Scott 1990, 45–63.
81. See for example *STQB*, 28 January 1994, 6; *STQB*, 14 January 1994, 6; *STQB*, 28 January 1994, 6; *SWB*, 13 February 1994, 3; *SWB*, 21 February 1994, 1; *Guangzhou Ribao*, 4 February 1994, 1; *STQB*, 4 February 1994, 6; *STQB*, 25 March 1994, 6; *STQB*, 22 August 1994, 6; Liang Yibo 1992, 4–6; Jie and Yang, eds. 1993, 67–71.
82. *STQB*, 25 January 1994, 9; *STQB*, 22 March 1998, 9; *STQB*, 22 March 1998, 9; *STQB*, 29 March 1998, 9; *SWB*, 24 February 1994, 7.
83. Zhang Li described three dominant modes of representation in the construction of the migrant other in Chinese cities: unifying and homogenizing; dehistoricizing and dehumanizing, and, thirdly, abnormalizing. Zhang 2001, 31–33. This would hold true in Shenzhen mainly for those categorized as the "three withouts" (*sanwu*), i.e., all those rural people who have come to cities and have no legal job, no legal residence, and no official identification documents. For a discussion of this category, see Florence 2004, 58–60.
84. It is worth emphasizing that in the "Song of *Dagong*," the author uses the exact same expression "to offer one's best years of youth" (*fengxian qingchun*) to describe the contribution he and migrant workers have made.
85. *STQB*, 29 March 1998, 6.
86. Scott 1990, 35–36.
87. Scott goes further into this idea: "For anything less than completely revolutionary ends the terrain of dominant discourse is the only plausible arena of struggle." Scott's development of this argument in his book has been most helpful in my analysis. Ibid., 103. The "public transcript" is specific to a social site and represents discourse, but also the practices of the dominant. For a further definition of the public transcript, see ibid., 14–15.
88. Again, in many other letters, as well as in many of my interviews with migrant workers, I find the expression of suffering and different forms of reactions related to the reality and constraints they experience.
89. See Pun 2002; Yu 2001.
90. I am grateful to Guy Massart for highlighting this point.
91. Scott 1990, 102–3, 105.
92. I came across a similar expression in an article in the *Shenzhen Special Zone Daily* on model migrant workers that takes a poetico-ideological form: "The reason why the production line is so beautiful is because it uses youthfulness to dress up. These ranges of youngsters sitting there are the green grass and flowers along the water, they are contending vigorously. The value of youth is flowing away smoothly along the production line." *STQB*, 8 March 1998, 6. The title of the article is "I sacri-

fice my youth to the running water," running water being shorthand for *liushuixian,* which means the production line.
93. Li 2003; Wang 1994; Xiang 2000; Solinger 1997.
94. O'Brien 2006, 84–86.
95. Thireau and Hua 2001a, 1283–312; Thireau and Hua 2003, 83–103.
96. Lee 2002, 68.
97. O'Brien 1996, 31.
98. Scott 1990, 102, 138. Scott raises here the difficult issue of the definition of an act of resistance by asking: "Does resistance…require recognition by the party being resisted?" For Steve Pile, "one of authority's most insidious effects may well be to confine definitions of resistance to only those that appear to oppose it directly, in the open, where it can be made and seen to fail." See Pile 1997, 3. As stressed above, I remain cautious about interpreting any relationship between a limited ideological critique and the supposed effects of the dominant discourse. See Scott 1990, 92. Another possible effect of power relations may be, as Steve Pile argues, to give the impression that it is everywhere. See Pile 1997, 27.
99. The category of migrant workers' rights may sometimes be dealt with in migrant magazines or in more mainstream media along the line of unfair treatment and harassment by police officers in the Delta, which would correspond to an extension of what the category originally embodied.
100. Rofel 1999, 123. See also Chen et al. 2001, 11. Zhao Yuezhi (2002, 129) observes that the category of "class" is taboo and there is no serious analysis of class formation in reform-era China.
101. I am grateful to Rachel Murphy for helping me to frame this argument.
102. Sayad 1991, 61–62.

Chapter 3 – Murphy

1. Lü 2000.
2. Examples of excellent contributions that examine diversification and liberalization in China's media include Lynch 1999; Zhao 1988; Lee 2003; Donald, Keane, and Yin 2002; Keane 2003; and Keane 2002.
3. These claims are clear in state-endorsed investigative journalism programs in which the journalists always investigate corrupt lower-level officials or factory managers and explain their malfeasance in terms of greed or weakness or backwardness. Such a focus in reporting encourages viewers to accept the official line that the central state policies are good but that lower quality officials at the lower levels distort implementation. Claims that corruption derives from failed individual ethics are likewise clear in media reports of corruption cases which focus on individual character failings and call for all individuals to engage in self-reflection. Such claims are also made explicit in slogans such as "the mainstream of cadres are good," implying that it is only a few bad apples that cause rot to the whole. See, for instance, Chu, in Fong and Murphy 2006, 68–95.
4. He Zhengke 2000, 243–70; Yao 2002, 279–99.
5. Lü 2000, 190–92, 249.
6. Gong 2002, 85–103; Shevchenko 2004, 161–85; Wedeman 2005, 93–116.
7. Lü 2000, 166–71, 188.
8. Ibid., 170.
9. Ibid., 220.
10. Ibid.; Cao 2004; Murphy, in Fong and Murphy 2006, 9–26.
11. Tao and Liu 2006; Zhang 2006.
12. Lü 2000, 220; Cao 2004.
13. Burawoy, in Smith and Thompson 1992, 180–200.
14. Lü 2000, 170.
15. He Zhengke 2000.
16. Lü 2000, 23.
17. Ibid., 22–23.

18. The material in this paragraph is drawn from Su, in Lee 1994, 75–88, and Wu 2000, in Lee 2000, 45–67.
19. McDonald 2005, 27. Professor Jiao Guobiao, formerly of Beijing University, published his criticisms of the Publicity Department in a 20-page article posted on the internet. His website has since been shut down.
20. Pan, in Lee 2000, 112–51.
21. Ibid.
22. Keane 2001, 783–98; Chen 2004; Luard 2004; China Cracks Down on Corruption, BBC NEWS, 24 October 2006.
23. See also He 2000; Cao 2004; Tao and Liu 2006.
24. Lü 2000, 172–73.
25. These letters come mainly from employees in schools and hospitals and from local officials.
26. Friedman, in Lee 1994, 129–46.
27. He Zhou 2000, in Lee 2000, 112–51; Wu 2000, in Lee 2000, 45–67.
28. He Zhou 2000, in Lee 2000, 112–51.
29. Tie 2005.
30. For a discussion about the use of "dominant assumptions that underpin social life" to encourage certain kinds of interpretations of media see Croteau and Hoynes 2002, 231–39. For an examination of this in relation to gender, see, Van Zoonen 2000, 5–15.
31. Peng Li 2000, 5.
32. *JA Daily*, 14 September 2000.
33. *China Youth News*, 23 August 2000.
34. Liu 2000, 2.
35. Levy 2002, in Link, Madsen, and Pickowicz 2002, 39–56.
36. John Corner, cited in Van Zoonen 2000, 12.
37. *China Youth News*, 23 August 2000.
38. Gu 2000, 4.
39. This gendered dichotomy is common in the political drama genre. Van Zoonen 2000, 9.
40. *China Youth News*, 23 August 2000.
41. *The Life and Death Decision*: A Forerunner of Domestic Epic Drama Films. 2003. http://lcqz.com/zuanti/xiaohuang/ssjz/2301.html. 8 January.
42. Gao and Liao 2000, 1; Ma 2000.
43. *The Life and Death Decision*: A Forerunner of Domestic Epic Drama Films. 2003. URL: http://lcqz.com/zuanti/xiaohuang/ssjz/2301.html. 8 January. *Jiangxi Daily*, 26 August 2000.
44. Corner 2000, 398. John Corner makes this point in relation to British media and U.S. presidential films. Neve 2000, 19–31.
45. China Anti-Corruption Film Tops Hollywood Imports at Box Office. 2000. URL: http://chinaonline.com/topstories/000825/c00082410.asp. 25 August; Pan 2000, 3.
46. *China Youth News*, 23 August 2000.
47. The "Three Represents" (*san ge daibiao*) are (1) the development trends of advanced productive forces; (2) the orientations of an advanced culture; and (3) the fundamental interests of the majority of the people in China.
48. Yang 2000, 4.
49. Schoenhals 1992.
50. *Jiangxi Daily*, 26 August 2000.
51. Ibid.
52. Ibid.
53. Townsend 1996, in Unger and Barmé 1996, 18.
54. *Jiangxi Daily*, 1 September 2000.
55. This idea of "gap" leading to cynicism is explored in Anagnost 1997, 94.
56. Abeles 1988, 391–404.

Notes

57. Though she herself is associated with rumors of accepting money in exchange for sexual liaisons with a leading figure in the Xiamen smuggling scandal!
58. Alexander and Jacobs 1998, in Liebes and Curran 1998, 23–41; Croteau and Hoynes 2002, 229–53; Friedman 1994, in Lee 1994, 129–46.
59. Anagnost 1997, 45–76.
60. Ibid., 94.
61. Yang 2004. Yang Dali documents some efforts to move away from pedagogic campaigns in favor of using systemic reforms to increase supervision over cadres' discipline thereby curbing corruption. These reforms, however, continue to be internal to the system and they fall short of independent and impartial supervision of state officials and institutions. Yang acknowledges that some scholars such as He Zhengke believe independent supervision, including a greater role for the media, is necessary for achieving significant improvements and that the efficacy of increased internal supervision remains to be seen. Certainly in Jiangxi in the early 2000s pedagogic campaigns rather than impartial supervision appeared to be central to efforts to improve governance. Moreover, several other studies document an increasing intensity of official corruption in China with "increasing intensity" being understood as more corruption cases, greater amounts of money lost through embezzlement and bribes, and the scope and number of people involved in corruption cases expanding with the emergence of ever larger networks of players. See Wedeman 2004, 895–921; Wedeman 2005, 93–116.
62. He Zhengke 2000.

Chapter 4 – Jeffreys

1. Altman 2000, 176.
2. Grewal and Kaplan 2001, 669–70.
3. Ibid., 665.
4. See Altman 2000, 174.
5. Martin 2000, 81, 84.
6. Wan Yanhai 1997.
7. Fu 2004; Xiao and Qin 2004. In this article, the expressions "Chinese mainstream media," and, subsequently, "the media," are used to refer to the traditional print media and the new media of the internet. During the Maoist period, newspapers and magazines were funded by the Chinese government (central or regional) and operated as "the voice" of the Chinese Communist Party. Since the introduction of economic reforms, newspapers and other print media forms have been authorized to become "self-sufficient" and, therefore, to commercialize and carry advertisements. This shift has encouraged provincial and municipal government newspapers to open branch papers and weekend editions under different names that appeal to broader readerships by selling advertisements and carrying more sensational news items, a trend that is even more pronounced in recent on-line editions and website forums. This article is based on qualitative information derived from searches of available on-line Chinese-language newspapers and news-related websites for "Li Ning." I conducted the searches between late 2004 and late 2005. Reflecting the highly specific nature of the web search — which was conducted outside of China — a qualitative media analysis was adopted as the preferred methodology on the grounds that it would be virtually impossible to obtain a stratified random sample.
8. Zhang Ning 2005. The nine other cases were: (1) the case of counterfeit baby formula in Anhui Province; (2) the case of corruption brought against the Vice-president of the Anhui Provincial Government; (3) the case of Ma Jiajue, a student at Yunnan University who murdered four of his roommates; (4) the case of a counterfeit winning ticket in a BMW lottery held in Xi'an; (5) the case of a Nanjing law firm that sued the Bureau of Industry and Commerce for failing to protect trademark legislation; (6) the case of internet pornography in Chengdu City; (7) the Guangzhou smuggling case; (8) the case of police corruption in Jilin, which entailed giv-

ing 10,000 driving licenses to people who had not been required to first take a driving test; and (9) the case of the International Music Products Association suing more than 10,000 karaoke dance venues for violating copyright and using MTV without paying requisite royalties.
9. Guo Xiaofei 2004; Lü Fuming 2004; Xiao and Qin 2004.
10. *Criminal Law of the PRC* 1997, Articles 358–59.
11. Quanguo renda changweihui 1991.
12. Jeffreys 2004, 96–102.
13. Quanguo renda changweihui 2005.
14. Jeffreys 2004, 138–49.
15. Historic liberation of Chinese women 2000.
16. Jeffreys 2004, 96–102.
17. This does not mean that the Li Ning case constitutes the first known case of homosocial prostitution in China. On 15 December 2001, two unspecified men in Beijing were sentenced to nine and six year's imprisonment respectively for running a male-male prostitution business. In July 2003, the Shanghai Changning District Court sentenced Wang Zhiming to three years imprisonment and a fine of 3,000 yuan for organizing four young men to sell sex from a rented residential premise. The court handed down a lenient sentence in this case because Wang Zhiming gave himself up to the police and admitted his guilt. And, on 12 January 2004, the Huangpu District People's Court in Shanghai sentenced Shao Wei to imprisonment for one year and a fine of 1,000 yuan for harbouring male prostitutes in a bar. See Fu 2004; Gong 2003; Liu Yaotang 2004; Yao Lan 2004, 3; Zhang Cenyi 2003.
18. Guo Xiaosong 2004; Liu Zhi (n.d.); Zong and Yang 2004.
19. Fan and Guo 2004; Guo Xiaosong 2004; Liu Zhi (n.d.).
20. Guo Xiaosong 2004.
21. Fu 2004; Xiao and Qin 2004.
22. Guo Xiaosong 2004; Wei 2004.
23. Liu Yaping 2004.
24. See Li Yinhe 2005.
25. Zong and Yang 2004.
26. Xiao and Qin 2004.
27. Zhonghua renmin gongheguo guowuyuan 1999.
28. For a discussion of the implications of this distinction with regard to the provision of male-male commercial sexual services in Thailand, see Malcolm McCamish et al. 2000, 167–82.
29. Zong and Yang 2004.
30. Xiao and Qin 2004.
31. Wei 2004; Yao Zixu (n.d.).
32. Liu Yaotang 2004; see also China: Law faces sex problems — Sichuan teahouse case 1999.
33. Wei 2004; Yang Tao (n.d.).
34. Guo Xiaofei 2004.
35. Yao Zixu (n.d.).
36. Guo Xiaosong 2004.
37. Wei 2004.
38. This "Reply" was made in response to requests from lower-level public security authorities in Guangxi Zhuang Autonomous Region for advice on how to deal with the phenomenon of same-sex prostitution, see Gong'anbu 2001.
39. Guo Xiaofei 2004; Yao Zixu (n.d.).
40. Liu et al. 2004.
41. Li Meiyi 2004.
42. Li Yang 2005; Lü and Deng 2005; Yang Liu 2005; Yuan 2005.
43. Fu 2004; Li Meiyi 2004.
44. Fu 2004.
45. Rofel 1999, 465.

Notes

46. Fu 2004; Zhang Beichuan et al. 2000a.
47. Fu 2004.
48. Zhang Beichuan et al. 2000a.
49. See Sigley and Jeffreys 1999, 50–58.
50. See Chou 2000; Geyer 2002, 262–64; Hinsch 1992; Li Yinhe 2006, 82–101.
51. Martin 2000, 81; Li Yinhe cited in McDonald 2005.
52. Li Yinhe cited in McDonald 2005, see also Friess 2004; Geyer 2002; He tongxinglian youguan de falü 2003; Rubin 2003.
53. Gao Feng 2003.
54. Ibid.; Gong 2003.
55. Although claims that "sex" disappeared during the Maoist period have been called into question (see Honig 2003, 143–75), it remains the case that public and academic discussions of issues of sex and sexuality have increased dramatically in the reform period, and that the provision of sex-related courses at Chinese universities is a recent phenomenon. Scholars and activists who are credited with opening public debates on homosexuality and gay rights in present-day China include Gong Guojiang 2003; Li Yinhe 1998; Wan Yanhai 1997; and Zhang Beichuan et al. 2000a, 2000b.
56. Fu 2004.
57. McDonald 2005; see also Gong 2003; Zhang Beichuan et al. 2000a; Zhang Beichuan et al. 2000b.
58. Fu 2004; see also Langfitt 2000.
59. Rofel 1999, 466.
60. Fu Jianfeng 2004.
61. Guo Xiaofei 2004.
62. Lü 2004.
63. The sexologist Alfred C. Kinsey is famous for conducting the largest quantitative studies of human sexual behaviors in the USA during the 1940s and 1950s. See Gong 2003; Rubin 2003; Zhang Beichuan et al. 2000a.
64. Zhang Beichuan et al. 2000a.
65. China cracks down on gay prostitution 2004; Police arrest 37 gays in social vice swipe 2000; Xiao and Qing 2004; Yao Zixu (n.d.).
66. Gong Guojiang 2003; Tongxinglianzhi de gongmin quanli he fazhi jianshe 2003.
67. Xie Wei et al. 2005.
68. Fu 2004.
69. Li Yinhe 2005; Pan Suiming 1998.
70. Zhu 2003.
71. Lü Fuming 2004.
72. Han Junjie 2005. These regulations constitute a formal advance on a controversial set of regulations that were introduced in Chengdu City, Sichuan Province, in 2000. See Chengdushi xingbing aizibing fangzhi guanli tiaoli 2000; Pomfret 2001; Rubin 2003.
73. Rofel 1999, 470, 464.

Chapter 5 – Damm

1. See also Taylor 1999, 12, 14, 24.
2. McIntyre 1997, 149–69; Qiu 1999/2000, 1–25; Chase and Mulvenon 2002; Kluver and Qiu 2003; Sohmen 2001, 17–26. Empirical data on the use of the internet and the most recent figures can be found at www.cnnic.com.cn, the website of the China Internet Network Information Center (CNNIC), which published the first statistical report to provide various data on the development of the internet in China; since 1998, these reports, which include information on user demographics, access locations and average on-line behavior, have been published twice yearly; see esp. CNNIC 2004, CNNIC 2006. For the problems of the data material, see Giese 2003b, 30–57, esp. 31–35.
3. See May 1999, A23. Falun Gong is a Chinese spiritual practice or "sect" that was founded in 1992 by Li Hongzhi; since 1999 Falun Gong has officially been declared

illegal in China and its supporters have been persecuted. The *Tiananmen Papers* are documents that were revealed to the world in January 2001 by a group of American Sinologists, translators, and publishers, who claim to have background information about the crack-down on the protest movement in 1989. These documents are available in both English and Chinese in electronic format. There is some doubt as to the authenticity of these documents, which were compiled by Zhang Liang (a pseudonym) and published in 2001 by Public Affairs, New York, edited by Andrew J. Nathan and Perry Link.
4. Griffin 1991.
5. Specker 2004.
6. Ibid.
7. Interestingly, while the Chinese government tries to restrict this easy access for everybody through a variety of regulations, we found the following sentence "On the Internet, being a publisher costs next to nothing" on the Sohu E-Learning page, which is part of an English-language learning program, learning.sohu.com/82/61/article210596182.shtml; accessed 12 February 2005.
8. URL: www.newsmax.com/archives/articles/2002/5/2/192846.shtml; accessed 17 February 2005.
9. Quoted in Kalathil 2000.
10. Kids, cadres and "cultists" — all love it: Growing influence of the Internet in China. A March 2001 report from U.S. Embassy, Beijing. URL: www. usembassy-china.org.cn/sandt/netoverview.html; accessed 5 June 2004.
11. Specker 2004. For a more detailed overview, see Introduction, in Damm and Thomas 2006, 1–11; Chase et al. 2006, 64–101.
12. Internet activism in Asia: "Dissident e-zine threatens China." URL: journalism.uts.edu.au/subjects/oj1/oj1_a2002/internetactivisminasia/china_activists_vip.html; accessed 12 February 2005.
13. Zittrain and Edelman 2003. For the newly established Berkeley China Internet Project, headed by Xiao Qiang, see journalism.berkeley.edu/projects/chinadn /en; accessed 12 February 2005.
14. Xiao 2004.
15. Leung 1999, 781–90; Kluver and Qiu 2003; for a critical view of simplistic and technology-deterministic approaches, see McCormick and Liu 2003; Fang 2004; see also MacKinnon 2006.
16. See, for example, Griffiths 2002.
17. See also International Institute for Democracy and Electoral Assistance 2001; the authors are unable to perceive a "third way" of achieving more transparency within authoritarian regimes without the transformation of these systems through democratizing processes. They seem to seek to polarize the argument by pointing out that "the information revolution has assisted pro-democracy activists to progressively chip away at authoritarian regimes' grip on power," while at the same time commenting on "the ability of those same regimes both to disseminate propaganda and monitor their own citizens' behavior."
18. Rheingold 1993.
19. Ibid.
20. Fernback and Thompson 1995.
21. Rheingold 1993.
22. Cohen 2003; Cohen 1984.
23. Tsui 2001; other examples for research on censorship are Xing 2001 and Wacker 2003.
24. Chase and Mulvenon 2002.
25. See, for example, Chinese reports on the closing down of cybercafes: Zhai et al. 2004; Wong 2004.
26. China: Cyber cafés closed in new clampdown. URL: europe.cnn.com/2001 /TECH/internet/07/20/china.internet.reut/index.html, 2001; accessed 20 April 2005.
27. Hyman 2003.

Notes

28. See, for example, the U.S. "Children's Internet Protection Act" (CIPA). URL: www.fcc.gov/cgb/consumerfacts/cipa.html; accessed 15 June 2004.
29. See also Dobson 1998.
30. Editorial of the *Xinhua News Agency*, 13 January 2002, Keji kuayue, zhicheng gongheguo de mingtian [The technological leapfrogging supports the tomorrow of the Republic]. URL: oic.seu.edu.cn/show.aspx?id=458; accessed 12 May 2005.
31. See, Internet to contribute more to China's transformation. URL: www. edu.cn /20011128/3012100.shtml; accessed 1 June 2004. The article "Futurist Toffler: China has seen 'astonishing changes'" was published on the official website of the Chinese Embassy in the United States, 28 November 2001. URL: www.china-embassy.org/eng/zt/mgryzdzg/t36523.htm; accessed 1 June 2004; see also Hong 2002, Yi Ming 2001. It is not clear whether "leap frogging" is an indigenous development or whether it has derived from outside China: "Any belief in the revolutionary potential of ICTs among the Chinese leadership is thus as likely to have been influenced and derived from the up-beat assessments that have been produced outside China as by the heritage of the country's own past," Dai 2003, 8.
32. For a critical evaluation of these approaches, see Introduction, in Hughes and Wacker 2003, 1–7.
33. Giese 2003a.
34. Xie 2006, 145–46.
35. China reaps big fruits for future internet. URL: http://english.people.com.cn /200609/26/eng20060926_306545.html; accessed 9 October 2006.
36. Bu Wei's research topics include "Digital divide and media gap in China"; "Gender and media"; "The influence of Internet on audience and media"; "NGO and media in IEC strategy"; "Media education" (literacy), and "Communication methodology." URL: www.culturebase.net/artist.php?1424; accessed 4 February 2004; see also Hachigian 2001.
37. URL: www.ccidnet.com; accessed 2 March 2006.
38. CNNIC 2006.
39. These qualitative interviews were carried out as part of an interdisciplinary research project funded by the DFG (Deutsche Forschungsgemeinschaft), May 2001 –April 2003, on China's internet policy at Freie Universität Berlin. My research was primarily focused on local e-government, but to gain a clearer picture of the users, interviews were also held with graduate students and assistant researchers who accessed the internet within the universities (library or dormitory) (Xiamen University; Sun Yatsen University, Guangzhou; Fuzhou University); users in internet cafes in university districts (mostly undergraduates, or high school students), and a sample of citizens in the Xijiao district of Nanhai city and in the Taijiang district of Fuzhou city.
40. CNNIC 2004.
41. CNNIC 2004, CNNIC 2006.
42. This usually does not apply to other Europeans because non-English web pages are considered irrelevant to Chinese users and are therefore not blocked.
43. Interview with a research assistant at Xiamen University, 2003.
44. During my research, for example, the *China Times* (www.chinatimes.com) and the *United Daily* (www.udngroup.com.tw) sites were blocked; it was possible, however, to access the pro-independent educational Lihbao site, www.lih bao.com.
45. It should be kept in mind that my interview partners were winners of the reform: Nanhai in Guangdong and Xiamen in Fujian both represent extraordinary success stories and there was prevailing optimism that, in the near future, personal computers would become widely available to the middle class. All the research assistants and students in Xiamen had just moved to new buildings, offering both research facilities and accommodation on the university campus, where broadband access was available. Many of them reported that they had also traveled to foreign places such as Thailand and South Korea, or — at least — had been to Shenzhen and Hong Kong,

46. At least at the time when I was carrying out my interviews, internet cafes in Fujian were subject to fewer restrictions than cafes in Beijing or Shanghai; nobody was required to show an ID card. The cafes were probably all illegal — I observed police officers entering the cafe who, then, instead of checking the age of the users playing games, disappeared with the *laoban* (boss, or manager) into a back room — probably to talk "business."
47. Another fact is that Xiamen as a Special Economic Zone has attracted a lot of foreign/joint-venture enterprises and suppliers; some of my interviewees who had already left university were working in small advertising agencies or in joint ventures and thus had left the traditional *danwei*-structure, which under the socialist regime had functioned as a sub-state community, guaranteeing working places, housing, welfare, and education. People at the university, however, still lived in danwei-like university flats and were subject to strict social control.
48. See also Nip 2003.
49. Guo 2003.
50. Bobson Wong (2004) described this as follows: "At the same time, government officials appear willing to continue detaining individuals for using the Internet to speak out on controversial topics, even as they also appear willing to release these individuals if enough public pressure is applied. The line that distinguishes acceptable and unacceptable on-line behavior in China is becoming increasingly blurred."
51. See Nathan 2003.
52. Finding quantitative data on these phenomena is difficult; there are Chinese articles that criticize these so-called red hackers (*hong ke*), although they are said to enjoy great popularity; see, for example, Tuijian Zhongguo fazhi jincheng — heike bu ying yong ci fangshi "ai guo" [Strengthening the process of juridification of China: Hackers should not use that kind of "patriotism"]. 4 April 2005. URL: news.xinhuanet.com/it/2005-04/04/content_2782865.htm; accessed 3 June 2005; and Lao Shi 2005.
53. See de Kloet 2003.
54. Another explanation of the "hacker" problem could be that, unlike the classical definition of a hacker as the ultimate free netizen whose movements are not restricted within national borders, there might be hackers who have been instrumentalized by governments. Thus, actions that appear to be hacker actions are sometimes carried out by secret services. See, for example, Chase and Mulvenon 2002, 74.
55. In this, I follow Arif Dirlik's and Xudong Zhang's (2000, 3-4) view: "Under conditions of a global capitalism, Chinese states and populations are no longer merely the 'objects' of forces emanating from Euro-America but are themselves significant contributors to the operations of capitalism; hence the seemingly contradictory representations of China and Chinese at once in conventional orientalist (or self-orientalist) terms as a location of the exotic other but also as the carriers of values expanding the frontiers of capitalism."
56. Some confusion exists regarding the terminology: the applications known today as BBSs, particularly in Japan and China, are considered to be the successors of the original "bulletin board systems," which were widespread in the 1980s and 1990s and required a dial-in, and also of USENET-newsgroups, which are not very common in China.
57. Giese 2005.
58. Giese 2003b.
59. Giese 2005.
60. Yang 2003; Giese 2003a.
61. Such as Sohu BBS, club.sohu.com; Netease *shequ* (http://bj.163.com/), and the semi-private Sina *luntan*, people.sina.com.cn/forum.html, which offer BBSs in addition to Chat (*liaotianshi*).

Notes

62. A list with well-known Chinese BBSs can be found at soho178.com/wz/luntan.htm; there are also some forums with more politically oriented content such as the "Strong country forum" (*qiangguo luntan*), hosted by the *People's Daily* (www.qglt.com/bbs/mlbrd?to=47); for an analysis, see Yang 2003. An official registration, however, is necessary; some local websites, which I researched in 2002/2003, such as the website of Taijang/Fuzhou once provided BBBs, but have stopped now.
63. There is no special section for men; "Sohu women" and "Sohu cars" are probably the appropriate sections, according to SOHU.
64. It should be kept in mind, however, that virtual communities that once emerged from one of these forums could easily discuss other topics as well.
65. The Sohu site, club.sohu.com, was accessed on 15 October 2004; the sub-site Women's Club was accessed on 25 May 2004. Other discussion sections include "lens on social life," "health life," "photo paradise," "Sohu women," "Sohu cars," "houses, property and flats," "space for finance and economics," "travel," "zone for culture and education," "music and film," "sports forum," "Sohu science," "cities and regions", and "college/school forum."
66. Other topic threads are "horoscope picture show," "picture-declaration by 12 girls from Nanjing," "sorrow is the only real test of friendship," "show children how to work," "frJeans — Korean label for leisure and sport," "let the past go, it should not disturb your dreams," and "seven years in Beijing — a story about growing up."
67. Other BBS topics are "women are afraid of ghosts," "male village," "chat station," "people who share the same," "wandering around Beijing," "clouds over Beijing," "life in a Hutong," "babies of Beijing," "Beijing fashion," "living in foreign cities," "looking for travel companions," "shopping forum," "astrology forum," "ticket forum," "food forum," "holiday forum," "plant forum," "animal forum," "collection forum," "stamp forum," "I love my home," "leisure time," and "toward the Olympics."
68. It would be probably too easy to equate the new "leap frogging" with the help of ICT with earlier attempts of Communist central planning, the most famous example probably being the Great Leap Forward at the end of the 1950s. However much the methods have changed, what is still inherent is a belief that humankind can easily change the world; see also Dai 2003, 8.
69. Lu 2000, 146; see also Lu 1997 and Lu 2001, 111–33.
70. In this context, authors such as Dirlik and Zhang (2000) make a clear case for the need to understand both the historical uniqueness of Chinese postmodernism and its particularities in order to be able to grasp fully the condition of postmodernity worldwide.
71. There has been some recent research on the use of the internet in "underdeveloped" regions. Research topics include qualitative methodologies for measuring the success of the internet in empowering underdeveloped regions, and ethnographical field studies focused on the attitudes of rural residents toward the internet; see the unpublished papers from the Fourth Chinese Internet Research Conference, 21–22 July 2006, Singapore: Wang Xiling, Network technology and social impacts: Investigation of farmers' internet application and social transformations in northwest rural areas; Zhang Mingxin, Chinese rural residents' adoption of an attitude toward the internet: An exploratory research; Chao Naipeng, Farmers' internet access and usage in western China: A case study; Zhao Jinqiu, Hao Xiaoming, and Indrajit Banerjee, The internet adoption and usage: A case study of rural users in China's Shandong Province.
72. Xu 1999, 1.
73. Hartley 2000, 4.
74. Ibid., 3.
75. For the involvement of various ministries in the internet business, starting from the mid-1990s, see Harwit and Clark 2001.
76. See also Thompson 1995, 75–80.
77. Hartley 1999, 141–43, 154–59.

78. Keane 2001b, 4; Yang 2004.

Chapter 6 – Latham

1. Mueller and Tan 1997.
2. See, for example, Huang 1993, 216–40; Rowe 1990; Strand 1990.
3. Pye 1979, 153–78
4. See, for example, Zhao 1998; Lynch 1999; Lee 2000; Hemelryk Donald, Keane, and Hong 2002.
5. MII 2006.
6. See, for example, Chu 1979.
7. Whyte 1979, 113–24; Lau 1979, 125–50.
8. See, for example, Latham 2001, 89–107; Li 1998; Zhao 1998, 2000; Hussain 1990; Huang, Y. 1994; Liu 1998; Huang, C. 2000.
9. See, for example, Yu 2004; Yin and Li 2004; Li and Yang 2004; Zhang 2005.
10. Latham 2000.
11. Assuming a population of 1.3 billion people and using official figures of 123 million internet users in July 2006, sending on average 3.6 emails per week CNNIC (2005) gives a figure of 0.25 emails per person per week compared to nearly 305 billion SMS messages sent in 2005, equivalent to approximately 4.5 messages per person per week.
12. Munro 1977.
13. Blecher 1983, 63–86; Chu 1979, 57–75.
14. Whyte 1979.
15. Bennet 1977, 121–39; Cell 1983, 25–46.
16. See, for example, Li 1991; Latham 2000.
17. See, for example, Yu 2004.
18. See, for example, Huang 2000.
19. Calhoun 1989; Lynch 2000, 195.
20. Lynch 2000, 181.
21. Ibid., 182.
22. See, for example, Hughes and Wacker 2003; Sun 2002; Hu 2002, 192–99; Harwit and Clark 2001; Hartford 2003, 177–95; Shen 2002, 223–38.
23. Apart from technical, business, and economic literature outlining the developments of telecommunications policy and markets, e.g., Yan and Pitt 2002; Lu and Wong 2003; Mueller and Tan 1997.
24. Yan and Pitt 2002, 125–27.
25. Yang and Li 2004.
26. China Radio International 2005.
27. See Erwin 2000, 145–70.
28. "Apart from the enhanced possibility of intertextuality, on-line journalism also facilitates individuated, everyday reading of news stories — in a way that is oppositional to how media events are watched — through means of interactivity....Online interactivity also means that conversations between news users are less scripted and more subject to the moods and desires of the participating individuals." Sun 2002, 174–75.
29. Blogging, for instance, is changing the rules of conventional news production and consumption in four key ways: (1) by opening up new ways of sourcing news; (2) as a supplementary forum for the discussion of conventional news reporting; (3) as an informal mechanism for the verification or supervision of news stories; and (4) as an alternative outlet for journalistic writing.
30. Very occasionally newspapers have been closed down. See, for example, Zhao 1998, 22, 159.
31. See, for example, Latham 2000.
32. See, for example, Anagnost 1997, 118–28
33. Lynch 2000, 186.
34. See Lu and Wong 2003, 44–46 and 56–60.
35. Mueller and Tan 1997, 45–60.

36. For instance, the notion of maintaining an "orderly" *youxude* market and promoting "orderly" competition has often been used to justify the control of telecoms tariffs, to limit or reorganize the number of companies in the marketplace, and generally intervene when order seemed to be breaking down. Examples include the setting up of China Unicom, the division of the old China Telecom, into the new China Telecom and China Netcom, the strict separation of the telecoms and broadcasting sectors, forbidding cable television operators from offering telephony services, for instance, and the movement toward regional and national internet cafe chains, over small independently operated establishments. See stories carried by China Media Intelligence, www.eight- and-eight.com/cmi, on all these issues.

37. The internet has become gradually more and more controlled in China (see Hughes and Wacker 2003) and shifted from the disorderly end of the spectrum toward the orderly end. In the early days, the mid-1990s, relatively few people used the internet and these users constituted a relatively narrow social group — computer specialists, technicians, and intellectuals. As the use of the internet has diversified and become more common and as the sociological characteristics of internet users have moved increasingly toward groups perceived to be more vulnerable or potentially volatile — the young, in particular — the authorities have taken a greater interest in controlling content in one way or another. For example, up until 1999 portals were often writing their own news stories, but new regulations then required them only to use news from recognized licensed news organizations. In the early 2000s the blocking of websites considered actually or potentially subversive was also stepped up and in 2003 more stringent regulations were introduced covering the use of internet cafes, stipulating a minimum size and number of computers as well as banning under-18-year-olds from using them. This trend of tightening regulation and government intervention has continued.

38. *South China Morning Post* 2005.

39. For instance, the development and organization of China's cable television networks building up from the local level is reminiscent of the decentralized organization of the telecommunications system. The emerging trend toward internet protocol television, the fragmentation of audiences, and the development of specialist television channels and broadband video-on-demand services all constitute moves toward the more disorderly end of the mass media spectrum.

40. See, for example, Morley 1992, 45–58.

41. It is also the very leakiness of this once relatively hermetic seal that now makes some of the core principles of Chinese media production anachronistic. See Latham 2000; 2001.

42. Of course in theory Mao's mass-line model of communication was really about communication up the hierarchy, from the masses to the leadership, as well as down it (see Blecher 1983; Chu 1979). However, even leaving aside the fact that in practice the traffic has generally been one way, this is still a vertical model of communication.

43. Hall 1980, 128–38.

44. Lull 1991.

45. See, for example, Huang et al. 1993; Link et al. 1989; 2002; Davis 1995, 1–19.

46. Latham 2005.

47. Lynch 1999 and 2000.

48. Lynch 2000, 179, emphasis in original.

49. "*Xianzai geming shi cong shouji laide.*" Mr. Wang (pseudonym), an educated middle-class professional in his early forties, recounted this story to me.

50. Yang and Li 2004.

51. A further indication of the potentially criminal use of SMS was revealed in November 2006 when two men were arrested in Guangzhou for sending thousands of blackmailing SMS messages threatening violence to people's children if they did not pay money into a named bank account.

52. Yang and Li 2004.

Chapter 7 – Chu

1. Hooper 2005; Keane 2001.
2. Yin 2002, 51–55.
3. Chen, Zhili 2002, 135–36.
4. Chen, Li 2002, 73–74.
5. You 2002, 30–32.
6. Kang 2004a.
7. Xu Guangcun at the National Broadcasting Conference in Beijing in 2004. See ibid.
8. "Encouraging the Development of Broadcasting Enterprises," published by the State Administration of Radio, Film and Television, Beijing. See Kang 2004a.
9. Interviews with Kang Ning, 13–16 April 2004.
10. Kang 2004a.
11. Other filmed subjects include real estate sales personnel, managers, drivers of trucks, taxis, buses, light and heavy rail, a site supervisor, policemen, a reporter, the head of a local government office, village leaders, folk artists, craftsmen, small businessmen and women, migrants in Beijing and Shanghai, security guides, archaeologists, school teachers and a private school principal, academics, university students, interior designers, air hostesses, airport engineers and mechanics, a private theatre manager, a model and a bar owner, an unemployed looking for jobs, high school students, a retiree, a hairdresser, a web designer, a neighborhood worker, foot masseur, TV program producer and a host, an insurance saleswoman, a sick peasant family, museum workers, social workers, dockers, a blind football team, rocket scientists, football players, a troupe on horseback, musicians, doctors, border soldiers, performers in a military parade, zoologists, entrepreneurs, custom officers, a male baby sitter, a building inspector, a psychologist, a lawyer, a beautician, a fitness trainer, a tourist guide, a wedding agent, firefighters, and others.

❑

REFERENCES

Abeles, Marc. 1988. Modern political ritual: Ethnography of an inauguration and a pilgrimage by President Mitterrand. *Cultural Anthropology* 29 (3): 391–404 (June).

Alcoff, Linda. 1988. Cultural feminism vs. post-structuralism: The identity crisis in feminist theory. *Signs* 13 (3): 405–36.

Alexander, Jeffrey C., and Ronald N. Jacobs. 1998. Mass communication, ritual and civil society. In Tamar Liebes and James Curran, eds. *Media, ritual and identity.* London: Routledge. 23–41.

Altman, Dennis. 2000. Talking sex. *Postcolonial Studies* 3 (2): 171–78.

Anagnost, Ann. 1997. *National past-times: Narrative, representation, and power in modern China.* Durham, N.C.: Duke University Press.

Anonymous. 1999. Dagongmei qunti shi xingbing de genyuan [Migrant women are the sources of STDs]. *Wen Zhai Bao.* 4 March.

Apter, David, and T. Saich. 1994. *Revolutionary discourse in Mao's Republic.* Cambridge, Mass., and London: Harvard University Press.

Bai, Hui. 2001. Nongmin ke dai tudi jincheng [Peasants can bring the land to the city]. *Dalian Wanbao.* 13 August: 29.

Bakken, Børge. 2000. *The exemplary society: Human improvement, social control, and the dangers of modernity.* Oxford and New York: Oxford University Press.

Barlow, Tani. 1997. Woman at the close of the Maoist era in the polemics of Li Xiaojiang and her associates. In Lowe and Lloyd, eds. 1997. 506–13.

Barmé, Geremie. 1999. *In the red.* New York: Columbia University Press.

Bayart, Jean-François. 2004. *Le gouvernement du monde: Pour une critique politique de la globalisation.* Paris: Fayard.

Beijing Daxue, Dongguan mingong keti zu. 1995. *Zhanlue yu guanli* 2.

Bennet, G. 1977. China's mass campaigns and social control. In A.A. Wilson, S.L. Greenblatt, and R. Wilson, eds. *Deviance and social control in Chinese society.* New York: Praeger.

Berger, John. 1972. *Ways of seeing.* London: British Broadcasting Corporation and Penguin Books.

Bian, Bian. 2001. Rang nanren yuanli sanpei [Let men stay far away from bar hostesses]. *Lisa Sheng Huo Chao* [Lisa Lifestyle] 3: 10–11.

Billeter, Jean-François. 1985. The system of "class status." In Stuart Schram, ed. *The scope of state power in China.* Hong Kong: The Chinese University Press. 127–69.

Blecher, Marc. 1983. The mass line and leader-mass relations and communication in basic-level rural communities. In G.C. Chu and F.L.K. Hsu, eds. *China's new social fabric.* London: Kegan Paul International.

Bourdieu, Pierre. 1991. *Language and symbolic power.* Cambridge: Polity Press.

Brownell, Susan. 1995. *Training the body for China: Sports in the moral order of the People's Republic.* Chicago: University of Chicago Press.

Burawoy, Michael. 1992. View from production: The Hungarian transition from socialism to capitalism. In Chris Smith and Paul Thompson, eds., *Labour in transition: The labour process in Eastern Europe and China.* London: Routledge. 180–200.

Butler, Judith. 1993. *Bodies that matter: On the discursive limits of "sex."* New York: Routledge.

Calhoun, C. 1989. Tiananmen, television and the public sphere: Internationalization of culture and the Beijing spring of 1989. *Public Culture* 2 (1): 54–70.

Cao Jingqing. 2004. *China along the Yellow River.* London: Routledge.

Cell, C.P. 1983. Communication in China's mass mobilization campaigns. In G.C. Chu and F.L.K. Hsu, eds. *China's new social fabric.* London: Kegan Paul International.

Chan, Anita. 1993. Revolution or corporatism? Workers and trade unions in post-Mao China. *The Australian Journal of Chinese Affairs* 29 (January): 31–61.

———. 1995. The emerging patterns of industrial relations in China and the rise of the new labor movements. *China Information* 9 (4): 36–59.

———. 1998. The conditions of Chinese workers in East Asian–funded enterprises. *Chinese Sociology and Anthropology* 30 (4): 1–101.

———. 2002. The culture of survival: Lives of migrant workers through the prism of private letters. In Perry Link et al., eds., *Popular China: Unofficial culture in a globalizing society.* Lanham, Md.: Rowman and Littlefield. 163–88.

———. 2003. Toujours plus bas! Les effets de la mondialisation sur les conditions de travail en Chine. *Perspectives Chinoises* 75: 43–52.

———. 2005. Recent trends in Chinese labour issues: Signs of change. *China Perspectives* 57: 23–32 (January–February).

Chan, Anita, and Zhu Xiaoyang. 2003. Disciplinary labor regimes in Chinese factories. *Critical Asian Studies* 35 (4): 559–84 (December).

Chapkis, Wendy. 1997. *Live sex acts: Women performing erotic labor.* New York: Routledge.

Chase, Michael S., and James C. Mulvenon. 2002. *You've got dissent! Chinese dissident use of the internet and Beijing's counter-strategies.* Washington, D.C.: Rand Corporation.

Chase, Michael, James C. Mulvenon, and Nina Hachigian. 2006. Comrade to comrade networks: The social and political implications of peer-to-peer networks in China. In Damm and Thomas, eds. 2006. 64–101.

Chatterjee, Partha. 1989. Colonialism, nationalism, and the colonialized women: The contest in India. *American Ethnologist* 16 (November): 622–33.

Chen, Hui. 2001. Jiemei "zhengfu" yinfa shaqin canju [Two sisters attempt to murder each other for a man]. *Bandao Chenbao.* 11 May: 20.

References

Chen, Li. 2002. Zhangwo lilun wuqi, shijian "sange daibiao" zhongyao shixiang [The use of theory in the application of the notion of the "Three Representatives"]. In Li 2002.

Chen, Ming. 2001a. Beiqiangjian juran shuotinghao [The woman likes to be raped]. *Gaobie chunü* [Farewell to Virginity] 43: 57–59.

———. 2001b. Nüzhuchi ren diyici shiyu taizhang zuojiaoyi [A migrant woman's sexual transaction with her employer]. *Gaobie chunü* [Farewell to Virginity] 43: 49–56.

Chen, Nancy N., et al., eds. 2001. *China urban: Ethnographies of contemporary culture*. Durham, N.C., and London: Duke University Press.

Chen, Yanru. 2004. Defining media's social roles. *China Daily*, 6 August.

Chen, Zhili. 2002. Rushi hou de Zhongguo jiaoyu yu chelüe [The impact on education of China's entry into the WTO and available strategies]. *Zhongguo Jiaoyu* [China Education]. 9 January.

Cheng, Tiejun. 1991. *Dialectics of control: The household registration (hukou) system in contemporary China*. PhD diss. (State University of New York at Binghamton).

Cheng, Tiejun, and Mark Selden. 1994. The origins and consequences of China's hukou system. *The China Quarterly* 139: 644–68.

Chengdushi xingbing aizibing fangzhi guanli tiaoli [City of Chengdu STIs and HIV/AIDS prevention and management regulations]. 2000. 27 October. Available on-line at www.tsinghua.edu.cn/docsn/shxx/site/chinac/liudb/aids/lanmu/qinghua/tzh/baogao/38.htm (accessed 21 July 2005).

China anti-corruption film tops Hollywood imports at box office. 2000. http://chinaonline.com/topstories/000825/c00082410.asp. 25 August.

China cracks down on corruption. 2006. BBC News Online. 24 October. http://news.bbc.co.uk/go/pr/fr/-/1/hi/world/asia-pacific/6079400.stm.

China cracks down on gay prostitution. 2004. UPI NewsTrack, 15 June.

China Radio International 2005. Text message novels to be auctioned. CRI website, http://en.chinabroadcast.cn/business/index.htm, 4 February (accessed 20 February 2005). Attributed to the *Shenzhen Daily*.

China Youth News [Zhongguo qingnian bao] 2000. 23 August (Chinese).

China: Law faces sex problems — Sichuan teahouse case. 1999. Sinofile Information Services, 15 May.

Chou, Wah-shan. 2000. *Tongzhi: Politics of same sex eroticism in Chinese societies*. Binghamton, N.Y.: Haworth Press.

Christiansen, Flemming. 1990. Hu kou in China. *Issues and Studies* 26 (4): 23–42.

Chu, G.C. 1979. The current structure and functions of China's mass media. In Chu and Hsu, eds. 1979.

Chu, G.C., and F.L.K. Hsu, eds. 1979. *Moving a mountain: Cultural change in China*. Honolulu: University Press of Hawai'i.

Chu, Yingchi. 2006. Legal report: Citizenship education through a television documentary. In Fong and Murphy, eds. 2006. 68–95.

Clark, Constance. 1998. The politics of place making in Shenzhen, China. *Berkeley Planning Journal* 12: 103–25.

CNNIC (China Internet Network Information Centre). 2004. *The 14th statistical survey report on the internet development in China* (July 2004). Available on-line at www.cnnic.cn/download/2004/2004 072003.pdf (accessed 5 January 2006).

———. 2005. *Statistical report of the development of the internet in China* (January 2005). Beijing: China Internet Network Information Centre.

———. 2006. *The 18th statistical survey report on the internet development in China* (July 2006). Available on-line at www.cnnic.cn/download/2006/18threport-en.pdf (accessed 18 December 2006).

Cohen, Myron. 1993. Cultural and political inventions in modern China: The case of the Chinese "peasant." *Daedalus* 122 (2): 151–70.

Cohen, Paul A. 1984. *Discovering history in China: American historical writing on the recent Chinese past.* New York: Columbia University Press.

———. 2003. *China unbound: Evolving perspectives on the Chinese past.* London and New York: RoutledgeCurzon.

Cook, James. 1996. Penetration and neocolonialism: The "Shen Chong" rape case and the anti-American student movement of 1946–47. *Republican China* 22 (1): 65–97.

Corner, John. 2000. Mediated persona and political culture: Dimensions of structure and process. *European Journal of Cultural Studies* 3 (3): 386–402.

Crane, Georges T. 1994. Special things in special ways: National economic identity and China's Special Economic Zones. *The Australian Journal of Chinese Affairs* 37: 71–92 (June).

Criminal Law of the PRC. 1997. Adopted by the Second Session of the Fifth National People's Congress on 1 July 1979 and amended by the Fifth Session of the Eighth National People's Congress on 14 March 1979. Available on-line at www/chinajnbook.com/business/criminal01.htm (accessed 21 July 2005).

Croteau, David, and William Hoynes. 2002. *Media/society: Industries, images and audiences.* Newbury Park, Calif.: Pine Forge/Sage. 231–39.

Dai, Xiudian. 2003. ICTs in China's development strategy. In Hughes and Wacker, eds. 2003. 8–29.

Damm, Jens, and Simona Thomas, eds. 2006. *Chinese cyberspaces: Technological changes and political effects.* London and New York: Routledge.

Davis, Deborah S., ed. 1990. *Chinese society on the eve of Tiananmen.* Cambridge: Harvard University Press.

———. 1995. Introduction: Urban China. In Davis et al., eds. 1985.

Davis, Deborah et al., eds. 1995. *Urban spaces in contemporary China: The potential for autonomy and community in post-Mao China.* Woodrow Wilson Center Series. Cambridge: Cambridge University Press.

Davis, Nanette J., ed. 1993. *Prostitution: An international handbook on trends, problems, and policies.* Westport, Conn: Greenwood Press.

de Kloet, Jeroen. 2003. Robin Hood in cyberspace — hacken, nationalisme en digitale politiek. In Jeroen de Kloet, Giselinde Kuipers, and Suzanne Kuik, eds. 2003. *Digitaal Contact/Amsterdam: Amsterdams Sociologisch Tijdschrift* 30 (1–2): 46–65.

Dean, Mitchell. 1999. *Governmentality: Power and rule in modern society.* London: Sage.

Dirlik, Arif. 1983. The predicament of Marxist revolutionary consciousness: Mao Zedong, Antonio Gramsci and the reformulation of Marxist revolutionary theory. *Modern China* 9 (9): 182–211 (April).

References

Dirlik, Arif, and Xudong Zhang, eds. 2000. *Postmodernism and China.* Durham, N.C., and London: Duke University Press.

Dobson, William J. 1998. Dissidence in cyberspace worries Beijing. *San Jose Mercury News.* 28 June. Available on-line at www.hartford-hwp.com/archives/55/428.html (accessed 5 April 2001).

Donald, Stephanie Hemelryk, Michael Keane, and Yin Hong, eds. 2002. *Media in China: Consumption, content, and crisis.* London: Routledge.

Dong, Benqi, et al. 1995. Fengkuang zuoai zai sharenhou [Make love crazily in Sharenhou]. *Se Cai Qi An* [Surprising Cases of Beauty and Money]. 3 June: 65–67.

Dutton, Michael. 1998. *Streetlife China.* Cambridge: Cambridge University Press.

Dworkin, Andrea. 1980. Why so-called radical men love and need pornography. In Lederer, ed. 1980.

Edwards, Louise. 2000. Policing the modern woman in Republican China. *Modern China* 26 (2): 115–47.

Erwin, K. 2000. Heart-to-heart, phone-to-phone: Family values, sexuality, and the politics of Shanghai's advice hotlines. In Deborah S. Davis, ed. *The consumer revolution in urban China.* Berkeley and Los Angeles: University of California Press.

Evans, Harriet. 1997. *Women and sexuality in China: Dominant discourse on female sexuality and gender since 1949.* London: Polity Press.

Fan, Huawei, and Guo Zhenyu. 2004. Nanjing tongxingmaiyin'an diaocha [An investigation of Nanjing's same-sex prostitution case]. 5 March. Available on-line at www.cyol.net (accessed 21 July 2005).

Fang, Weigui. 2004. *Das Internet und China. Digital Sein, Digitales Sein im Reich der Mitte.* Hannover: Heise.

Fernback, Jan, and Brad Thompson. 1995. Virtual communities: Abort, retry, failure? Available on-line at www.rheingold.com/texts/techpolitix/VCcivil.html (accessed 2 June 2004).

Feuerwerker, Yi-tsi Mei. 1998. *Ideology, power, text: Self-representation and the peasant "other" in modern Chinese literature.* Palo Alto, Calif.: Stanford University.

Finnane, Antonia. 1996. What should Chinese women wear. *Modern China* 22 (2): 99–131.

Florence, Eric. 2004. Migrant workers in the Pearl River Delta: Between discursive inclusion and exclusion. In Hans Entzinger et al., eds. *Migration between states and markets.* Aldershot: Ashgate. 42–63.

Fong, Vanessa L., and Rachel Murphy, eds. 2006. *Chinese Citizenship: Views from the margins.* London: Routledge.

Foucault, Michel. 1972. *The archaeology of knowledge and the discourse on language.* London: Tavistock Publications.

———. 1978. Vol. I. *History of sexuality.* New York: Random House.

Friedman, Edward. 1994. The oppositional decoding of China's Leninist media. In Lee, ed. 1994. 129–46.

Friess, Steve. 2004. Gay men, lesbians in China attend Tongzhi Conference. *Chicago Tribune.* 9 May.

Fu, Jianfeng. 2004. Fayuan panjue: Tongxingmaiyinzui chengli [Court decision: the crime of same-sex prostitution exists]. *Nanfang Dushi Bao.* 18 February.

Gaetano, Arianne, and Tamara Jacka, eds. 2004. *On the move: Women and rural to urban migration in contemporary China.* New York: Columbia University Press.

Gao, Jiehua, and Liao Yijiang. 2000. Public reaction on the first day of *Life and Death Decision. Jiangxi Daily,* 29 August: 1 (Chinese).

Gao, Feng. 2003. Zhongguo tongxinglian quanjilu [A complete record of homosexuality in China]. *Jinyang Wang.* Available on-line at http://heritage.tom.com/Archive/2001/7/30-86494.html (accessed 18 December 2003).

Geoffry, Taubman. 1998. A not-so World Wide Web: The internet, China and the challenges to nondemocratic rule. *Political Communication* 2 (15): 255–72.

Geyer, Robert. 2002. In love and gay. In Link et al., eds. 2002. 251–74.

Giese, Karsten. 2003a. Construction and performance of virtual identity in the Chinese internet. In Ho, Kluver, Yang, eds. 2003. 193–210.

———. 2003b. Internet growth and the digital divide: Implications for spatial development. In Hughes and Wacker, eds. 2003. 30–57.

———. 2005. Surfing the virtual minefield. Doing ethnographic research on the Chinese internet. In Bettina Gransow, Pál Nyíri, Shiaw-Chian Fong, eds. *China: New faces of ethnography.* Berlin: Lit. 20–43.

Gong, Ting. 2002. Dangerous collusion: Corruption as a collective venture in contemporary China. *Communist and Post-Communist Studies* 35: 85–103.

Gong, Guojiang. 2003. Jiaqiang woguo de tongxinglian fazhi jianshe [Strengthen China's legal system with regard to same-sex love]. 8 October. Available on-line at http://www.chinag.org/shownews.asp?news_id+ 335 (accessed 18 December 2003).

Gong'anbu guanyu dui tongxing zhijian yi qiancai wei meijie de xingxingwei dingxing chuli wenti de pifu [A reply from the Ministry of Public Security on how to define and handle the exchange of same-sex sexual conduct for money or property]. 2001. Order 4 (accessed 23 August 2002).

Grewal, Inderpal, and Caren Kaplan. 2001. Global identities: Theorizing transnational studies of sexuality. *GLQ* 7 (4): 663–79.

Griffin, Em. 1991. *A first look at communication theory.* New York: McGraw-Hill.

Griffiths, Richard T. 2002. History of the internet, internet for historians. 11 October. Available on-line at www.let.leidenuniv.nl/history/ivh/frame_theorie.html (accessed 5 January 2005).

Gu, Yuyun. 2000. Emotions on playing a mayor's wife who accepts bribes. *JA Daily,* 1 October: 4 (Chinese).

Guan, Huya, et al. 2001. Jie kai san pei nu "rong sheng" xuan chuan bu fu bu zhang de hei mu [Unveiling the secret of a bar hostess promoted to general manager of press and propaganda department] *Jia Ting* [Family] 12: 50–52.

Guldin, Gregory E. 2001. *What's a peasant to do? Village becoming town in southern China.* Boulder: Westview Press.

Guo, Liang. 2003. *Approaching the internet in small Chinese cities.* Beijing: Research Center for Social Development, Chinese Academy of Social Sciences. Available on-line at 199.239.233.76/downloadable_assets/chinainternet_case studies.pdf (accessed 24 May 2004).

Guo, Shutian, and Liu Chunbin. 1991. *Shiheng de Zhongguo.* Tangshan: Hebei renmin chubanshe.

Guo, Xiaofei. 2004. Tongxingmaiyin'an tuxian falü kongbai [Same-sex prostitution case reveals gaps in the law]. 8 April. Available on-line at www.civil law.com.cn (accessed 21 July 2005).

Guo, Xiaosong. 2004. *Jiangsu shouli tongxingmaiyin'an zhong kaiting* [The court hearing of the first case of same-sex prostitution in Jiangsu finally begins]. *Dongfang Weibao*. 13 February.

Hachigian, Nina. 2001. China's cyber-strategy. *Foreign Affairs* 80 (2): 118–33 (March/April).

Hall, S. 1980. Encoding/decoding. In S. Hall, ed., *Culture, media, language: Working papers in cultural studies, 1972–79*. London: Hutchinson, in association with the Centre for Contemporary Cultural Studies, University of Birmingham.

Han, Junjie. 2005. Henan yule changsuo shishi shimingzhi shanggang qian xu jieshou aizibing jiance [Henan Province implements a proper name system in entertainment venues: Workers must have an HIV/AIDS test before commencing employment]. *Zhongguo Qingnian Bao*. 20 February.

Hartford, K. 2003. West Lake wired: Shaping Hangzhou's information age. In Lee Chin-Chuan, ed. 2003.

Hartley, John. 1999. *Uses of television*. London and New York: Routledge.

———. 2000. *The indigenous public sphere: The reporting and reception of aboriginal issues in the Australian media*. Oxford and New York: Oxford University Press.

Harwit, E., and D. Clark. 2001. Shaping the internet in China: Evolution of political control over network infrastructure and content. *Asian Survey* 41 (3): 377–408.

He, Shang. 2001. Shaonu nonggao gong'an suopei 81 wan [A young migrant woman angrily sued the public security bureau and claimed 810,000 yuan for the compensation fee]. *Xinshang Bao* [New Commerce Newspaper] 8 August: 18.

He tongxinglian youguan de falü [Laws pertaining to homosexuality]. 2003. 20 November. Available on-line at http://www.qianlong.com/2955/2003/11/20/41@1723211.htm (accessed 18 December 2003).

He, Zhengke. 2000. Corruption and anti-corruption reform in China. *Communist and Post-Communist Studies* 33 (2): 243–70 (June).

He, Zhou. 2000. Chinese Communist Party press in a tug-of-war. A political-economy analysis of the *Shenzhen Special Zone Daily*. In Lee Chin-Chuan, ed. 2000. 112–52.

Hemelryk Donald, Stephanie, Michael Keane, and Yin Hong, eds. 2002. *Media in China: Consumption, content, and crisis*. London: Routledge.

Hershatter, Gail. 1997. *Dangerous pleasures: Prostitution and modernity in twentieth-century Shanghai*. Berkeley and Los Angeles: University of California Press.

Hinsch, Bret. 1992. *Passions of the cut sleeve: The male homosexual tradition in China*. Berkeley and Los Angeles: University of California Press.

Historic liberation of Chinese women. 2000. Information Office of the State Council of the People's Republic of China, Beijing. White paper available on-line at http://www.china.org.cn/e-white/chinesewoman/index.htm.

Ho, K.C., Randolph Kluver, Kenneth C.C. Yang, eds. 2003. *Asia.com: Asia encounters the internet.* London and New York: RoutledgeCurzon.

Hoffman, Lisa. 2001. Guiding college graduates to work: Social constructions of labor markets in Dalian. In Chen et al., eds. 2001. 43–66.

Hong, Zhigang. 2002. Wo xuni, suoyi wo cunzai [I virtualize, therefore I am]. *People's Daily Online.* April 2002. Available on-line at www.people.com.cn/GB/paper85/6056/604017.html (accessed 3 June 2004).

Honig, Emily. 1992. *Creating Chinese ethnicity: Subei people in Shanghai, 1850–1980.* New Haven: Yale University Press.

———. 2003. Socialist sex: The Cultural Revolution revisited. *Modern China* 29 (2): 143–75.

Hooper, Beverley. 2005. The consumer citizen in contemporary China. *Working Paper,* no. 12, www.ace.lu.se/images/Syd_och_sydostasienstudier/ working_papers/Hooper.pdf.

Hu, X., 2002. The surfer-in-chief and the would-be kings of content: A short study of Sina.com and Netease.com. In Hemelryk Donald et al. 2002.

Huang, C. 2000. The development of a semi-independent press in post-Mao China: An overview and a case study of *Chengdu Business News. Journalism Studies* 1 (4): 669–74.

Huang, Hong. 1990. *Chaosheng youjidui* [The over-quota rural family]. Beijing: CCTV Spring Festival Evening.

Huang, Jincheng. 1999. Anmonu fuwu shangmen, dapaisong zhufu huyu qudi [Sauna hostess offer services at the door, wives appeal for a crackdown]. *Guangzhou Ribao* [Guangzhou Daily]. 5 September: 3.

Huang, Jun. 1988. Chao sheng de dan you [Worry of over-quota]. *Renmin Ribao.* 14 January: 3.

Huang, P. 1993. "Public sphere"/"civil society" in China? The third realm between state and society. In P. Huang et al. 1993.

Huang, P., et al. 1993. Symposium: "Public sphere"/"civil society" in China. Paradigmatic Issues in Chinese Studies III. Special issue of *Modern China* 19 (2).

Huang, Y. 1994. Peaceful evolution: The case of television reform in post-Mao China. *Media Culture and Society* 16: 217–41.

Hughes, Christopher R., and Gudrun Wacker, eds. 2003. *China and the internet: Politics of the digital leap forward.* London and New York: Routledge.

Hussain, A. 1990. *The Chinese television industry: The interaction between government policy and market force.* London: London School of Economics and Political Science.

Hyman, Gretchen. 2003. Violence breaks out in Los Angeles cyber cafés. Internet news.com. Available on-line at www.internetnews.com/bus-news/article.php/1564001. 3 January (accessed 1 February 2004).

International Institute for Democracy and Electoral Assistance (International IDEA). 2001. *Democracy and the information revolution: Values, opportunities and threats, democracy forum 2001 report.* Available on-line at www.idea.int/2001_forum/Democracy_Forum_2001_Report.pdf (accessed 5 January 2003).

JA Daily. See *Jiangxi Daily.*

Jacka, Tamara. 2000. "My life as a migrant worker": Women in rural-urban migration in contemporary China. *Intersections: Gender, history and culture in the Asian context* 3. URL: http://www.sshe.murdoch.edu.au:inter sections/issues4.

References

Jeffreys, Elaine. 2004. *China, sex and prostitution*. London and New York: Routledge Curzon.

Jian, Ping. 2001. Caifang shouji: Jingyan Dalian [Interview memoirs in Dalian]. *Xinzhoukan* [New Weekly] 10: 44.

Jiang, Fengqing. 2001. Zise jiushi liliang [Beauty is power]. *Dalian Ribao* [Dalian Daily]. 17 February: 11.

Jiangxi Daily, 26 August 2000 (Chinese).

Jiangxi Daily, 14 September 2000 (Chinese).

Jie, Pinru, and Yang Shen, eds. 1993. *Xiongyong mingongchao*. Guangzhou: Guangzhou chubanshe.

Kalathil, Shanthi. 2000. Cyber censors: A thousand web sites almost bloom. *Asian Wall Street Journal*. 29 August: 1.

Kang, Ning. 2004a. Kang Ning tongzhi zai Zhongguo jiaoyu dianshi tai 2004 nian xinwen xuanchuan gongzuo huiyi shang de jianghua [Comrade Kang Ning's speech on reasons for CETV reform at news conference of the Propaganda Ministry of 6 February 2004]. Beijing: CETV Documents.

―――. 2004b. *Zhongguo jiaoyu dianshi tai 2004 nian jiemu gaiban zongti qingkuang* [CETV program reform 2004]. Beijing: CETV Documents.

Keane, Michael. 2001a. Redefining Chinese citizenship. *Economy and Society* 30 (1): 1–17 (February).

―――. 2001b. Broadcasting policy, creative compliance and the myth of civil society in China. *Media, Culture and Society* 23 (6): 783–98 (November).

―――. 2002. As a hundred television formats bloom, a thousand television stations contend. *Journal of Contemporary China* 10 (30): 5–16.

―――. 2003. Creativity and complexity in post-WTO China. *Continuum* 17 (3): 291–302.

Keane, Michael, ed. 1994. *China's media, media's China*. Boulder, Colo.: Westview Press.

―――, ed. 2003. *Chinese media, global contexts*. London: Routledge.

Khan, Azizur Rahman, and Carl Riskin. 1998. Income and inequality in China: Composition, distribution and growth of household income, 1988–1995. *China Quarterly* 154 (June): 221–53.

Kjellgren, Bjorn. 2002. The Shenzhen experience or the city of the good cats: Memories, dreams, identities and social interaction in the Chinese showcase. *Stockholm East Asian Monographs* 66.

Kluver, Randy, and Jack. L. Qiu. 2003. The internet and democracy in China. In Indrajit Banerjee, ed. 2003. *The internet and democracy in Asia*. Singapore: Times Academic Press.

Lancaster, Roger N., and Micaela Di Leonardo, eds. 1997. *The gender/sexuality reader: Culture, history, political economy*. New York: Routledge.

Langfitt, Frank. 2000. Out of closet, onto internet. *Baltimore Sun*. February.

Lao, Shi. 2005. Aiguo jiu yingdang zunshou falü; wo bu lijie hongke de "aiguo qinggan" [Patriotism should respect the law; I do not accept the "patriotic feelings" of the red hackers]. *People's Daily Online*. 24 February. Available on-line at it.people.com.cn/GB/42891/42895/3199365.html (accessed 3 June 2005).

Latham, Kevin. 2000. Nothing but the truth: New media, power and hegemony in South China. *The China Quarterly* 163: 633–54 (September).

———. 2001. Between markets and mandarins: Journalists and the rhetorics of transition in southern China. In Brian Moeran, ed. *Asian media productions.* Richmond: Curzon Press. 89–107.

———. 2002. Rethinking Chinese consumption: Social palliatives and the rhetorics of transition in postsocialist China. In C.M. Hann, ed. *Postsocialism: Ideals, ideologies and practices in Eurasia.* London: Routledge. 217–37.

———. 2005. Media and the limits of cynicism in post-socialist China. Unpublished paper presented to the Department of Anthropology and Sociology Seminar, SOAS, University of London. March.

Lau, S.K. 1979. The People's commune as a communication network for the diffusion of agritechnology. In Chu and Hsu, eds. 1979.

Lederer, Laura, ed. 1980. *Take back the night: Women on pornography.* New York: William Morrow.

Lee, Chin-Chuan. 2000. *Power, money, and media: Communication patterns and bureaucratic control in cultural China.* Evanston, Ill.: Northwestern University Press.

Lee, Chin-Chuan, ed. 1994. *China's media, media's China.* Boulder, Colo.: Westview Press.

———, ed. 2003. *Chinese media, global contexts.* London: Routledge Curzon.

Lee, Ching-Kwan. 1995. Production politics and labour identities: Migrant workers in South China. *The China Review* (CD Rom version).

———. 1998. *Gender and the South China miracle: Two worlds of factory women.* Berkeley and Los Angeles: University of California Press.

———. 2002. Three patterns of working-class transition in China. In Jean-Louis Rocca and F. Mengin, eds. *Politics in China: Moving frontiers.* New York: Palgrave/Macmillan. 62–92.

Leshknowich, Anne Marie, Carla Jones, and Sandra Niessen, eds. 2003. *Re-orienting fashion: The globalization of Asian dress.* Oxford and New York: Berg.

Leung, Louis. 1999. Lifestyles and the use of new media technology in urban China. *Telecommunications Policy* 22 (9): 781–90.

Levy, Richard. 2002. Corruption in popular culture. In Link, Madsen, and Pickowicz, eds. 2002. 39–56.

Li, Lianjiang, and Kevin O'Brien. 1996. Villagers and popular resistance in contemporary China. *Modern China* 22 (1): 28–61.

Li, Meiyi, ed. 2004. Yatou caokong nanji maiyin: Guangdongsheng zuzhi tongxingmaiyin'an [Guangdong gives a verdict on the first case of organized male same-sex prostitution in the province]. Southcn.com. 12 June.

Li, Min. 1999. Shishang zazhi shidabing [The ten ills of fashion magazines]. *Xin Zhou Kan* [New Weekly] 7: 43–45.

Li, Ming. 2000a. Meikuangli gongren paiduigan nuren [Mine workers line up to engage sex with the women]. *Zhongguo Hongdengqu* [The Red Light District in China] 83: 42–44.

———. 2000b. Siji, xunhuawenliu zhulijun [Drivers constitute the main force to search for sexual partners]. *Zhongguo Hongdengqu* [The Red Light District in China] 83: 70–75.

Li, Peng, ed. 2002. Vol. 2. *Zhongguo jiaoyu dianshi tai wenji* [Collection of papers on the CETV]. Beijing: National Broadcasting Television University Press.

References

Li, Qiang. 2003. Policy issues concerning the informal employment of rural-urban migrants in China. *Social Science in China* 4: 126–37 (winter).

Li, Xiaoping. 1991. The Chinese television system and television news. *China Quarterly* 126: 340–55.

Li, Xiaojiang, Hong Zhu, and Xiuyu Dong, eds. 1997. *Pingdeng yu fazhan* [Equality and development]. Beijing: Sanlian shudian.

Li, Yaling. 1999. Kaojin mingpai daxue liangcaizi bei xiaojie yinyou ranshang linbing [An outstanding student in a key university is seduced by a hostess and contracted a STD]. *Chengdu Shangbao* [Chengdu Commerce Newspaper]. 12 August: 2.

Li, Yang. 2005. Xi'nan diqu shouli qiangbi nanzimaiyin'an "laobao" zhou shoushen [Yesterday the southwestern region heard the first case concerning an organizer who forced men into prostitution]. *Chongqing Shangbao*. 25 March.

Li, Yinhe. 1998. *Tongxinglian yawenhua* [The subculture of homosexuality]. Beijing: Jinri Zhongguo chubanshe.

———. 2005. Woguo yinggai ba maiyin dang daode wenti chuli [China should handle prostitution as a moral (not legal) issue]. *Jinyang Wang*. 14 May. Available on-line at http://www.yfs.gov.au (accessed 21 July 2005).

———. 2006. Regulating male-male love in the People's Republic of China. In Elaine Jeffreys, ed. *Sex and sexuality in China*. London and New York: Routledge Curzon. 82–101.

Li, Yu. 1999. *Wai lai mei [Maids from the outside]*. Directed by Hao Cheng. Guangzhou: Shidai Yingyin Chubanshe.

Li, Zhurun. 1998. Popular journalism with Chinese characteristics: From revolutionary modernity to popular modernity. *International Journal of Cultural Studies* 1 (3): 307–28.

Li, Z.G., and S.K. Yang. 2004. Dangqian zhongguo dianshi meiti de san da quexian ji duice sikao [Three large failings in China's contemporary television industry and strategic thinking]. *South China Television Journal* 45: 38–42.

Liang, Yibo. 1992. Mingongmen de sheng yu si [The life and death of migrant workers]. *Shehui* 5: 4–7 (May).

Life and Death Decision: A forerunner of domestic epic drama films. 2003. http://lcqz.com/zuanti/xiaohuang/ssjz/2301.html. 8 January (Chinese).

Life and Death Decision: Shouting out for the people. 2000. *People's Daily*, 19 August: 5 (Chinese).

Lin, Georges S. 2001. Flexible production in the Hong Kong-Pearl River Delta region: Regionalization of industry and transformation of a local Chinese economy. *CURS Paper Series* 6: 1–29.

Link, Perry, Richard P. Madsen, and Paul G. Pickowicz, eds. 1989. *Unofficial China: Popular culture and thought in the People's Republic*. Boulder: Westview Press.

———, eds. 2002. *Popular China: Unofficial culture in a globalizing society*. Lanham, Md.: Rowman and Littlefield.

Liu, Chi. 2000. Beautiful women and corrupt officials. *Jiangxi Daily*. 5 September: 2 (Chinese).

Liu, Dalin. 1995. *Zhongguo dangdai xingwenhua: Zhongguo wanli "xingwenming" diaochabaogao* [Sex culture in Chinese contemporary society: The survey of sex culture in China]. Shanghai: Sanlian Shudian.

Liu, H. 1998. Profit or ideology? The Chinese press between party and market. *Media, Culture and Society* 20 (1): 31–41.

Liu, Hongbo. 2000. Chunümo de shengli [The triumph of hymen]. *Nan Feng Chuang* [Windows to the South] 184: 27.

Liu, Jianlin. 1999. Sanpeinü chengwei fanzui gaofa qunti [The highest crime rate is found in the group of bar hostesses]. *Zhongguo Qingnianbao* [Chinese Youth Newspaper]. 20 August: 3.

Liu, Li. 1998. Liao xi yuan an [The case of injustice in Liaoxi]. *Zhi Yin* [Bosom Friend]. 10: 33–35.

Liu, Lydia. 1995. *Translingual practice: Literature, national culture and translated modernity — China, 1900–1937.* Palo Alto, Calif.: Stanford University Press.

Liu, Meiyuan. 2001. Bao ernai yu fanfubai [Keeping second-wives and anti-corruption]. *Can Kao Xiao Xi* [Information and News]. 9 August: 8.

Liu, Nianxian, Zhang Yumei, and Guo Ying. 2004. Jilin shouli tongxingmaiyin'an xuanpan [A verdict is reached on Jilin's first case of same-sex prostitution]. *Jilin Ribao.* 26 May.

Liu, Yaotang. 2004. Jiaofeng: "Tongxingmaiyin" duo wenlun [Confrontation: Different perspectives on "same-sex prostitution"]. Available on-line at http://www.148china.com/ReadNews.asa?NewsID=1112 (accessed 1 June 2005).

Liu, Yaping. 2004. Cong Nanjing shouli tongxingmaiyin'an kan zuixing fading [The first case of same-sex prostitution in Nanjing reveals the legal definition of a crime]. 18 March 2004. Available on-line at http://www.148china.com/ReadNews.asa?NewsID=1112 (accessed 1 June 2005).

Liu, Zhi (n.d.). Nanjing tongxinglian maiyin'an [Nanjing's homosexual prostitution case]. *Fenghuang Zhoukan* 141.

Lowe, Lisa, and David Lloyd, eds. 1997. *The politics of culture in the shadow of capital.* Durham, N.C.: Duke University Press.

Lü, Xiaobo. 2000. *Cadres and corruption: The organizational involution of the Chinese Communist Party.* Palo Alto, Calif.: Stanford University Press.

Lu, Ding, and C.K. Wong. 2003. *China's telecommunications market: Entering a new competitive age.* Cheltenham: Edward Elgar.

Lü, Fuming. 2004. Zhongguo shouci gongbu nantongxinglian renshu [First public statistics on male homosexuality in China]. Xinhuanet.com. 1 December. Available on-line at http://news.xinhuanet.com/health/2004-12/01/content-22 80 536.htm (accessed 6 June 2005).

Lü, Jian, and Deng Jian. 2005. Jin shen quansheng shouli qiangpo tongxingmaiyin'an [The first case of forced male-male prostitution in (Sichuan Province) is heard today]. *Chengdu Shangbao.* 24 February.

Lu, Sheldon Hsiao-peng. 1997. Art, culture, and cultural criticism in post-new China. *New Literary History* 28 (11): 111–33.

———. 2000. Global POSTmodernIZATION: The intellectual, the artist and China's condition. In Dirlik and Zhang, eds. 2000: 145–74.

———. 2001. *China, transnational visuality, global postmodernity.* Palo Alto, Calif.: Stanford University Press.

Lu, Xinning. 1998. Xiandai ren, hechu shi jiaxiang? Liudong zhong de xiangqing he qinqing [Modern people, where is the hometown? The sentiment for family and hometown]. *Renmin Ribao.* 24 January: 11.

References

Lu, Xueyi. 2000. Zouchu "chengxiang fenzhi, yiguo liangce" de kunjing [Out of the city-countryside dichotomy in a nation]. *Du Shu* [Reading] 5: 3–10.

Luard, Tim. 2004. China slow to loosen media muzzle. *BBC News Online*. 13 January.

Lull, J. 1991. *China turned on: Television, reform, and resistance*. London: Routledge.

Lynch, Daniel C. 1999. *After the propaganda state: Media, politics and "thought work" in reformed China*. Palo Alto, Calif.: Stanford University Press.

———. 2000. The nature and consequences of China's unique pattern of telecommunications development. In Lee Chin-Chuan 2000, 179–207.

Ma, Yingbing. 2000. Fighting corruption — On life and death decision of the administration and party. Xinhua News Agency. 26 August.

Ma, Zhongdong, and Yuantao Qu. 2001. Da nai fanghuo shao ernai [The first wife sets fire to burn the second wife]. *Dalian Wanbao* [Dalian Evening Newspaper], 11 July: 14.

MacKinnon, Catharine. 1987. *Feminism unmodified: Discourses on life and law*. Cambridge, Mass., and London: Harvard University Press.

MacKinnon, Rebecca. Chinese blogs: censorship and civic discourse. Available on-line at rconversation.blogs.com/rconversation/files/mackinnon_chinese_blogs_chapter.pdf (accessed 28 March 2006).

Manalansan IV, Martin F. 2003. *Global divas: Filipino gay men in the diaspora*. Durham, N.C., and London: Duke University Press.

Marcus, Steven. 1966. *The other Victorians: A study of sexuality and pornography in mid-nineteenth-century England*. New York: Basic Books.

Martin, Fran. 2000. From citizenship to queer counterpublic: Reading Taipei's New Park. *Communal/Plural* 8 (1): 81–94.

May, Greg. 1999. Spamming for freedom. *The Washington Post*. 19 February: A23.

McCamish, Malcolm, Graeme Storer, and Greg Carl. 2000. Refocusing HIV/AIDS interventions in Thailand: The case for male sex workers and other homosexually active men. *Culture, Health and Sexuality* 2 (2): 167–82.

McClintock, Anne. 1992. Gonad the barbarian and the Venus flytrap. In Segal and McIntosh, eds. 1992, 111–31.

McCormick, Barrett L., and Qing Liu. 2003. Globalization and the Chinese media: Technologies, content, commerce and the prospects for the public sphere. In Lee Chin-Chuan, ed. 2003, 139–58.

McDonald, Hamish. 2005. Critic of Chinese censors sacked. *West Australian Newspaper*. 30 March: 27.

———. 2005. Gay revolution puts red China in the pink. *Sydney Morning Herald*. 27 August.

McIntyre, Bryce T. 1997. China's use of the internet: A revolution on hold. In Paul S.N. Lee, ed. *Telecommunications and development in China*. Cresskill, N.J.: Hampton Press, 1997. 149–69.

MII (Ministry of Information Industries). 2006. MII website: www.mii.gov.cn (accessed 20 December 2006).

Moore, Henrietta. 1994. *A passion for difference*. Bloomington: Indiana University Press.

Morley, D. 1992. *Television, audiences and cultural studies*. London: Routledge.

Mueller, M., and Z. Tan. 1997. *China in the information age: Telecommunications and the dilemmas of reform.* Washington, D.C.: Center for Strategic and International Studies.

Munro, D. 1977. *The concept of man in contemporary China.* Ann Arbor: University of Michigan Press.

Murphy, Rachel. 2002. *How migrant labour is changing rural China.* Cambridge: Cambridge University Press.

———. 2004. Turning peasants into modern Chinese citizens: "Population quality" discourse, demographic transition and primary education. *China Quarterly* 177: 1–20 (March).

———. 2006. Citizenship education in the countryside: Technical and dispositional training for cadres and farmers. In Fong and Murphy, eds. 2006. 9–26.

Nathan, Andrew J. 2003. Authoritarian resilience. *Journal of Democracy* 14 (1): 6–17.

Neve, Brian. 2000. Frames of presidential and candidate politics in American films of the 1990s. *Javnost — The Public* 7 (2): 19–31.

Nip, Joyce Y.M. 2003. The queer sisters and its electronic bulletin board: A study of the internet for social movement mobilization. Available on-line at www.hkbu.edu.hk/~jour/documents/joyce/paperJuly03.pdf (accessed 12 March 2005).

O'Brien, Kevin O. 1996. Rightful resistance. *World Politics* 49 (1): 31–55.

Ong, Aihwa. 1999. *Flexible citizenship: The cultural logics of transnationality.* Durham, N.C., and London: Duke University Press.

Pan, Fan. 2000. What does the enthusiastic screening of *Life and Death Decision* show? *People's Daily.* 17 September: 3 (Chinese).

Pan, Suiming. 1998. Zhongguo de jinchang zhengce yu shiji qingkuang fenxi [An analysis of China's policy of banning prostitution and its effects]. *Bamian Laifeng.* November.

Pan, Zhongdang. 2000. Improvising reform activities: The changing reality of journalistic practice in China. In Lee Chin-Chuan 2000, 112–51.

Parker, Andrew, et al. 1992. Introduction. In Andrew Parker, Mary Russo, Doris Sommer, and Patricia Yaeger, eds. *Nationalisms and sexualities.* New York: Routledge.

Peng, Li. 2000. The mission of film — Looking at *The Life and Death Decision. Beijing Evening News.* 31 August (Chinese).

Pile, Steven. 1997. Opposition, political identities and spaces of resistance. In Steve Pile and Michael Keith, eds. *Geographies of resistance.* London: Routledge.

Police arrest 37 gays in social vice swipe. 2000. *China News Digest.* 10 July.

Pomfret, John. 2001. Chinese city is first to enact law on AIDS: Controversial rules set for infected people, high-risk groups. *Washington Post Foreign Service.* 15 January: A16.

Pun, Ngai. 2002. Am I the only survivor? Global capital, local gaze, and social trauma in China. *Public Culture* 14 (2): 341–48 (spring).

———. 2004. The precarious employment and hidden costs of women workers in Shenzhen Special Economic Zones in China. *Journal of Oxfam.* http://www.cwwn.org/download/The%20Precarious%20Employment%20and%20 Hidden%20 Costs.doc.

Pye, L.W. 1979. Communication and political culture in China. In Chu and Hsu, eds. 1979.

Qiu, Jack L. 1999/2000. Virtual censorship in China: Keeping the gate between the cyberspaces. *International Journal of Communications Law and Policy* 4: 1–25.

Quanguo renda changwu changweihui, xingfashi, fazhi gongzuo weiyuanhui [Criminal Law Office and the Legal Council of the Standing Committee of the National People's Congress]. 1991. Guanyu yanjin maiyin piaochang de jueding he guanyu yancheng guaimai banjiafunü, ertong de fanzui fenzi de jueding shiyi [An explanation of the decision on strictly forbidding the selling and buying of sex and the decision on the severe punishment of criminals who abduct and traffic in or kidnap women and children]. Beijing: Zhongguo jiancha chubanshe.

Quanguo renda changwu weiyuanhui [Standing Committee of the National People's Congress]. 2005. Zhonghua Renmin Gongheguo Zhi'an Guanli Chufa Fa [Security Administration Punishment Law of the People's Republic of China]. Available on-line at http://news.xinhuanet.com/newscenter/ 2005-08/28/content_3413618.htm (accessed 16 November 2006).

Rheingold, Howard. 1993. *The virtual community: Homesteading on the electronic frontier.* Reading, Mass.: Addison-Wesley 1993. Available on-line at www.rheingold.com/vc/book (accessed 1 June 2004).

Rofel, Lisa. 1999a. *Other modernities: Gendered yearnings in China after socialism.* Berkeley and Los Angeles: University of California Press.

———. 1999b. Qualities of desire: Imagining gay identities in China. *GLQ* 5 (4): 451–74.

Rose, Nikolas S. 1999. *Powers of freedom: Reframing political thought.* Cambridge: Cambridge University Press, 1999.

Rowe, W. 1990. The public sphere in modern China. *Modern China* 16 (3): 309–29. July.

Rubin, Kyna. 2003. How to be gay in Beijing. *The Gay and Lesbian Review Worldwide* 10 (3): 29–33.

Ruhlen, Rebecca N. 2003. Korean alterations: Nationalism, social consciousness, and "transnational" clothing. In Leshknowich et al., 2003, 117–39.

Sayad, Abdelmayek. 1991. *L'immigration ou les paradoxes de l'altérité.* Paris and Brussels: De Boeck Université.

Scharping, Thomas, ed. 1997. *Floating population and migration in China: The impact of economic reforms.* Hamburg: Mitteilungen des Instituts für Asienkunde.

———. 1999. Selectivity, migration reasons and backward linkages of rural-urban migrants: A sample survey of migrants to Foshan and Shenzhen in comparative perspective. In Frank Pieke and Hein Mallee, eds. *Internal and international migration: Chinese perspectives.* Surrey: Curzon Press. 73–102.

Scharping, Thomas, and W. Schultze. 1997. Labour and income developments in the Pearl River Delta: A migration survey of Foshan and Shenzhen. In Scharping, ed. 1997. 98–118.

Schein, Louisa. 2000. *Minority rules: The Miao and the feminine in China's cultural politics.* Durham, N.C.: Duke University Press.

———. 2001. Urbanity, cosmopolitanism, consumption. In Chen et al., eds. 2001. 225–41.

Schoenhals, Michael. 1992. *Doing things with words in Chinese politics: Five studies.* Berkeley, Calif.: Institute of East Asian Studies.

Scott, James C. 1990. *Domination and the arts of resistance: Hidden transcripts.* New Haven: Yale University Press.

Segal, Lynne. 1992. Sweet sorrows, painful pleasures: Pornography and the perils of heterosexual desire. In Segal and McIntosh, eds. 1992. 65–91.

Segal, Lynne, and Mary McIntosh, eds. 1992. *Sex exposed: Sexuality and the pornography debate.* London: Virago Press.

Shen, J.J. 2002. Computer-mediated communication: Internet development and new challenges in China. In W. Jia, X. Lu, and D.R. Heisey, eds. *Chinese communication theory and research: Reflections, new frontiers, and new directions.* Westport, Conn.: Ablex.

Shen, Ping. 1999. Guxi gangke baoyang miaolingnu: Xiangxia "jinwu" nan cang jinsique [The elderly Hong Kong man keeps a young woman: The countryside house cannot hide the caged bird]. *Nanfang Ribao* [South Daily], 6 August: 6.

Shevchenko, Alexei. 2004. Bringing the Party back in: The CCP and the trajectory of market transition in China. *Communist and Post-Communist Studies* 37: 161–85.

Shi, Xianmin. 1999. Zhongguo yanhai jingji zhongxin chengshi laodongli liudong yu tizhi xuanze. *Shehuixue yanjiu* 3: 112–25.

Sigley, Gary, and Elaine Jeffreys. 1999. On "sex" and "sexuality" in China: A conversation with Pan Suiming. *Bulletin of Concerned Asian Scholars* 31 (1): 50–58.

Siu, Helen. 1989. *Agents and victim.* New Haven: Yale University Press.

———. 1990a. *Furrows: Peasants, intellectuals, and the state.* Palo Alto, Calif.: Stanford University Press.

———. 1990b. The politics of migration in a market town. In Davis, ed. 1990.

Sohmen, Philip. 2001. Taming the dragon: China's efforts to regulate the internet. *Stanford Journal of East Asian Affairs* 1: 17–26. Available on-line at www.stanford.edu/group/sjeaa/journal1/china1.pdf (accessed 4 January 2005).

Solinger, Dorothy J. 1995a. The Chinese work unit and transient labor in the transition from socialism. *Modern China* 21 (2): 155–83.

———. 1995b. The floating population in the cities: Chances for assimilation. In Davis et al., 1995.

———. 1997. Migrant petty entrepreneurs and a dual labour market. In Scharping, ed. 1997, 98–118.

———. 1999. *Contesting citizenship in urban China: Peasant migrants, the state, and the logic of the market.* Berkeley and Los Angeles: University of California Press.

South China Morning Post. 2005. Special force tackles negative chat. At www.scmp.com, 20 May 2005 (accessed 23 May 2005). Attributed to Reuters, Beijing.

Specker, Roland. 2004. China und das internet: Bringt die "Technology of freedom" die Demokratie ins Reich der Mitte? Available on-line at socio.ch/intcom/t_rspeck01.htm (accessed 7 August 2004).

Strand, D. 1990. "Civil society" and "public sphere" in modern China: A perspective on popular movements in Beijing, 1919–1989. *Working Papers in Asian/Pacific Studies.* Durham, N.C.: Duke University Press, Asian/Pacific Studies Institute. 90–101.

Su, Shaozhi. 1994. Chinese communist ideology and media control. In Lee Chin-Chuan 2000, 75–88.
Sun, Wanning. 2002. *Leaving China: Media, migration, and transnational imagination.* Lanham, Md.: Rowman and Littlefield.
Sun, Shaozhen. 2001. Lun meinu de wuqi [A discussion of the weapon of beauty]. *Dalian Ribao* [Dalian Daily]. 3 February: 11.
Tan, Shen. 2000. The relationship between foreign enterprises, local governments, and women migrant workers in the Pearl River Delta. In Loraine A. West and Yaohui Zhao, eds. *Rural labor flows in China.* Berkeley and Los Angeles: University of California Press. 292–309.
Tan, Sheng. 1996. Gender difference in the migration of rural labor force. Paper read at the Conference on Migrant Labor in China, Chinese University of Hong Kong.
Tao, Ran, and Liu Mingxing. 2006. Urban-rural income disparity, local government spending and fiscal autonomy in China. Paper presented at the conference on Rethinking the Rural-Urban Cleavage in Contemporary China, Harvard University, Fairbank Center, 6–8 October.
Taylor, Peter James. 1999. *Modernities: A geohistorical interpretation.* Cambridge: Polity Press.
Thireau, Isabelle, and Hua Linshan. 2001a. En quête d'un nouveau droit du travail. *Annales HSS* 6: 1283–312 (November–December).
———. 2001b. Ouvriers migrants et "écoles du soir" à Shenzhen. *Perspectives chinoises* 65: 36–48 (May–June).
———. 2003. The moral universe of aggrieved Chinese workers: Workers' appeal to arbitration committees and letters and visits to offices. *The China Journal* 50: 83–103 (July).
Thompson, John. 1995. *The media and modernity.* Cambridge: Polity Press.
Tie, Ming. 2005. The construction of civilization is further developed. http://jaglw.com.cn/Article_Print.asp?ArticleID=109 (downloaded 23 March 2005) (Chinese).
Tong, Xing. 1995. *Kaifang dachao xia de shenghuo fangshi* [The lifestyles in the tide of opening]. Beijing: Zhongguo Qingnian Chubanshe.
Tongxinglianzhe de gongmin quanli he fazhi jianshe [Homosexual rights and rule of law]. 2003. Sina.com. 5 December. Available on-line at http://www.sina.com.tw/man/n/2003-12-05/4851.html (accessed 18 December 2003).
Townsend, James. 1996. Chinese nationalism. In Jonathan Unger and Geremie Barmé, eds. *Chinese nationalism.* Armonk, N.Y.: M.E. Sharpe, 1–30.
Tsui, Lokman. 2001. *Internet in China: Big Mama is watching you.* Available on-line at www.lokman.nu/thesis (accessed 5 June 2003).
Unger, Jonathan. 2002. *The transformation of rural China.* Armonk, N.Y.: M.E. Sharpe.
Van Zoonen, Liesbet. 2000. Popular culture and political communication. *Javnost — The Public* 7 (2): 5–15.
Vance, Carole. 1997. Negotiating sex and gender in the attorney general's commission on pornography. In Lancaster and Di Leonardo, eds. 1997, 440–52.
Wacker, Gudrun. 2003. The internet and censorship in China. In Hughes and Wacker, eds. 2003. 58–82.

Wakeman, Frederic. 1995. Licensing leisure: The Chinese nationalists' attempt to regulate Shanghai, 1927-1949. *Journal of Asian Studies* 54 (1): 19–42.

Wan, Yanhai. 1997. Sexual work and its public policies in China. International Conference on Prostitution: an interface of cultural, legal and social issues. California State University, Northridge, and COYOTELA (www.coyotela.org/index1.html): The Centre for Sex Research. 13–16 May.

Wang, Chunguang. 1994. *Shehui liudong he shehui chonggou: Jingcheng, zhejiang-cun yanjiu.* Hangzhou: Zhejiang renmin chubanshe.

Wang, Hui. 2003. *China's new order: Society, politics, and economy in transition.* Ed. Theodore Huters. Trans. Rebecca E. Karl. Cambridge, Mass., and London: Harvard University Press.

Wang, Jinling, and Sisun Xu. 1997. Xinsheng maiyinnu xinggoucheng, shenxin tezheng yu xingwei zhiyuanqi [The psychological and physical characteristics of sex workers]. In Li et al., eds., 1997, 276–97.

Wang, Shaoguang. 1995. The politics of private time: Changing leisure patterns in urban China. In Davis et al., eds., 1995, 149–73.

Wang, Xiaoyan. 2001. Dalian liangchu renkou dipai [Dalian publicizes its population]. *Bandao Chenbao* [Bandao Morning Post]. 18 April: 2.

Wang, Xuetai. 1999. *Youmin wenhua yu zhongguo shehui* [Drifters' culture and Chinese society]. Beijing: Xueyuan chubanshe.

Wedeman, Andrew. 2004. The intensification of corruption in China. *China Quarterly* 180: 895–921 (December).

———. 2005. Anticorruption campaigns and the intensification of corruption in China. *Journal of Contemporary China* 14 (42): 93–116 (February).

Wei, Yi. 2004. Zhanzai zuixingfading de lichang wei Nanjing tongxinmaiyin'an bianhu [Using the perspective of criminal law to defend the Nanjing same-sex prostitution case]. *Shanghai Faxue Wang*. 20 June. Available on-line at http://www.yfzs.gov.cn (accessed 6 June 2005).

Wen, Yue, and Ma, Zhong, 1991. Zoujin dushi de nongjia nu [Rural women entering the city]. In Jifang Zhan and Tianpeng Luo, eds. *Jingtou zai yanshen* [Extending focus]. Chengdu: Sichuan minzu chubanshe. 221–26.

Whyte, M.K. 1979. Small groups and communication in China: Ideal forms and imperfect realities. In Chu and Hsu, eds. 1979.

Wong, Bobson. 2004. The tug-of-war for control of China's internet. China Rights Forum. 25 February. Available on-line at www.bobsonwong.com/research/china/tug-of-war (accessed 5 January 2005).

Wong, Linda, and Huen Wai-Po. 1998. Reforming the household registration system: A preliminary glimpse of the blue chop household registration system in Shanghai and Shenzhen. *International Migration Review* 32 (4): 974–94.

Woon, Yuen-Fong. 1993. Circulatory mobility in post-Mao China: Temporary migrants in Kaiping County, Pearl River Delta Region. *International Migration Review* 27 (3): 578–604 (fall).

———. 1999. Labor migration in the 1990s. *Modern China* 25 (4): 475–512.

Wu, Guoguang. 2000. One head, many mouths: Diversifying press structures in reform China. In Lee Chin-Chuan 2000, 45–67.

Wu, Xianghan. 2001. Xinghuilu weihai you duoda? [How much harm does sex bribery produce?] *Zhongguo Qingnian Bao* [Chinese Youth Newspaper]. 22 April: 2.

References

Xiang, Biao. 2000. *Kuayue bienjie de shequ: Beijing Zhejiang cun de shenghuoshi.* Beijing: Xin zhi sanlian shudian.

Xiao, Jie, and Qin Xing. 2004. Jiangsu shouli tongxingmaiyin'an yi shen panjue [A verdict is reached on Jiangsu's first same-sex prostitution case]. Available on-line at http://www.lawbase.com.cn/consult%5Cclassic_lawcase_view.asp?op=4&classic_lawcase_id=196 (accessed 25 March 2004).

Xiao, Liu. 2001. Siwang yinying longzhao "xiaojie" qunti [Hostesses are shadowed by death]. *Dalian Wanbao* [Dalian Evening Newspaper]. 9 September: 18.

Xiao, Qiang. 2004. The "blog" revolution sweeps across China. *New Scientist* (Print Edition). 24 November 2004. Available on-line at www.newscientist.com/article.ns?id=dn6707 (accessed 3 December 2004).

Xie, Kang. 2006. Industrialization supported by informatization: The economic effects of the internet in China. In Damm and Thomas, eds. 2006. 132–47.

Xie, Wei, Shen Jianli, and Lia Wenhua. 2005. Liu Baiju weiyuan: Tongxing xingqinfan yingding "weishezui" [Liu Baiju (a member of the Chinese People's Political Consultative Conference) says same-sex sexual violence should be defined as "molestation crime"]. *Guangming Ribao.* 6 June.

Xing, Fan. 2001. *Communications and information in China: Regulatory issues, strategic implications.* Lanham, Md., New York, and Oxford: University Press of America.

Xu, Ben. 1999. *Disenchanted democracy: Chinese cultural criticism after 1989.* Ann Arbor: University of Michigan Press.

Xu, Feng. 2000. *Women migrant workers in China's economic reform.* New York: St. Martin's Press.

Xu, Ren. 1993. China. In Davis, ed. 1993, 87–107.

Xu, Ting. 2001. Wanbei nongcun "zuo chuang nu" zou cun cuan hu ["Bed-sitting women" in Wanbei countryside]. *Bandao Chenbao* [Bandao Morning Post]. 15 November: 20.

Yan, Hairong. 2003. Neo-liberal governmentality and neo-humanism: Organizing *suzhi*/value flow through labor recruitment networks. *Cultural Anthropology* 4 (18): 493–523.

Yan, Xu, and Douglas C. Pitt. 2002. *Chinese telecommunications policy.* Norwood, Mass.: Artech House.

Yang, Bin. 2001. Ma Dandan jianchi suopei 500 wan [Ma Dandan insists on the compensation fee of 5 million yuan]. *Xin Shang Bao* [New Commerce Newspaper]. 18 July: 7.

Yang, Dali. 2004. *Remaking Leviathan.* Palo Alto, Calif.: Stanford University Press.

Yang, David Da-Hua. 2004. Civil society as an analytic lens for contemporary China. *China: An International Journal* 2 (1): 1–27.

Yang, Guobin. 2003. The internet and the rise of a transnational cultural sphere. *Media, Culture, Society* 25: 469–90.

Yang, Liu. 2005. Sichuan shenpan shouli qiangpo nanzi maiyin'an beigao beipan liunian tuxing [Sichuan comes to a verdict on the first case of forced male prostitution: The defendant is sentenced to six years imprisonment]. *Chengdu Wanbao.* 3 March.

Yang, Peiqin. 2000. *The Decision* will go on and on. *JA Daily.* 5 September: 4 (Chinese).

Yang, Tao (n.d.). Cong "Zhengqiba" zuzhi tongxingmaiyin'an kan "ge'an qingshi" [The "Zhengqi Bar" same-sex prostitution case raises questions about the practice of asking for instructions on specific cases]. Available on-line at http://www.148china.com/ReadNews.asa?NewsID=1112 (accessed 1 June 2005).

Yang, W.J., and P.H. Li. 2004. Bacheng shouji yonghu zeng shou saorao, wangzhan duanxin fuwu ying cengqiang [Eight in ten mobile subscribers have received harassment, website SMS services need to be strengthened]. *People's Daily* website: http://www.people.com.cn/GB/it/index.html, 9 April 2004 (accessed 10 April 2004).

Yao, Lan. 2004. Gay pimp gets one year in prison. *China Daily* (North American ed.). 13 January: 3.

Yao, Shutian. 2002. Privilege and corruption: Problems of China's socialist market economy. *American Journal of Economics and Sociology* 61 (1): 279–99 (January).

Yao, Zixu (n.d.). Tongxingmaiyin de zui yu fa [Same-sex prostitution: Crime and punishment]. Available on-line at http://www.fmedsci.com/printpage.asp?ArticleID=1852 (accessed 21 March 2005).

Yi, Ming. 2001. Tuofule yuyan: "Disici langchao" yi renlei jinru taikong juzhu wei tedian de shidai [Toffler's prediction: "The fourth wave" characterized by the time when human beings reside in outer space]. *Beijing qingnianbao*. 28 November. Available on-line at http://www.people.com.cn/GB/kejiao/42/155/20011128/614385.html; accessed 3 June 2004.

Yin, H., and D.G. Li. 2004. 2003: Zhongguo dianshi chanye beiwang [2003: Reflections on China's television industry]. *South China Television Journal* 45: 32–37.

Yin, Hong. 2002. Zhongguo de jiaoyu dianshi yu shehui fazhang [Teaching via television and social development in China]. In Li 2002, 51–55.

You, Chun. 2002. Zihao, gankai, qipan [Proud, sighing with emotion and looking forward]. In Li 2002, 30–34.

Yu, G.M. 2004. 2004: Zhongguo chuanmeiye fazhan dashi tuixiang [2004: Thoughts on the general situation of development in China's broadcasting industries] *South China Television Journal* 45: 28–31.

Yu, Jiexi. 2001. Bei cha tan guan zhong jiu cheng "bao er nai" [Corruption and "keeping the second wife"]. *Dalian Wanbao* [Dalian Evening Newspaper]. 10 January: 10.

Yu, Xiaomin. 2001. *Kuayue jieji de bianjie: Zhujiang sanjiaozhou shangcan nongmingong "qunti yishi" de poubai*. Hong Kong: The Chinese University of Hong Kong, Universities Centre for China Studies.

Yuan, Xin. 2005. Tongzhi chalouli de exing [Evil conduct in a homosexual teahouse]. *Minzhu Yu Fazhi Bao*. 9 May.

Zhai, Wei, Lutao Shen, Wei Zhou. 2004. Guanzhu wei chengnianren jiankang chengzhang wangluo "duliu" qiefu zhi tong [Concerns about the healthy development of adolescents: to suffer personal pain from the net "tumor"]. *People's Daily Online*. Available on-line at www.people.com.cn/GB/jiaoyu/1053/2515724.html (accessed 5 June 2004).

Zhang, Beichuan, Li Xiufang, Hu Tiezhong, Liu Dianchang, and Shi Tongxin. 2000. Dui nannanxingjiechuzhe de aizibing ganyu: lilun yu shijian [Theory and practice: AIDS intervention concerning men who have sex with men]. Zhongguo Xingbing Aizibing Fangzhi 3.

Zhang, Beichuan, Liu Dianchang, Li Xiufang, and Hu Tiezhong. 2000. A survey of men who have sex with men: Mainland China. *American Journal of Public Health* 90 (12).

Zhang, Chenyi. 2003. Shanghai fayuan panchu yizuzhi tongxingmaiyin'an beigaoren panxing sannian [Shanghai court rules on a case of organized same-sex prostitution: The organizer is sentenced to three years]. Chinanews.com. 9 July. Available on-line at http://www.chinanews.com.cn/n/ 2003-07-09/26/322 309.html (accessed 25 March 2004).

Zhang, H.J. 2005. Shenhua tizhi gaige, dazao wenhua pinpai [Deepen structural reform, forge a cultural brandname]. *South China Television Journal* 51: 27–29.

Zhang, Junzhang, and Gao Xiao. 1998. *Hong zhi zhu* [Red spider]. Guangzhou: Guangzhou yinxiang chubanshe.

Zhang, Li. 2001. *Strangers in the city: Reconfiguration of space, power, and social networks within China's floating population.* Palo Alto, Calif.: Stanford University Press.

Zhang, Ning. 2005. 2004 Zhongguo shida anjian [China's 10 biggest legal cases in 2004]. Xinhua News Agency. 10 January. Available on-line at http://www/dps.In-gov.cn/zazj/Print.asp?ArticleID=3666 (accessed 29 April 2005).

Zhang, Xiaoshan. 2006. Deepening reform, promoting the construction of the new countryside. Eighth European Conference on Agricultural and Rural Development in China, Yiwu, Zhejiang, China, 31 August–2 September (in Chinese).

Zhao, Donghui, and Hongcan Liu. 2001. Shanxi yi "wu nu" dang shang fa guan [A hostess becomes a court judge in Shanxi]. *Bandao Chenbao* [Bandao Morning Post], 16 October: 19.

Zhao, Yuezhi. 1998. *Media, market, and democracy in China: Between the party line and the bottom line.* Champaign, Ill.: University of Illinois Press.

———. 2000. From commercialization to conglomeration: The transformation of the Chinese press. *Journal of Communication* 50 (2): 3–26.

———. 2002. The rich, the laid-off and the criminal in tabloid tales: Read all about it! In Perry Link et al., eds., *Popular China: Unofficial culture in a globalizing society.* Lanham, Md.: Rowman and Littlefield. 111–35.

Zheng, Tiantian. 2003. Consumption, body image, and rural-urban apartheid in contemporary China. *City and Society* 15 (2): 143–63.

———. 2004. From peasant women to bar hostesses: Gender and modernity in post-Mao Dalian. In Gaetano and Jacka, eds. 2004.

Zhonghua renmin gongheguo guowuyuan [State Council of the PRC]. 1999. *Yule changsuo guanli tiaoli* [Regulations concerning the management of public places of entertainment]. Beijing: Wenhua chubanshe.

Zhu, Jiaolong. 2003. Saohuang yinggai zhua jinü haishi piaoke? [Should campaigns against prostitution and illegality target the sellers or buyers of sex?]. *Nanfang Dushi Bao.* 2 December.

Zittrain, Jonathan, and Benjamin G. Edelman. 2003. Internet filtering in China. Available on-line at cyber.law.harvard.edu/filtering (accessed 20 September 2006).

Zong, Yiduo, and Yang Fan. 2004. Zhongshen weichi banian xingqi: Nanjing "yaba" maiyin'an chen'ai luoding [Final verdict confirms eight years' imprisonment in

Nanjing's "male prostitution" case]. URL: http://news.xinhuanet.com/legal/2004-05/11/content_1461593.htm. Xinhua Wang, www.news.cn (accessed 14 December 2006).

CONTRIBUTORS

Yingchi Chu is a senior lecturer in Media Studies and the Business School at Murdoch University. She is a member of the Asia Research Centre at Murdoch, with a research specialization in Chinese media. She currently holds an ARC Discovery Grant for research on Chinese documentaries. She is the author of *Hong Kong Cinema: Coloniser, Motherland and Self* (RoutledgeCurzon, 2003) and *Chinese Documentaries: From Dogma to Polyphony* (Routledge, 2007). Email: Y.Chu@murdoch.edu.au.

Jens Damm is a research associate at the Institute of East Asian Studies, Free University Berlin. His research interests include the new media in China, the Chinese diaspora, and gender studies. Email: jensdamm@gmx.net.

Eric Florence is a researcher at the Center for Ethnic and Migration Studies (CEDEM) of the University of Liège (Belgium). A graduate in Chinese studies and political science, he is doing research in the field of ethnic and migration studies and has been conducting fieldwork research in Guangdong Province for the last eight years. He is also a lecturer in Chinese Studies at the University of Liège. His recent publications include "Migrant workers in the Pearl River Delta: Between discursive inclusion and exclusion," in Hans Entzinger et al., eds., *Migration between States and Markets* (Ashgate, 2004), and "Debates and classification struggles regarding the representation of migrant workers," *China Perspectives* 65 (May–June 2006): 15-27. Email: Eric.Florence@ulg.ac.be.

Vanessa L. Fong is an assistant professor in the Graduate School of Education at Harvard University. She is the author of *Only Hope: Coming of Age under China's One-Child Policy,* which won the Francis Hsu Prize in Asian Studies, coeditor (with Rachel Murphy) of *Chinese Citizenship: Views from the Margins,* and author of articles in *American Anthropologist, American Ethnologist, City and Society,* and *Ethos.* Her research focuses on a cohort of youth born under China's one-child policy, which began in 1979. She is in the early phases of a longitudinal project that follows members of this cohort throughout the course of their lives. Email: v@vfong.com.

Elaine Jeffreys is senior lecturer in China Studies at the Institute for International Studies at the University of Technology, Sydney. She is the editor of *Sex and Sexuality in China* (RoutledgeCurzon, 2006) and author of *China, Sex and Prostitution* (RoutledgeCurzon, 2004). Her current research is on the regulation of new sexual behaviors in the People's Republic of China. Email: Elaine.Jeffreys@uts.edu.au.

Kevin Latham is a lecturer in Social Anthropology and Anthropology of Media at the School of Oriental and African Studies (SOAS), University of London. His research interests include, in particular, Chinese newspapers and journalism, television, film, and other media in China, Chinese consumption, and popular culture. He has also worked on Cantonese opera in Hong Kong and more recently started research on new media in China including the internet and telecommunications. Email: kl1@soas.ac.uk.

Rachel Murphy is senior lecturer in East Asian Studies and associate senior lecturer in Social Policy, University of Bristol (UK). Her research interests are in the sociology of development, rural society, population, and media. Recent publications include *How Migrant Labor Is Changing Rural China* (Cambridge, 2002), *Chinese Citizenship: Views from the Margins,* coedited with Vanessa L. Fong (Routledge, 2006) and articles in *China Quarterly, Journal of Peasant Studies,* and *Population and Development Review.* Email: Rachel.Murphy @bristol.ac.uk.

Tiantian Zheng received her PhD in anthropology at Yale University in 2003, and currently teaches as an assistant professor in the Department of Sociology/Anthropology at SUNY Cortland. Her dissertation is an ethnographic study of the confluence of rural migrant women seeking to survive through sex work, the urban men seeking their services for power exchanges, and the evolving Chinese patriarchal state. Her recent work is on HIV/AIDS and condom use in China. She has contributed chapters in several books published by Columbia University Press, Routledge, and Shanghai Wenhui Press, and written articles, including forthcoming ones, in *China Quarterly, Journal of Contemporary China, City and Society,* and *Yale Journal of Student Anthropology.* Email: ZhengT@cortland.edu.

❏

INDEX

A

Absolute Power (Juedui quanli), 62
administrative sanctions, Chinese system of, 68
Aibai (gay website), 73
All-China Women's Federation, 13
anticorruption campaigns, cadres and, 61
authority, forms of, 57

B

Bulletin Board Systems (BBSs), 83; content on, 92, 95
Beijing Youth Daily, 55
Broadcasting Bureau, 15

C

cadre competition, impact of, 48
cadres, integrity and discipline of, 49
categories of the dominant discourse, malleability of (Scott), 41
CCID Saidi-consultant, 88
censorship, 83, 86, *See* media
Central State Office of Civilization, 60
Central Television University (CTU), 111
China Education Television network (CETV), 110; identity problems of, 113; impact of, 112; policy reforms and, 114; pressures on, 112; program content, 117; reputation of, 113
China Mobile, 99
China Unicom, 99
Chinese Academy of Social Sciences (CASS), 91
Chinese Communist Party (CCP), 6, 27, 62, 68, 84, 89, 97
Chinese intellectuals, and women, 15
Chinese Internet Network Information Center (CNNIC), 89
Chinese Ministry of Education, 110
Chinese People's Political Consultative Conference, 80
Chinese Psychiatry Association, 77
citizenship, media and, 96, 97, 104, 106, 110. *See* media
civil society discourses, 94
classification schemes, changes in the reform era, 28; state use of, 28
collective corruption *(jiti fubai)*, 57
commercial sex, consumption of in reform era, 6; restrictions against, 79
communication hierarchies, 104
Communist Youth Corps, 49
Communist Youth League, 60
consumerist postmodernity, 83
control discourse, emergence of, 86
copyright protections, 83
core tasks (top-down), demonstrating achievements of, 48
corruption (black gold politics), 90
corruption (official), Party-state portrayals of, 55
creative society *(chuangxin shehui)*, 116
criminal code, prostitution and, 67, 68
Criminal Law of the PRC, 67, 70, 73
crusade against failed individual ethics, Party-state's role in, 60
cults, 90
Cultural Revolution, 40, 102, 111
Culture Bureau, 15
cybercafes, 86–87, 90
cyber-dissidents, 91

D

dagong, 27, meaning of, 45; media discourse about, 45
dagong experience *(dagongjingli)*, 33
Dalian, 6–8, 24
Dazhai, 117
democratic life groups *(minzu shenghuo hui)*, 59
Deng Xiaoping, 38, 43, 48, 61, 97, 111
Department of Disease Control, 81
Department of Health and Hygiene, 79
Departments of Health and Hygiene, Industry and Commerce, and Culture (Henan Province), 80
didacticism (political and ideological), 118
Discipline Inspection Commission, 63
discourse (state-sponsored), changes in, 29
discourse and power, relationship between, 9
discourse on wealth, in reform era, 37
discourses, composition of (Foucault), 9
disorderly media, 97, 101, 103, 108–9
docile bodies (Foucault), 111

E

economic reforms, post-1978, 8, 29

F

Falun Gong, 83, 84, 89, 102, 108
flexible citizenship (Ong), 23
floating population, 8
flow of communication, structure of, 84
Ford Foundation, 80

G

gay and gender studies, 78
gay subculture, growth of, 76
gays and lesbians in China, lifestyles, 81; numbers of, 79
gender, assumptions about, 54–55
gender as a performance (Butler), 19
globalization, image-shaping power of, 37
governing strategy (Party-state), impact of, 50
Great Leap Forward, 48
Guangdong, same-sex prostitution in, 74
Guangzhou, 31, 33, 99
guanxi, 7, 23

H

harassment, concerns about, 107
harmonious society *(hexie shehui)*, 116
Hello, Little Xiaoping, 61, 62
hierarchies of citizenship, 31
HIV/AIDS, 13, 66, 67, 79, 80, 81
homophobia, 67
homosexuality in China, history of, 77; legal status of, 77, 79
hooliganism *(liumangzui)*, 73, 77
hostesses, 6; abusive treatment of, 22; agency of, 18, 19, 25; character detachment, 21; clients and, 20; economic power of, 23; emergence of, 7; identity construction, 22, 26; identity switching, 21; images of, 7; intellectuals and, 16; marketing of, 21; rural origins of, 7; victimization of, 18
hothouse horticulture, 117
household registration cards, 8, 24
household registration system, 8, 28, 30; impact on migrant workers, 31
human rights, conceptions of, 66; internet use and, 84

I

ideological control, transformation of, 29
individual consciousness, corruption and, 54; media focus on, 56
individual rights, protection of, 72
individuals, education and surveillance of, 55. *See* censorship
information, disposability of, 105
intellectuals, subordination of science to the state, 16
internet, commercialization of, 85–86, 95; contents analysis of, 88–89, 94; economic development and, 87; effects of use, 85, 88; government controls on, 84; liberating potential of, 86, 93; research on use in China, 85, 88; use of in China, 83, 89, 91–92; user profiles in China, 89, 90, 94, 96; Western discourses on, 93
Internet Protocol Version 6, 88
internet users, trust in government, 91
involution, sources of, 48
involutionary regime, cadres in, 49

J

JA Daily, 50, 53; content of, 51; Party-state power and, 50; reliability of, 51
JA Evening News, 53
JA Prefecture, 50

Index

Japanese war crimes, protests against, 106, 108
Jiang Zemin, 59
Jiangsu Television, 112
Jiangxi Daily, 53
Jiangxi Province, 47
Jinniu District People's Court (Chengdu City), 74

K

Kang Ning, 113, 114
karaoke bars *(liange ting),* 7, 62, 81
Kinsey, Alfred C., 79

L

Legal Affairs Committee (NPC), 69
Li Ning (legal case), 67, 69, 70; conviction and sentencing, 71–72; media coverage of, 69, 74
liberation discourse, internet use and, 84
The Life and Death Decision, cadre education and, 59; compulsory screenings of, 58, 60; content of, 54; mode of exhibition, 54; language used in, 59; market competitiveness of, 58; Party-state power and, 58; popular success of, 58; role in mobilization, 62; textual analysis of, 58

M

Maids from the Outside (Wai lai mei), 13
male-male commercial sexual services, prices of, 76
male-male prostitution, 66–67
Mao Zedong, 97, 117
market reforms, 8, 104, 115
marriage law, 13
mass line, principle of, 98
mass mobilization campaigns, media and, 98
massage, forms of, 81
McLuhan, Marshall, 83
media, assumptions and presuppositions about, 103, 105; censorship of, 89; diversification of, 32; durable value and, 103; effects of, 104; framing of issues, 44; Party-state control of, 32, 49, 102, 110, 115, 119; production of, 97; reconceptualizations of, 108; role of, 97, 98
media and citizen, relationship between, 107
media and communications, transformation of, 96
media discourse, role of, 9
media events, public participation in, 119
media organizations, state ownership of, 104
media output, nature and content of, 107, 121
media reform, 97, 120
media studies, 104
migrant women, fertility of, 10; perceived threat of, 12
migrant work, benefits of, 35
migrant workers, attitudes of public workers toward, 42; cultural construction of, 27; discourses about, 27, 44; exploitation of, 30; legal rights of, 42, 43; media portrayals of, 35, 40; narratives of, 44; police and, 42; sacrifices of, 40; salaries of, 30; vulnerability of, 30, 31
migrant workers magazines, nature and status of, 31; pedagogical function of, 32
migrant workers' rights, violations of, 33
migration, 8
migration (rural-urban), reasons for, 33
Ministry of Education, 112, 115
Ministry of Information Industries (MII), 96, 102
Ministry of Public Security, 73, 78
Ministry of Publicity, 115
mobile phones, use of in China, 88
mobility restrictions, 8
modes of socializing, SMS text messaging and, 99
money boys, 75; categorizing of, 78
monopoly on power (Party-state), 54
Monthly Comment, 53
morality and sexuality, regulation of, 17
multiple identities, construction of (Chapkis), 21
municipality labor bureau, migrant workers and, 43
My Sun (Wode taiyang), 110, 115, 118

N

Nanguan District People's Court (Changchun City), 74
Nanjing same-sex prostitution case, 69
narrative modes, 34

narrative techniques, 28
National Broadcasting Conference, 113
national minorities, discriminatory representations of, 10
National People's Congress, 69; Li Ning case and, 72
Netease.com (stock-listed portal), 89, 99
new Chinese citizen, 114; characteristics of, 110–11
new modes of professionals (Hoffman), 29

O

orderly media, 97, 101–3, 105–9
Organization Bureau, 53
Organization Department, 46
organizational involution, 54, 60, 65; Party-state and, 49
organizational involution (Lü Xiaobo), 46
over-quota guerrilla force *(chaosheng youjidui)*, 10

P

P2P (peer-to-peer) technologies, 83
Party committees, role in media management, 50
Party members, role in disciplining families, 55
Party newspapers, accountability of, 53; cadres and, 53; compulsory sales of, 53; financial pressures on, 52; role and function of, 50–52
Party-state institutions, pedagogic role of, 58; role in naturalizing a social order, 56
paternal authority, need for, 55
patrimonial authority, 56
patriotic films *(aiguo pian)*, 54
Pearl River Delta, 27, 29–31, 34, 38; disciplinary controls in, 29; investments in, 30; migrant women workers in, 33; migrant workers in, 29, 30; socioeconomic and institutional context of, 29; working conditions in, 41
peasantry, derogatory portrayals of, 8, 10, 16
pedagogic media, role and impact of, 46, 49
pedagogic mode of governance, 53, 60
pedagogic products, use by Party-state, 47
People's Daily, 50
performance, as constitutive and political act, 19
Petitions Administration, 63
policing of sex (Foucault), 18
political citizenship, acquisition of, 24
political language (Schoenhal), 59
political subjectivity, construction of, 96
poor governance, Party-state and, 47; reasons for, 47, 48
population control, 9, 27
pornographic magazines, portrayal of migrant women in, 14
pornography, censorship of, 11
postmodern consumerist society, 91
power-sex transactions *(quanse jiaohuan)*, 14
practices of domination and exploitation (Scott), 41
Press Bureau, 15
Procuratorial Department, 63
propaganda *(xuanchuan)*, meaning of, 110; orderly model of, 103, 106; reality and, 64
Propaganda Department, 15
propaganda materials, cadres and, 61, 64
propaganda media, role of celebrities in, 62
propaganda messages, criticisms of, 62
prostitution industry, definition of, 70; efforts to eradicate, 68; reemergence in reform era, 68
prostitution law, elements of, 68
protests (in rural areas), 8
public sphere (Habermas), 96, 111
Publicity Bureau (Rivercounty), 52, 53
Publicity Department, 46, 49; role in naturalizing a social order, 56

Q

quality of the population *(renkou suzhi)*, 29
queer theory, 66

R

Red Spider, 12–13
Regulations concerning the Management of Public Places of Entertainment, 71
reinterpretative techniques, 28
rightful resistance (O'Brien), 43
Rivercounty, 47; reactions to *The Life and Death Decision*, 56

rule of law, 72
rural migrant women, discourses about, 17; government corruption and, 14; marginalization and degradation of, 18; media depictions of, 17; media naturalization of, 7; portrayals of, 14, 17
rural migrants, categories of, 31; discrimination against, 9; number of, 9, 76; political identities of, 7
rural women, portrayals of, 11; state media control of, 12, 21

S

same-sex prostitution, 72; media commentary on, 75
same-sex sexual behaviors, pathologization of, 81
same-sex sexual conduct, legal aspects of, 69; media coverage of, 67
sanpei xiaojie, 7
Sanyuanzhu (Shangdong), 117
SARS, 120
satellite publishers, 52
second wives *(ernai),* 12, 14
Security Administration Punishment Law, 68
sex industry, 6; governance of, 81
sexual behavior, in rural areas, 10
sexual bribery *(xing huilu),* 14
sexual violence, 80
sexuality, governmental regulation of, 67; state cultural control of, 15
sexuality in China, history of, 76
sexually transmissible infections (STIs), 13, 80
Shenzhen, 27, 33; building of, 40; model of national economic development, 38; Party newspapers in, 52; population of, 30
Shenzhen Daily, 52
Shenzhen Evening News, 35
Shenzhen Special Economic Zone, 38
Shenzhen Special Zone Daily, 32, 35, 40
shishiqiushi (look for truth in facts), 43
short messaging service (SMS), 97. *See* SMS
Sichuan Television, 112
Sina.com (stock-listed portal), 89, 99
SMS industry, market value of, 99

SMS messages, characteristics of, 103; content of, 100, 106; impact of, 99; volume of, 97, 99, 106
SMS text messaging, emergence of, 99
social mobility and stratification, mode of rationalization, 34
social stratification, 44
socialist market economy, 110
sodomy *(jijianzui),* 73
Sohu.com (stock-listed portal), 89, 92, 99
Special Economic Zones (SEZs), 7
Springtime Story, 62
State Administration of Radio, Film and Television, 60, 113
state involution (Siu), 15
state nationalism, role of, 60
state pedagogy, reforming governance and, 63
State Press and Publications Administration, 49
stock-listed portals, 89, 92, 99
structural disparities, 37
The Structural Transformation of the Public Sphere (Habermas), 111
studies of sexuality, Euramerican, 66; non-Western, 66
Supreme Court (China), Li Ning case and, 69

T

technological leap frogging, 87
telecommunications, new uses of, 98
telecommunications services, 97
televised education programs, effects of, 112; public approval and, 112
The Decision. See *The Life and Death Decision*
third parties *(disanzhe),* 13
The Third Wave (Toffler), 87
three principles of closeness, 114
three represents (Jiang Zemin), 59
three stresses, 59
Tiananmen (incident), 102
Tiananmen Papers, 83
Today I Am at Home (Jintian wo zai jia), 120
tongxinglian (same-sex love), 75
tongxingmaiyin (same-sex sex seller), 75
tongzhi love, 93

township household registration system, 8
transgressive behavior, 16
transgressive sexuality, 14, 15
transgressive sexuality (Foucault), 17

U
urban-rural gap, 8
Usenet, 85

V
vertical communications hierarchy. *See* communication hierarchies
violence and sexuality, 11

W
Western imperialism, hackers' actions and, 91
The Women behind Corrupt Officials, 59
women migrant laborers, 9
women workers, depictions of, 16
Women's Federation, 49
World Health Organization, 79
World Trade Organization, 80, 112, 113
World Wide Web, 85, 92

X
Xiaogang (Fengyang), 117

Y
Yuanhua Export Company (Fujian Province), corruption in, 59
Yuexiu District People's Court (Guangdong), 74

Z
Zhong Yang Textile Factory, 63; corruption in, 54
zuotai xiaojie, 6